Praise for *Fixing American Politics*

"*Fixing American Politics*, writes its editor Roderick P. Hart in the opening chapter, 'is based on two premises: (1) Politics is a terrible thing because (2) only politics can solve our most vexing problems.' The authors of the subsequent 29 chapters take these premises and, drawing on their collective years of research and practice, run with them – in different directions, but always with insight, passion, creativity, and hope. Hart calls this book 'distinctive.' It is to be sure. But it is also timely, needed, and an example of what scholarship is ultimately for."

Michael X. Delli Carpini, *University of Pennsylvania, USA*

"Hopeful. Provocative. Thoughtful. This lively and accessible collection is all that and more. It speaks to our current distressed moment but advocates, both concretely and audaciously, for ways it could be different. The essays here deserve to be widely read, taught, and debated – on college campuses, in book clubs, and among professionals in journalism and politics."

Peter Simonson, *University of Colorado Boulder, USA*

"In this timely and important volume, Roderick P. Hart has assembled a collection of essays offering contrasting opinions, assessments, and solutions regarding the twin crises of legitimation and polarization challenging contemporary politics and elections in the United States. The essays include philosophical and historical discussions as well as practical and strategic calls for action, and they cover diverse issues such as political advertising, journalistic practices, civic engagement, and legislative and regulatory reforms. Readers are offered lively and engaging perspectives that will stimulate robust conversations that may help us improve our political deliberations and learn to listen and communicate with each other again."

Thomas A. Hollihan, *University of Southern California, USA*

"*Fixing American Politics* achieves the elusive Goldilocks standard. Instead of an inflated cure-all or a shallow laundry list, Hart assembles a highly diverse *and* substantive set of prescriptions for healing our republic. Instead of naive fantasies or complacent band-aids, the proposals embody both passion *and* perspective. Instead of Cassandra or Dr. Pangloss, we meet sober optimists, ready to guide us through the strong, slow boring of hard boards that is political reform."

Michael A. Neblo, *Ohio State University, USA*

Fixing American Politics

Fixing American Politics: Solutions for the Media Age brings together original chapters from 34 noted scholars from two disciplines – political science and communication – asked to identify the most pressing problems facing the American people and how they can be solved. Authors address the questions succinctly and directly, with their favored solutions featured in chapter titles that exhort and inspire.

The book gives the reader much to think about and debate. Should news outlets be funded with public money rather than by private enterprise? Are the new social media a boon or a bane to political elections? Is the American past dead, or is it living once again? Do churchgoers and environmentalists have anything to discuss? Is the FCC doing its job? Can political ads be made less toxic? Should Fox News be "cancelled?" Should cancel cultures be cancelled? Can we become more civil to one another and, if so, how? *Fixing American Politics* poses all the best questions . . . and offers some concrete answers as well. This book is perfect for students, citizens, the media, and anyone concerned with contemporary challenges to civic life and discourse today.

Roderick P. Hart holds the Shivers Chair in Communication and is Professor of Government at the University of Texas at Austin, USA. He is also the founding director of the Annette Strauss Institute for Civic Life based in the Moody College of Communication where he was Dean from 2004–2015.

MEDIA and POWER

Media and Power
David L. Paletz, Series Editor

Media and Power is a series that publishes work uniting media studies with studies of power. This innovative and original series features books that challenge, even transcend, conventional disciplinary boundaries, construing both media and power in the broadest possible terms. At the same time, books in the series are designed to fit into several different types of college courses in political science, public policy, communication, journalism, media, history, film, sociology, anthropology, and cultural studies. Intended for the scholarly, text, and trade markets, the series should attract authors and inspire and provoke readers.

Published Books

Presidents and the Media
The Communicator in Chief
Stephen E. Frantzich

Star Power
American Democracy in the Age of the Celebrity Candidate
Lauren Wright

Politics, Journalism, and the Way Things Were
Martin Tolchin

The Political Voices of Generation Z
Laurie L. Rice and Kenneth W. Moffett

Fixing American Politics
Solutions for the Media Age
Edited by: Roderick P. Hart

Spectacle and Diversity
Transnational Media and Global Culture
Lee Artz

www.routledge.com/Media-and-Power/book-series/MP

Fixing American Politics
Solutions for the Media Age

Edited by Roderick P. Hart

NEW YORK AND LONDON

First published 2022
by Routledge
605 Third Avenue, New York, NY 10158

and by Routledge
2 Park Square, Milton Park, Abingdon, Oxon, OX14 4RN

Routledge is an imprint of the Taylor & Francis Group, an informa business

© 2022 Taylor & Francis

The right of Roderick P. Hart to be identified as the author of the editorial material, and of the authors for their individual chapters, has been asserted in accordance with sections 77 and 78 of the Copyright, Designs and Patents Act 1988.

All rights reserved. No part of this book may be reprinted or reproduced or utilised in any form or by any electronic, mechanical, or other means, now known or hereafter invented, including photocopying and recording, or in any information storage or retrieval system, without permission in writing from the publishers.

Trademark notice: Product or corporate names may be trademarks or registered trademarks, and are used only for identification and explanation without intent to infringe.

Library of Congress Cataloging-in-Publication Data
Names: Hart, Roderick P., editor of compilation.
Title: Fixing American politics : solutions for the media age / edited by Roderick P. Hart.
Description: First Edition. | New York : Routledge, 2022. | Series: Media and Power | Includes bibliographical references and index.
Identifiers: LCCN 2021024114 (print) | LCCN 2021024115 (ebook) | ISBN 9780367858230 (Paperback) | ISBN 9781032080109 (Hardback) | ISBN 9781003212515 (eBook)
Subjects: LCSH: United States—Politics and government—21st century. | Politics, Practical—United States. | Mass media and public opinion—United States.
Classification: LCC JK275 .F59 2022 (print) | LCC JK275 (ebook) | DDC 320.973—dc23
LC record available at https://lccn.loc.gov/2021024114
LC ebook record available at https://lccn.loc.gov/2021024115

ISBN: 978-1-032-08010-9 (hbk)
ISBN: 978-0-367-85823-0 (pbk)
ISBN: 978-1-003-21251-5 (ebk)

DOI: 10.4324/9781003212515

Typeset in Sabon
by Apex CoVantage, LLC

Contents

List of Tables	xi
List of Contributors	xii

Introduction	1
1 Make Politics Your Passion RODERICK P. HART	3

PART 1
Make History Functional	11
2 Let's Find a Usable Past JILL A. EDY	13
3 Understand Your Moment in Time DAVID A. CROCKETT	21
4 Heed the Prophetic Voice THEON E. HILL	29
5 Experiment With Playful Protest TIFFANY LEWIS	37

PART 2
Exploit Human Capacities	47
6 Let Consensus Overcome Polarization MARC C. HETHERINGTON	49

viii Contents

7 Use Emotion Wisely   56
   BETHANY ALBERTSON

8 Explore the Reasons for Incivility   64
   EMILY SYDNOR

9 Tell the Story of Poverty   73
   EUNJI KIM

10 Imagine New Political Coalitions   80
   VINCENT N. PHAM

PART 3
Open Your Mind   89

11 Listen to the First Amendment   91
   LISBETH A. LIPARI

12 Hear the Presidency Differently   100
   VANESSA BEASLEY

13 Fix the "Cancel Culture" Mentality   108
   SHAWN J. PARRY-GILES

14 Cultivate Empathy for Outgroups   117
   NICHOLAS A. VALENTINO

PART 4
Confront the Establishment   127

15 Counter a Reactive Media System   129
   DHAVAN SHAH, YINI ZHANG, JON PEVEHOUSE, AND SEBASTIÁN
   VALENZUELA

16 Create a Watchdog Branch of Government   137
   J. H. SNIDER

17 Modernize Health-Care Decision-Making   147
   AMY BUNGER

18 Give Election Apps More Integrity   153
    JESSICA BALDWIN-PHILIPPI

19 Shake Up the FCC   161
    BARTHOLOMEW H. SPARROW

PART 5
Upgrade Political Campaigns   173

20 Study the Electorate Thoroughly   175
    DARON R. SHAW

21 Talk About Voters Thoughtfully   185
    SHARON E. JARVIS

22 Vote When Voting Really Counts   193
    JOHN C. TEDESCO

23 Make Ads Safe for Democracy   201
    GLENN W. RICHARDSON JR

24 Let's Outperform Super PACs   209
    ROBERT KLOTZ

PART 6
Reimagine Traditional Journalism   217

25 Address Journalism's Crisis Boldly   219
    REGINA G. LAWRENCE

26 Measure Newsroom Effectiveness Differently   227
    NATALIE (TALIA) JOMINI STROUD AND YUJIN KIM

27 Publicly Subsidize Journalism   235
    DAVID M. RYFE

28 Report on Terrorism Responsibly   244
    SCOTT L. ALTHAUS

x *Contents*

29 Challenge Fox News   251
    JEFFREY P. JONES

Conclusion   261

30 Enliven Your Civic Capacities   263
    SUSAN NOLD

Index   275

Tables

20.1 Swing Voting in Presidential Elections, 2012–2016   181
24.1 Producers of Most-Viewed Senate Campaign Videos on YouTube   213

Contributors

Bethany Albertson is Associate Professor of Government at the University of Texas at Austin.

Scott L. Althaus is Merriam Professor of Political Science and Professor of Communication at the University of Illinois.

Jessica Baldwin-Philippi is Associate Professor of Communication and Media Studies at Fordham University.

Vanessa Beasley is Associate Professor of Communication Studies and Vice-Provost for Academic Affairs at Vanderbilt University.

Amy Bunger is Assistant Designated Institutional Official and Assistant Professor in the College of Medicine at the University of Cincinnati.

David A. Crockett is Professor of Political Science at Trinity University.

Jill A. Edy is Associate Professor of Communication at the University of Oklahoma.

Roderick P. Hart holds the Shivers Centennial Chair in Communication and is Professor of Government at the University of Texas at Austin.

Marc C. Hetherington is Raymond Dawson Distinguished Bicentennial Professor of Political Science at the University of North Carolina, Chapel Hill.

Theon E. Hill is Associate Professor of Communication at Wheaton College.

Sharon E. Jarvis is Professor of Communication Studies at the University of Texas at Austin.

Jeffrey P. Jones is Lambdin Kay Professor of Entertainment & Media Studies at the University of Georgia.

Eunji Kim is Assistant Professor of Political Science at Vanderbilt University.

Yujin Kim is a doctoral candidate in Communication Studies at the University of Texas at Austin.

Robert Klotz is Associate Professor of Political Science at the University of Southern Maine.

Regina G. Lawrence is Professor and Associate Dean of Journalism and Communication at the University of Oregon.

Tiffany Lewis is Assistant Professor of Public and International Affairs at Baruch College.

Lisbeth A. Lipari is Professor of Communication at Denison University.

Susan Nold is Senior Lecturer and Director of the Annette Strauss Institute for Civic Life at the University of Texas at Austin.

Shawn J. Parry-Giles is Professor of Communication at the University of Maryland.

Jon Pevehouse is Vilas Distinguished Professor of Political Science at the University of Wisconsin, Madison.

Vincent N. Pham is Associate Professor of Civic Communication and Media at Willamette University.

Glenn W. Richardson Jr. is Professor of Political Science at Kutztown University.

David M. Ryfe is Professor and Director of the School of Journalism and Mass Communication at the University of Iowa.

Dhavan Shah is Maier-Bascom Professor of Journalism and Mass Communication at the University of Wisconsin, Madison.

Daron R. Shaw holds the Frank C. Erwin, Jr. Chair of State Politics and is Professor of Government at the University of Texas at Austin.

J. H. Snider is President of iSolon.org.

Bartholomew H. Sparrow is Professor of Government at the University of Texas at Austin.

Natalie (Talia) Jomini Stroud is Professor of Communication Studies & Journalism at the University of Texas at Austin.

Emily Sydnor is Assistant Professor of Political Science at Southwestern University.

John C. Tedesco is Professor of Communication at Virginia Tech University.

Nicholas A. Valentino is Professor of Political Science and Professor of Communication Studies at the University of Michigan.

Sebastián Valenzuela is Associate Professor of Communications at Pontificia Universidad Católica de Chile.

Yini Zhang is Assistant Professor of Communication at the State University of New York at Buffalo.

Introduction

1 Make Politics Your Passion

Roderick P. Hart

This is a preposterous title for a book chapter. Who in their right mind would want to become passionate about politics? From time immemorial, politics has been the bane of human existence. People trying to help their fellow human beings, people like Moses, were chased across the desert by their Egyptian overlords. Jesus, too, reached out to the downtrodden, only to be killed in a ghastly manner by the Romans. In our own times, Father Ricardo Antonio Cortéz, seeking only to end violence in El Salvador, was dispatched for his meddling ways, a fate also suffered by Sister Lydie Oyanem Nzoughe for her work with poor people in Gabon (Guidos, 2021; Williams, 2020). Hold out a helping hand, some would say, and you will be crushed by a political establishment wanting to keep things just as they are.

Politics. The very word calls up a host of sins – graft, manipulation, double-dealing, expediency. There are worse things, too – agitation, revolution, bedlam, war. Some say that politics brings out the worst in us – our greed, our untrustworthiness, our lust for dominance. Politics attracts an entire class of undesirables, people who cannot live a quiet life but who must superimpose themselves on others, promising one thing today and another thing tomorrow and delivering on neither next week. Look at a politician's bank account, and you will find only ready cash. Long-term fiduciaries like Honesty, Trust, Dependability, and Responsibility are nowhere to be found. On its best days, politics is a trauma.

To make matters worse, politics never ends. All wars have been started by one kind of politician or another, some wearing priestly garb. As soon as one politician is defeated, another arises from the ashes. Surely, it was Satan himself who sired the political class, purchasing their souls at birth. When they were ready to run for office, their bodies had been primed for the task – a checkbook instead of a heart, eyes that could see only the bottom line, Silly Putty instead of a backbone. On Election Day, everyone wins – the winners take office and the losers become lobbyists. Some voters cheer, others are crestfallen, but either way, another election looms. You can kill hope and you can kill kindness, but you cannot kill political campaigns.

DOI: 10.4324/9781003212515-2

And yet . . . And yet . . . And yet we humans are wedded to politics, at least those among us with a memory. Politics has been part of every misadventure since Adam struck a sorry bargain with Eve, but it has also produced human marvels. Politics starts wars, but it also ends them, albeit too late. Politics and religion can be unhappy bedfellows, but they often navigate their ways to a common space. Diseases have plagued us since the beginning of time, but then politics enters the picture – working with private corporations to create vaccines, investing in health campaigns to encourage double-masking, tasking the National Guard to assist those waiting to be vaccinated. Politics gets ready for hurricanes each spring – its storm trackers issuing dire warnings, police escorting folks from low-lying areas, FEMA sending in heavy equipment to help with the cleanup. It is easy to hate politics until we hear the sound of sirens.

Politics is a big and brawny thing involving muscle and might. But politics is also a delicate thing that searches for middle ground between dueling antagonists. Should we end all abortions? Perhaps, but what about back-alley butchery? Should we ban all homeless encampments? Perhaps, but then where would the evicted go? Should we quadruple the cost of gasoline to save the ozone layer? No doubt, but then how would we get around, and who would give Johnny's dad a job? Politics is about war and pestilence, but it is also about something worse – compromise. Who can trust a politician who won't stand still? Why do politicians always settle for half a loaf of bread instead of delivering the whole thing? What is the exact distance between My Space and Your Space, and how long will it take to get from here to there? Compromise, a slithery creature.

Politics is also about time, something that none of us wants to waste. We are, for example, constantly hectored by the campaign calendar – presidents, senators, governors, mayors, the county commissioner. Will politics never stop? When speaking, will politicians never get to the point quickly? Will congressional debates never end? Must legislative decisions always be made at the last minute? Why does it take months – decades if you live in the Middle East – to sign a peace treaty? Patience, like compromise, is a dirty word, and politicians have more of it than most. Politics requires patience because the combatants so often detest one another. As a result, there's a lot of waiting around in politics.

This book is about politics and the problems it confronts. However, it is also a book about solutions. The book is based on two premises: (1) Politics is a terrible thing because (2) only politics can solve our most vexing problems. You and I can rant and rave about the government – about the injustice it ignores, about the tragedies it stumbles into – but it takes only a moment to realize that the only solution to bad politics is more politics. That brings us to another curiosity: Throughout human history, there has never been a shortage of politicians. Why? The cynical answer is that politics is about power, and everyone wants it. A less cynical answer is that some people, a small number perhaps, have both

Hope and Patience and one additional trait: Idealism. They believe that problems can be solved. These people are called politicians.

This book is about just such people – people with Hope, Patience, and Idealism. The authors of this book possess such traits as well. They have Hope and Patience in abundance, which is why they became teachers in the first place. Painful though it is, they are willing to wait and wait and wait until the lights go off in students' heads. But unlike many college professors who endlessly anguish about society's problems, this book's authors want to make things better.

Looking at the verbs in the titles of the forthcoming chapters tells you something about its authors (and about politics as well). Some of the verbs are actional – *build, make, heed, subsidize, fix, try*. Here we see the business side of politics, of getting practical things done for practical reasons. But other verbs are more cerebral – *study, create, find, imagine* – verbs showing that politics takes time to function effectively. Some verbs highlight the relational aspects of politics and thus the need to be patient – *hear, listen, cultivate, explore, care*. Yet other verbs – *experiment, modernize, challenge, counteract, shake up* – show that politics always involves risk, thus requiring courage. In short, the authors see politics as a necessary, even grand, tool for improving people's lives, but they also know it is imperfect. Before considering how politics can be fixed, then, let's consider why its imperfections seem so obvious.

Why Is It Easy to Hate Politics?

Politics will be central to your life, whether you like it or not. Politics will determine whether your student loans are paid, deferred, or canceled altogether. Politics will determine your personal income tax rate and whether your company of choice can afford to hire you. Politics will decide whether the economic climate is right for having kids, and politics will affect how your 401(k) performs. Politics will impinge on everything else as well: the traffic situation on your way to work, the kinds of people moving into your neighborhood, whether your garbage is picked up regularly. So politics will always be there, which leaves only two questions: (1) Will you make politics intellectually central to your life, and (2) will you make politics emotionally central as well? Only you can answer those questions.

Why is it so easy to dismiss politics? That is a short question requiring a long answer. Here is a sketchy one:

- **Substance.** People are afraid of earthquakes and rightly so. Earthquakes are rumbling monsters of death and destruction. They can be massive in scale, undermining entire cities and changing treasured topographies in a nanosecond. People detest earthquakes, but they do not shake their fists at them. Wildfires are a different story. Wildfires, too, cost lives and devastate communities, but they are quickly met with angry denunciations at the town meeting. Earthquakes get off scot-free, but wildfires take the heat: Why hadn't the brush fueling the fire been cleared away by the Department of Public Works? Why hadn't state officials read the impending signs of climate change and taken precautionary measures? Why did local officials let developers build subdivisions in an ecologically fragile area? Earthquakes versus wildfires. Innocence versus politics.

- **Performance.** There is much about politics that deserves our censure. Citizens send their hard-earned tax dollars to Washington, and then Washington goes bankrupt, requesting more money. Bridges fall down, income inequality soars, schools fail, farm subsidies prove insufficient, soldiers die in battle, and riots break out in the cities. There are currently 456 federal agencies in the nation's capital, and every one of them makes mistakes each day. All of these agencies say they would do better if they only had more money, but, like clockwork, we hear of under-the-table payoffs, lavish Washington offices, fancy trips abroad, and overpaid secretaries. Virtually every unsavory headline in every newspaper can be tracked to a faulty political decision. Or so it seems.
- **Personnel.** Whenever folks in the entertainment business get lazy, they make a show about politics: *The West Wing, The Wire, Parks and Recreation, The Good Wife, Veep, House of Cards, Madam Secretary.* How could Hollywood go wrong? Politics has all of the raw materials needed for great drama: overweening egos, constant clashes of opinion, questionable ethics, a supply of colorful hangers-on, a panoply of dark motives, and dramatic outbursts performed at high decibel levels. Although politics deals with the most important things in our lives – the kind of job we get, the safety of our neighborhoods – politicians consistently fail us. We are supposed to look up to our leaders, but all too often, we look down at them.
- **Coverage.** Politicians and journalists often detest one another, and some citizens say that is fine. Politicians dislike the press because reporters constantly embarrass them, asking hard questions about complex matters and demanding immediate answers. But the problem goes deeper: Reporters are poorly paid, while politicians eat at the best restaurants. That is enough to make reporters jealous, and it does. Reporters notice politicians' fancy cars, tailored suits, and swanky vacations. Politicians are envious in return: about how often journalists appear on television, journalists' hundred thousand Twitter followers, and journalists' ability to "choreograph" the news by using this video clip rather than that one. Politicians and reporters are a match made in hell.
- **Culture.** When describing Weimar Germany, Peter Sloterdijk (1987, p. 484) said, "the expectation of being deceived . . . had become a universal state of consciousness." Destitute and demoralized, the

German people had come to believe in nothing and, hence, could believe in one great thing – Adolph Hitler. Definitionally, cynicism is a belief in human frailty and institutional corruption, along with an overwhelming need to predict mass unhappiness (Hart, 1994). That sounds depressing, but popular culture nevertheless peddles cynicism avidly, resulting in the late-night TV formula: (1) Here's what the president did today; (2) he said he did it for these reasons, but we know he did it for those reasons; (3) so he's still the same old dissembler; (4) cue laugh track. Cynicism makes us feel good about ourselves (we're clever; we're cool) and feel bad about our leaders (they're corrupt; they're unworthy). Cynics are never wrong, but they are also never joyous.

- **Socialization.** Think about moving to a new town alone. Eventually, you meet one or two people and go for a drink. What do you discuss? The job, the local sports team, the latest on TikTok, the fate of Bitcoin, who's dating whom at the office. You do not talk about religion, of course, and you do not talk about politics given today's polarization. But that's only part of the story. You can, of course, talk about politics if you do so correctly: "They've done it to us again; they said they wouldn't, but they did; they'll do it again tomorrow; let's have another beer." This sort of (cynical) talk is always culturally available. Politics, with its inevitable disappointments and high-profile fights, contains all the raw ingredients needed for conversation. Talking about politics in these ways helps us fit in to almost any venue.

Trashing politics makes us feel contemporary, on the cutting edge. It becomes cultural coinage to be spent freely, helping us manage almost any social situation. But cynicism also has a cost. In fact, it has three costs: Hope, Patience, and Idealism. This book describes more than two dozen ways to stave off the sickening sweetness of cynicism. Its authors do not have all the answers, but each has at least one solution, and that's a start. They, too, are afraid of earthquakes, but they also think that wildfires can be whittled down to size. Hence this book.

Conclusion

Some of the solutions presented here are speculative, and some are quite practical, ready to be implemented immediately . . . if people would only listen. That might not happen tomorrow, so, being the Idealists they are, the authors are also Patient, willing to wait until the time is right. Mostly, though, the authors are Hopeful, convinced that politics is worthy of their most creative efforts.

Part 1 looks to the past to find a better future. Theon E. Hill points to some of the oldest voices in society – the prophets – noting that they still move among us and still have important things to say. David A. Crockett looks to the past as well but in a more strategic sense, arguing that leaders become lost when forgetting they are history's heirs. Press too hard or shrink from the fray? Both are errors but errors of a contrary sort. Tiffany Lewis takes us on an interesting trip to the early days of women's suffrage. Instead of finding prim and proper ladies, however, she finds outrageous women willing to shake things up via their colorful parades and delightful outspokenness. Above all, says Jill A. Edy, we must reap the past to sow the future, and that requires heeding the lessons of those who have gone before, especially those who were unheard when living among us.

Part 2 contains a set of eclectic chapters urging us to do things that are hard to do. Bethany Albertson, for example, tells us not to shrink from political emotions, especially when the stakes are high. We should treat emotion as both a bounty and an incentive, says Albertson, a sign that change is needed. Emily Sydnor agrees, noting that the incivility found in social media is often beneficial (and justifiable), a barometer of which issues need addressing and which social groups must be heard. From different vantage points, Marc C. Hetherington and Vincent N. Pham ask us to reach out to those who are different from us but who share our social space. It takes creativity to do so, says Pham, as when environmentalists and civil rights groups find common cause, or, as Hetherington notes, when environmentalists link arms with military leaders to change public attitudes about climate change. Finally, Eunji Kim urges us to "read against" popular entertainment when it ignores the dangerous economic inequality now stalking the United States.

Part 3 focuses on the cleavages of American society, cleavages of race, gender, class, and ethnicity, asking the simple question: Can we do better? Of course we can, says Vanessa Beasley, by demanding that the nation's leaders "call us together," which is to say, "call *all* of us together," a possibility that seemed to defy Donald Trump when he served as the nation's chief executive. We can "cancel" offending voices, says Shawn J. Parry-Giles, but that is foolish in a country distinguished by its massive size and brilliant diversity. Far better, she suggests, to risk being intimidated by new ideas, very few of which will strike us a fatal blow. Really listening to such voices, says Lisbeth A. Lipari, is what the First Amendment was all about – sounding-off freely, yes, but also granting sufferance to others. Until we stretch ourselves in these ways, says Nicholas A. Valentino, we will find it hard to make a nation that works, a nation that gathers in the promises of its founders.

Part 4 hunts the big game – the mass media, the health-care industry, the FCC, and government itself. With the proliferation of media outlets, says Dhavan Shah, it has become hard to know whom to trust, requiring that we build our own media menus. The Federal Communications Commission does not help much in that regard, says Bartholomew H. Sparrow, and so "news deserts" pop up, as conglomerates gobble alternative media properties. We may need to get radical in this touchy area, says

J. H. Snider, creating a federal watchdog agency to monitor government operations and reporting to its citizen-employers in a detailed annual audit. While we are at it, says Jessica Baldwin-Philippi, let's redesign our digital platforms to make campaigns fairer. Why not, she asks, impose transparency requirements on election apps to counteract the disinformation now proliferating? When in the redesigning mood, says Amy Bunger, let's not forget health care. Surely, we can find better ways of delivering medical information to the computer illiterate, a need amplified recently by the COVID-19 crisis.

Part 5 discusses how voter turnout in 2020 was both a blessing and a curse. The good news: People came to the polls in massive numbers. The bad news: They came angry as hornets. "That's because of super PAC videos," says Robert Klotz in Part 5. "That's because of toxic political ads," says Glen W. Richardson Jr. "That's because of misleading polling data," says Daron R. Shaw. Should we regulate such things or double-down on civic literacy training? If the former, what laws should be passed, and would they respect free speech rights? If the latter, who would provide the needed training, and would it be objective? However, let's not spend all our time on presidential elections, says John C. Tedesco. True, cable news, campaign debates, and talk radio grab our attention, but they also divert us from the local race for mayor and city council member. Sharon E. Jarvis agrees. "Going local" is important because everyday voters are so often ignored. Who shows up to vote? What do they really want from their government? What sorts of people ignore politics completely? There is a lot of misinformation about voters, says Jarvis, and we need to change that state of affairs.

Part 6 reimagines traditional journalism. The economic model supporting the news no longer works, says Regina G. Lawrence, with more and more reporters being laid off. One of Lawrence's suggestions is more hyperlocal reporting, getting news to people where they live. We must also operate on a larger scale, says David M. Ryfe, perhaps using public funds to subsidize news operations. Would that infringe on press objectivity? Would the founders roll over in their graves at such a thought? There are less revolutionary options, say Natalie (Talia) Jomini Stroud and Yujin Kim. Why not look at the news text itself? Expose focus groups to Story-type #1 vs. Story-type #2 and then see which they find most interesting, memorable, and informative. While we are at it, says Scott L. Althaus, let's examine reporting on terrorism, an arena in which reporters get emotionally caught up, inadvertently reinforcing terrorists' incentives for creating mass havoc. Terrorists are dangerous, Jeffrey P. Jones admits, but Fox News is worse. In fact, says Jones, Fox News is not news at all, or if it is, it is news that gives news a bad name. While all of these authors worry about different facets of journalism, they agree that all of us must become our own news curators, using every ounce of our brainpower to sift the wheat from the chaff.

Although this book focuses on solutions, it has no panaceas. Some of its ideas may be impractical. Others may disrupt democratic traditions. Still others may be too abstract or too hard to accomplish. But this is a book about American politics, and Americans, after all, have always been willing to try out new ideas . . . simply because they can. The experiments suggested here might not work as planned, but the experimenting must continue. It is this experimental mindset, this American mindset, that is most needed today. In an age of emotional overload, we need fresh ways of sorting things out. In an age surfeited with bad information, dangerous information, evil information, we must show up on Election Day as fit as possible. Carrying this book with you to the voting booth would make a grand statement, identifying you as an experimental citizen looking for answers.

Bibliography

Guidos, R. (2021, January 14). In clergy killings in El Salvador, a priest who knew them asks for justice. *The Tablet.* https://thetablet.org/clergy-killings-el-salvador-priests-justice/

Hart, R. P. (1994). *Seducing America: How television charms the modern voter.* New York: Oxford University Press.

Sloterdijk, P. (1987). *Critique of cynical reason* (M. Eldred, Trans.). Minneapolis: University of Minnesota Press.

Williams, T. D. (2020, March 24). African nun found brutally murdered in Gabon. *Breitbart News.* www.breitbart.com/africa/2020/03/24/african-nun-found-brutally-murdered-in-gabon/

Part 1
Make History Functional

2 Let's Find a Usable Past

Jill A. Edy

Polarization gets a lot of attention in discussions of how American politics has gone awry. We think of politics in terms of political parties, and we know that the United States' two parties have evolved into warring camps. But American politics isn't just polarized; it is also shattered (Edy & Meirick, 2019). Issues of identity have become central, and the struggle to be recognized and respected has fragmented the nation, each faction united by shared memories of unshared grievances. Lilliana Mason (2018) suggests that our factional identities are now subsumed by our partisan identities, creating this dilemma for American politics: We no longer recognize the ties that bind us together as a people.

To see how badly the nation has been shattered, one need only look at the turmoil over how to remember NBA basketball legend Kobe Bryant following his untimely death in a helicopter crash in January 2020. American sports culture has, in many respects, become the last bastion of popular culture in our fragmented media system, a place where, unlike politics, heroic achievement still seems possible. After Bryant's death, however, a struggle broke out. Should he be remembered as one of the greatest players of all time or as a man once accused of sexually assaulting a teenaged woman? Remembering his greatness makes you a misogynist. Remembering the sexual assault case makes you a racist. Twitter wars and death threats ensued, and a toxic politics of recognition overwhelmed the potential to find common ground in shared memory.

To fix American politics, we need a sense of ourselves as a people, and one way to attain that is to recognize our common past. Not only that, we must share that past publicly, celebrating the old-but-new ties that bind us together. Alas, none of this is easy.

The American Experiment

The problem of crafting common ground amid diversity is not a new problem. The liberal historian Henry Steele Commager once described the challenges of creating an American national identity when the United States became a political entity:

> The problem which confronted the new United States then was radically different from that which confronted, let us say, Belgium, Italy, Greece, or Germany in the nineteenth century, or Norway, Finland, Iceland, and Israel in the twentieth. These "new" states were already amply equipped with history, tradition, and memory . . . Of them it can be said that the nation was a product of history. But with the United States, history was rather a creation of the nation.
>
> (1965)

In other words, there was not much in the beginning of the nation that gave its inhabitants a sense of themselves as a people sharing common interests and a common fate. Other nations had a shared past, a collective memory, which proved foundational to cultural (Assmann, 2008; Halbwachs, 1992; Hobsbawm & Ranger, 1983) and national (Bodnar, 1992; Zerubavel, 1995) identity. The United States, lacking such traditions and already eminently diverse, had to invent its own history. Commager described how we did so, using popular and literary culture to forge a manufactured sense of who we were. Today, however, the literary canon Commager praised has itself been decried for its narrow view of the American experience, a view featuring the relentless progress of White men pursuing their Manifest Destiny.

It is reasonable to ask, of course, whether the nation really needs a shared identity or a sense of common cause. After all, American politics is founded on the ideals of John Locke, whose approach to democracy was grounded in his profound belief in individualism. Given how frequently nationalism has incited wars and genocides throughout the world, perhaps the United States was better off without such a belligerent and confining sense of itself. On the other hand, a nation without the sense of a shared past invites political conflict without limits, sacrifices legitimacy to power, encourages individualistic self-regard, and prioritizes personal interests over a common good. Such a lack of cohesion would be unsustainable, and it has already infected the nation's politics to an alarming degree. We still need what Commager called (1965) a "usable past," but both conservative and liberal versions of our national past have fundamental flaws that make them unsuitable for telling a cohesive national story. We will need to look elsewhere to find common ground.

The Case Against Conservative Nostalgia: The Limited Charms of the Past

Conservatism, by its nature, embraces the past, its traditions and ideals. In our current polarized politics, such traditionalism has been condemned as racist, sexist, homophobic, and altogether intolerant. Soft targets for such censure are defenders of the Confederate battle flag and supporters of monuments to Confederate leaders. As Erika Doss (2010) points out, it is a strange nation indeed that venerates a failed insurgency. Yet the critique is broader than that. Jill Lepore (2010) documents Tea Partiers' use of the American Revolution as a means of authenticating their political philosophy. She accuses them of "historical fundamentalism," of idealizing an entirely imaginary world of heroic White men and wishing that such a world, which in fact never existed, still reigned supreme. Lepore's critique gets at the heart of conservative nostalgia and its failings as a source of common ground.

Nostalgia is a longing for an idealized past that can never be recovered. By its nature, nostalgia recalls the joys and triumphs and forgets the sorrows and failures. Public memory grounded in conservative nostalgia aims at bringing people together in a patriotic embrace, a shared love of country. It raises monuments to great men and heroic deeds, with stories of freedom, justice, and progress. But nostalgia is also vulnerable to historical facts, to a record of sorrows and failures, to memories of justice delayed and freedom denied.

Conservative nostalgia works by telling some parts of the story and not others and, by so doing, erasing some citizens' experiences. Conservative nostalgia, for example, furthers the fiction that North America was uninhabited before the arrival of Europeans, brushing aside the paradox that the very same men who demanded freedom also profited by enslaving others. Not everyone longs to return to the past conservatives idealize. As Jill Lepore observes:

> In eighteenth-century America, I wouldn't have been able to vote. I wouldn't have been able to own property, either. I'd very likely have been unable to write, and, if I survived childhood, chances are that I'd have died in childbirth. And no matter how long or short my life, I'd almost certainly have died without having once ventured a political opinion preserved in any historical record.
>
> (2010, p. 124)

Because it is selective and idealized, conservative nostalgia denies the complexities and imperfections of social history in favor of fairy tales reinforcing traditional forms of civil order and legacy values.

Conservative nostalgia proposes a common ground in which we surrender our distinctive social identities, either by imagining ourselves as heroic White men of the past (in order to share in the glories of their deeds) or by conceding that we owe a shared debt to their heroism. For example, Doss (2010, p. 55) documents that in 2005, the landing page of the National Park Service's website for Mount Rushmore read in part: "The four presidents [George Washington, Thomas Jefferson, Abraham Lincoln, and Theodore Roosevelt] represent all Americans. They represent our courage, dreams, freedom and greatness." Subsuming our national identity in the carved features of four White men, three of whom were fabulously wealthy, is clearly a limited vision of national greatness.

Yet dismissing conservative nostalgia as barely repressed sexism and racism also oversimplifies things. While some conservatives may be nostalgic for a world in which women and people of color knew their place, this is not a necessary feature of conservative nostalgia. And the kind of past longed for by conservatives clearly had its charms, as did the wish to relive the joys of the past without reliving its sorrows. Nostalgia for your high school days does not mean that you wish to return to cafeteria lunches, oodles of homework and complexion problems, and borrowing your parents' car for the evening. Still, best friends, first dates, new freedoms, and finding your passion may well be moments you wish to live again.

Conservative nostalgia reminisces about a world that is ordered and predictable, where choices are validated by outcomes. Such a world can only be imaginary, of course, since its logic becomes clear only when the end of the story becomes known. But nostalgia is particularly useful when the world seems to be falling apart. Selective and idealized, conservative nostalgia recalls moments of national unity and shared sacrifice, moments that become clear only when details have been forgotten (Bodnar, 2010). Yet such imaginings may be necessary for creating the kind of imagined political community (Anderson, 1983) democracies need in order to function effectively. So conservative nostalgia has its benefits even though its shortcomings are obvious as well.

The Problem With Progressivism: The Overwhelming Burdens of History

The political left, whether liberal or progressive, tends to censure rather than glorify the past. Embracing reforms that address social inequity and marginalization, progressivism sees the past in terms of its injustices. Even though conservatives are normally thought to be the standard-bearers of individualism, when it comes to history and identity, it is the Left that celebrates individuals and their distinctiveness. Progressives are especially prone to articulating the unique historical experiences of distinct groups of Americans, often highlighting the terrible darkness of the nation's past. When concentrating heavily on marginalized groups, however, progressives preclude the possibility of finding common ground, of celebrating a shared sense of purpose for the nation writ large.

Examples abound. Struggles to memorialize both Franklin Roosevelt and Martin Luther King near the National Mall in Washington, D.C., have been marked by the politics of recognition. Disability advocates demanded that there be a depiction of Roosevelt in a wheelchair (something he himself assiduously avoided). Meanwhile, the appointment of a Chinese sculptor to render the statue of King at his memorial sparked impassioned debate over whether any artist who was not African American was capable of depicting the fabled civil rights leader (Doss, 2010). In California, an effort to produce more multicultural and inclusive history textbooks encompassing the diversity of the American experience foundered – not because conservatives deemed them unpatriotic but because various marginalized communities felt that not enough attention had been paid to their historical experiences. As a result, different regions of the state adopted different textbooks. Ironically, some school systems wound up adopting the old, White-dominated textbooks (or no textbooks at all) because they could not agree on newer, more progressive alternatives (Gitlin, 1995).

Other memory struggles have also pitted marginalized groups and their pasts against one another. Recognizing the nation's deep Hispanic roots, New Mexico erected a statue of 16th-century conquistador Juan de Onate, who brought European settlement to the area. Native Americans chopped a foot off the statue to protest Onate's vicious treatment of indigenous people (Doss, 2010). For groups such as these, the line between integration into a common national story and continued sublimation of their unique history has been razor thin.

Another challenge is that the stories of these group-centric pasts are framed in opposition to a cohesive, national story. In 2020, for example, the story of women's suffrage was frequently told as a nearly century-long struggle of women against the US government, hardly a story of national cohesion. Civil rights remembrances of other groups similarly distinguish them from the larger American public. The story of Japanese Americans interned by the US government during World War II is another example of setting the experiences of one group of Americans against the whole. Such narratives, by acknowledging a history of discrimination, paradoxically distance these groups from a larger and more cohesive national story.

The memory of grievance creates a dynamic of blame between groups, as well as unambiguous divisions within the public – "your story" cannot possibly be "my story." Such divisions are constructed on both the Right and the Left. Reece Peck (2017, p. 687) documents "how – in an effort to breed political dissensus – Fox News fashioned populist antagonisms to *unravel* the public's memory of the Great Depression" by highlighting class division instead of widespread hardship. In 2020, Oklahoma's senior US senator, Republican Jim Inhofe, ran campaign ads distinguishing "real Oklahomans" from those not part of that imagined community. Conservative values distinguished "us" from "not us." Whether originating on the left or the right, these group-based memories surely make the sharing of a common past difficult if not impossible.

Yet other progressive versions of the past simply invert conservative nostalgia, turning heroic White men into villains who commit genocide against indigenous people, participate in the enslavement of African

Americans, subjugate women, and are generally oblivious to the interests, concerns, and rights of others. While recalling the sorrows and losses of the past rather than its glories, such histories nonetheless grant agency to the same dominant group heralded by conservatives. In such a scenario, the rest of us become bit players, persons victimized by the Joker rather than saved by Batman.

In so many versions of national public memory, the dominant story remains fixated on the (mis)deeds of the few, yet asking citizens to share the burden of a blighted past and a legacy of injustice encourages many Americans to abandon the project completely. Some do so by identifying with the oppressed and by refusing to recognize that, in other contexts, the oppressed were indeed the oppressors. Others embracing a progressive agenda declare: Many in the past were racist, sexist, and homophobic but not me. Some must acknowledge their shame and change their ways but not me. Some are responsible for this legacy of shame but not me. And so the problem with the progressive alternative becomes obvious: The flight from a shameful past inevitably divides the public into two groups, with one claiming moral authority at the expense of the other. This is a hard way to make a nation truly national.

Conclusion

Under ideal circumstances, the contrast between liberal and conservative versions of the national past could generate productive tensions. The conservative vision of a triumphal past would be moderated by a liberal challenge to own up to the nation's legacies of injustice. The liberal tendency to highlight former wrongs would be tempered by the conservative recognition that the nation's truest legacy lies in its continuing willingness to redress the wrongs of the past. Unfortunately, such a symmetry of viewpoints has not yet been reached.

Two strands of scholarship suggest how we might navigate between these extremes. First, studies of online social activism repeatedly find that people commonly negotiate their own relationship to the larger movement organization (Bennett & Segerberg, 2013; Papacharissi, 2015), embracing *portions* of the movement's philosophy to make sense of their lives. Historians Roy Rosenzweig and David Thelen (2000) find that people do something analogous with American history, looking for parts of the national fabric that connect to their personal and family histories. Some contemporary designers of national memorials think similarly, creating works that help visitors find themselves in the past being depicted.

Applying this "patchwork" approach to national memory would feature a shared past but one that builds upon the personal histories of the national polity. In such a model, the national story would not be a unified narrative featuring the deeds of great men but an assemblage of individual stories building upon one another continually. Such a shared memory would balance the stories of famed decision-makers with the stories of those who lived the consequences of those decisions. This would be a dynamic and complicated past nicely suited to the dynamic and complicated nation it is meant to serve.

Second, studies of collective memory in an age of globalization have given rise to a concept of cosmopolitan memory (Levy & Sznaider, 2002), memory that travels across group boundaries, that features our shared humanity, and that adopts a moral perspective on the past. In such a national memory, empathy rather than blame would light our path, emphasizing our common values (as ideals but not always as lived realities) and our constant struggle to live out those values. Imagining ourselves in the circumstances of others does not negate the possibility of blame, but it does constrain the facile tendency to make our shared past the responsibility of others and not of ourselves. Such a public memory would respect but not be intimidated by the difficulties of assimilation and the subjugation of others. It would be a past featuring *identity* – "you are you and I am not you" – but a past that also leaves room for *empathy* – "I am human and hence can imagine your circumstances."

However we approach the problem of fixing American politics, restoring a sense of the national "us" must surely be our goal. The American problem is an old one, dating back to the nation's founding, but contemporary politics has moved it to the crisis stage. Seeing ourselves as a people with a shared past and a shared fate sustains us as a polity, setting limits on political conflict so that those who win elections can actually govern. Without it, there is little chance of recognizing a common good during moments when we must act together, as we saw during the 2020 pandemic. Fostering national public memory need not mean sacrificing one's identity to some inferior form of homogenized citizenship, but it does mean recognizing ourselves as part of a rich diversity of people whose common past cannot be denied but must constantly be reimagined.

Bibliography

Anderson, B. (1983). *Imagined communities: The origin and spread of nationalism*. London: Verso.

Assmann, J. (2008). Communicative and cultural memory. In A. Erll, A. Nunning, & S. B. Young (Eds.), *Cultural memory studies: An international and interdisciplinary handbook* (pp. 109–118). Berlin: Walter de Gruyter.

Bennett, W. L., & Segerberg, A. (2013). *The logic of connective action: Digital media and the personalization of contentious politics*. New York: Cambridge University Press.

Bodnar, J. (1992). *Remaking America: Public memory, commemoration, and patriotism in the twentieth century*. Princeton: Princeton University Press.

Bodnar, J. (2010). *The good war in American memory*. Baltimore, MD: Johns Hopkins University Press.

Commager, H. S. (1965). The search for a usable past. *American Heritage, 16*(2), 4–9. www.americanheritage.com/search-usable-past (accessed July 6, 2020).

Doss, E. (2010). *Memorial mania: Public feeling in America*. Chicago: University of Chicago Press.

Edy, J. A., & Meirick, P. C. (2019). *A nation fragmented: The public agenda in the information age*. Philadelphia: Temple University Press.

Gitlin, T. (1995). *The twilight of common dreams: Why America is wracked by culture wars*. New York: Metropolitan Books.

Halbwachs, M. (1992). *On collective memory* (L. Coser, Trans.). Chicago: University of Chicago Press.

Hobsbawm, E. J., & Ranger, T. O. (1983). *The invention of tradition*. New York: Cambridge University Press.

Lepore, J. (2010). *The whites of their eyes: The tea party's revolution and the battle over American history*. Princeton, NJ: Princeton University Press.

Levy, D., & Sznaider, N. (2002). Memory unbound: The Holocaust and the formation of cosmopolitan memory. *European Journal of Social Theory, 5*(1), 87–106. doi: 10.177/1368431002005001002

Mason, L. (2018). *Uncivil agreement: How politics became our identity*. Chicago: University of Chicago Press.

Papacharissi, Z. (2015). *Affective publics: Sentiment, technology and politics*. New York: Oxford University Press.

Peck, R. (2017). Usurping the usable past: How Fox News remembered the Great Depression during the Great Recession. *Journalism, 18*(6), 680–699. doi: 10.1177/1464884916636139

Rosenzweig, R., & Thelen, D. (2000). *The presence of the past: Popular uses of history in American life*. New York: Columbia University Press.

Zerubavel, Y. (1995). *Recovered roots: Collective memory and the making of Israeli national tradition*. Chicago: University of Chicago Press.

3 Understand Your Moment in Time

David A. Crockett

American politics is situated in a historical context that typically places significant constraints on the exercise of presidential leadership, particularly the office's agenda-setting function. Epoch-shaping trigger events such as economic collapses (the Great Depression) or constitutional crises (the Civil War) tend to advantage one political party over the other, giving the advantaged party a generation-long ability to define the parameters of political debate in its favor and thereby establish a new partisan regime. We can think of the advantaged party in this context as the "governing party" of the era and of the disadvantaged party as the "opposition party." In a separation of powers system, as opposed to a parliamentary one, it is possible for the opposition party to win the presidency, but absent a trigger capable of establishing a new regime, the opposition-party president is unable to steer politics in a new direction. In such circumstances, the governing party retains definitional control and, when its candidate recaptures the White House, the new president restores the governing-party agenda to its dominant place (Crockett, 2002). As we will see in this chapter, understanding one's moment in time, knowing what history permits, often spells success during such changeful political moments.

Viewing American politics from this perspective lets us assign presidents to different categories, which helps us understand when politics can change and when it cannot. *Regime builders* are those presidents who repudiate a vulnerable and collapsing tradition and that establish a new era of politics – Andrew Jackson, Abraham Lincoln, Franklin Roosevelt, Ronald Reagan. *Regime managers* follow the regime builders and attempt to adapt the new orthodoxy to changing times – Martin Van Buren, Ulysses Grant, Harry Truman, George H.W. Bush. Sometimes the opposition party captures control of the presidency, sending the governing party into metaphorical exile, even though it remains relatively robust. *Opposition presidents* like William Henry Harrison, Grover Cleveland, Dwight Eisenhower, and Bill Clinton would be included in this latter grouping. But the governing party always comes back from exile to recapture control of the White House, with *restoration presidents*

DOI: 10.4324/9781003212515-5

working to restore the old orthodoxy to what they believe is its rightful place – James K. Polk, Benjamin Harrison, John F. Kennedy, and George W. Bush (Skowronek, 1993; Crockett, 2012).

This four-part taxonomy is hardly exhaustive, and each era adds its own complications to the nation's political story. But this account also puts the lie to the notion that all presidencies are created equal or with an equal opportunity to accomplish their agendas. In fact, presidents do not come to power on level playing fields. The regime builders have the greatest flexibility to leverage their position in what Stephen Skowronek calls "political time" to redefine American politics. The regime managers are forced to operate in the shadow of the regime builder, heavily constrained by the new orthodoxy. Opposition presidents *desire* to move in their own direction but are constrained to play by the rules established by the regime builder, while restoration presidents work excessively hard when returning from exile to restore the governing party's agenda to its proper place.

In short, a president's agenda-setting efforts are necessarily situated in this larger context of political time, a context that remains outside of the leader's control. In order to be successful, however success is defined, the president must be "stubbornly realistic" and "reflective" in understanding his position in the larger government (Jones, 1994, p. 294). Indeed, the central task of the president is to understand what is possible given the constraints of his historical context (Hargrove & Nelson, 1984, p. 78). Some presidents learn this lesson and some do not.

The Problem: Misreading Context

Unfortunately, presidents all too often fail to understand their constraints. It is probably natural, after having won the biggest prize in American politics, to think that you have a mandate to begin the world anew, to recreate politics on your terms – to be a regime builder. A president's ambition typically is not to go down in history as simply a "capable manager of the regime." Presidents often overinterpret the election results, leading to policy overreach and eventual backlash from voters and members of Congress. Political scientist George Edwards has written two books chronicling the presidencies of George W. Bush and Barack Obama. In both cases, these very different presidents sought transformational policy change without being situated in the needed transformational context, leading to a loss of control of Congress and to a diminished agenda-setting capacity (Edwards, 2007; Edwards, 2012).

In today's political climate of partisan polarization, the consequences of this repeated failure are higher than ever. The sorting of liberals and conservatives in the electorate into their partisan homes has made the two major parties more ideologically consistent and homogeneous. These divisions intensify the conflict at the worldview level, with diverse policy areas like economic welfare, foreign affairs, civil rights, and cultural values collapsing into single-issue alignments. The issues then become nationalized, and the result is a level of polarization not seen since just after the Civil War.

To make matters worse, we know that voters' perceptions are heavily influenced by these partisan perspectives. Republicans, toward the end of the Obama presidency, for example, thought that things were horrible, while Democrats remained relatively positive about life in the United States. With the election of Donald Trump, however, these perspectives reversed themselves, even before Trump accomplished something (Abramowitz &Saunders, 1998; Hetherington, 2001; Hunter, 1991; Shafer, 2016; Campbell, 2016).

As the political parties grow further apart, it becomes increasingly difficult to forge agreements about the facts on the ground or how to respond to the crises of the day. The room for compromise disappears as people see one another not as mere political opponents but as enemies who are dangerous to the republic. We have long known that there is an "expectations gap" in the American presidency, a gap between promise and fulfillment (Lowi, 1985; Tulis, 1987; Waterman et al., 2016). That gap widens during a period of increasing polarization. That is, as each new president gets elected, his co-partisans expect him to be the second coming of Franklin Roosevelt (if a Democrat) or Ronald Reagan (if a Republican). Each new president is expected to have the power to vanquish his foes and reset the political universe on the right track – to be another regime builder. Their fraught efforts to do so then increase polarization, and their resulting failures increase citizen disappointment. In this account, polarization exacerbates the tendency of presidents to misunderstand their historical context, which, in turn, exacerbates the failure that comes from being misled.

Misreading one's historical context is not a recent phenomenon. Whig victory in 1840 prompted Henry Clay to overinterpret the election results and plan a grand repudiation of the Jacksonian governing philosophy. The premature death of William Henry Harrison and elevation of closet-Democrat John Tyler to the presidency foiled Clay's plans. When James K. Polk recaptured the presidency for Democrats in 1844, he proceeded to vigorously pursue the completion of the Jacksonian revolution, leading to his party's defeat in 1848. Franklin Pierce's similar restoration to power of the Democratic Party in 1852 encouraged him to reset the political universe on the slavery question. The result was popular sovereignty, the Kansas-Nebraska Act, and a hastening of the secession crisis.

In parallel fashion, opposition president Grover Cleveland sought to repudiate the reigning Republican Party in 1888 by making the tariff a central theme of his reelection campaign. His defeat encouraged the victorious Republicans to pursue their entire ambitious agenda, leading to one of the most disastrous midterm election defeats in American history – and loss of the White House two years later. We can see a similar dynamic at play in the presidency of Woodrow Wilson, followed by the "return to normalcy" under Warren G. Harding, which ended with the GOP's repudiation in the Great Depression (Crockett, 2012, 2019).

Contemporary Manifestations

The historical pattern described already persists in our own era. The opposition president-to-restoration president pattern has been repeated twice in the Reagan era – four presidencies comprising 28 years (thus far). Each president misread his context, contributing to and then dramatically increasing polarization.

Clinton-Bush

Bill Clinton came to office in the wake of a 12-year period during which Reagan and Bush established the contours of a conservative era. Clinton ran for office as a moderate Southern governor, a member of the "New Democrat" faction of the party that consciously sought to reorient the party in a more centrist direction to account for the reality of life in a more conservative era. When he entered office, however, Clinton seemingly forgot that context and chose to wage a frontal assault on Reagan conservatism. His goal was to reverse and undo the previous 12 years, to establish a new regime. Early executive orders on abortion and personnel decisions focused on identity politics sent a threatening message to social conservatives, as did his attempt to reverse the military's ban on homosexuals. His economic plan, which included public-works spending and tax increases, were also clearly contrary to the Reagan doctrine.

Most important, Clinton's effort to enact universal health care, complete with homages to FDR and Social Security, as well as a veto threat, signaled to conservatives of all stripes that it was time for all-hands-on-deck in opposition. As a result, a juggernaut arose to bury Clinton's plan without a vote. Although Clinton's presidency survived this early overreaching, his larger plan was never realized, with Clinton shifting toward the center for political survival and being compelled to govern very much as a moderate Republican for the remaining six years of his presidency. Clinton's early misreading of his context earned him the implacable opposition of the governing party, leading eventually to his impeachment (Crockett, 2002, pp. 175–200).

In turn, George W. Bush promised "to restore honor and dignity to the White House" – in other words, to restore the Reagan agenda as the driving force in American politics. Despite the exceptionally narrow margin of his election victory, Bush governed as though he had a mandate. He used executive orders to restore Reagan-era policies on abortion, appealed to social conservatives by establishing a White House Office of

Faith-Based and Community Initiatives, and banned federal funding of future embryonic stem-cell research.

Suddenly, though, the terrorist attacks of September 11, 2001, altered the national security stance of Bush's administration. Reagan's "evil empire" quickly became the "axis of evil," leading to military campaigns in both Afghanistan and Iraq. After winning another very narrow victory in 2004, Bush declared that he had "earned capital in the campaign, political capital. And now I intend to spend it." Successes on free trade and Supreme Court vacancies were low-hanging fruit on that agenda, but his effort to transform the Social Security system by introducing personal accounts – a conservative ambition that predated the Reagan presidency – ran into a buzz saw of opposition and went nowhere.

Similarly, his intervention in the tragic case of Terri Schiavo, a Florida woman who had lived in a vegetative state for 15 years, appealed to some religious conservatives but struck most of the public as inappropriate meddling in a private family affair. Bush's policy overreach was compounded by perceptions of incompetence when he failed to respond with alacrity to the devastation wrought by Hurricane Katrina or to bring the wars in the Middle East to a successful conclusion. With the financial crisis of 2008, Republican candidate John McCain felt compelled to run against his own party and president, declaring, "Change is coming!" This second attempt to enact Reagan 2.0 ended in failure (Baker, 2013).

Obama-Trump

Barack Obama entered the presidency in 2009, promising "change we can believe in" and marketing himself as a transformational leader who would alter the trajectory of American politics and become another regime builder. Following Bush, a man who had become the most polarizing president in the modern era, Obama inherited an economic crisis and two lingering wars in the Middle East. He also had a goal to enact universal health-care reform, with a 60-seat Senate majority to help him. Despite these advantages, Obama had trouble crafting an ideal bill. His efforts generated unprecedented levels of party-line voting in Congress, and he lost his filibuster-proof Senate majority in January 2010 when Republican Scott Brown won a special election to take the seat occupied by the late Edward Kennedy. Clever parliamentary maneuvering squeezed out a partisan victory on health care, but the measure remained unpopular with the public and cost Obama the House in the midterm election of 2010. He spent the next six years struggling with a divided government (Edwards, 2012).

Needless to say, the next president failed to learn Obama's lesson. Donald Trump came to power promising to "make America great again." His slogan served as a reminder of Reagan, even as he rhetorically distanced himself from over a dozen Reagan heirs to claim the nomination. His populist presidential campaign represented an effort to align the party with his image, redefining the Reagan era in the process. In many ways, from tax cuts to deregulation to court nominations, Trump governed as a conventional conservative Republican. His style, however, was too transgressive to gain the popular support needed to establish a new era. For all his efforts to reshape and redefine American politics, Trump never enjoyed a positive approval rating, ultimately becoming the most polarizing president of the modern era (Herbert et al., 2019), a distinction that led to his defeat in 2020.

Conclusion

Given the consistency of the historical patterns described here, one might well wonder whether there is a way out of history's trap. Perhaps the combination of political time and presidential psychology is too difficult a nut to crack. There is, however, at least one example of presidential pairing that serves as a counterbalance to this grim history – two presidents who were unusually attuned to the constraints of their presidencies – Dwight Eisenhower and John F. Kennedy.

Eisenhower was the first opposition president in the New Deal era. Personally conservative on domestic issues, he desired to "unseat the New Deal-Fair Deal bureaucracy in Washington." However, he was also quite aware of his party's disadvantaged status in the New Deal era. Despite an electoral victory that brought him unified government in Congress, Eisenhower understood that the New Deal had become a permanent part of the American system and that any attempt by Republicans to abolish popular programs like Social Security would be foolhardy. Accordingly, Eisenhower consciously moderated his political agenda to avoid a frontal assault on the New Deal order, pursuing instead a more tempered agenda.

Eisenhower consistently resisted, for example, congressional Republicans' efforts to reverse the basic foreign policy commitments inherited from Roosevelt and Truman. Instead of attempting to rescind the New Deal, Eisenhower focused on fiscal and budget politics. He saw his pursuit of balanced budgets in national security terms, and his fiscal restraint tempered the growth of the New Deal system, even as he expanded Social Security coverage, raised the minimum wage and unemployment benefits, and supported construction of the Saint Lawrence Seaway. When Republicans lost control of Congress in 1954, Eisenhower emphasized his non-partisan image, meeting regularly with Democratic House Speaker Sam Rayburn and Senate Majority Leader Lyndon Johnson to pursue a constructive policy agenda.

In short, Eisenhower remained aware throughout his presidency of the limitations of his historical context. The combination of budget politics, use of his veto, and above-the-fray personal style enabled him to manage capably and successfully a presidency that ran in opposition to the dominant forces of the times. He understood that changing the trajectory of American politics was not possible for him, and that recognition allowed him to remain effective throughout his two terms. Making no attempt at regime building, his deliberate pursuit of "hidden-hand leadership" and his more tempered agenda and style frustrated his allies, who wanted him to aggressively attack the New Deal. This approach also frustrated his opponents, who longed for advancement along more progressive lines (Greenstein, 1982; Crockett, 2002, pp. 130–150).

Democrats got their chance to restore the New Deal agenda with the election of John F. Kennedy in 1960. His promise to "get the country moving again" was a clear reference to the pre-Eisenhower world of Roosevelt and Truman, promising to catch up after being in exile for eight years. Kennedy, however, won one of the narrowest popular-vote victories in American history, and his party lost ground in both chambers of Congress upon his election. Instead of claiming a mandate for change, Kennedy remained particularly attuned to the narrowness of his victory (he even carried a piece of paper on his person detailing his thin margin). Kennedy also remained cautious on domestic and economic policy and, after being burned in the Bay of Pigs fiasco, on national security policy as well.

Kennedy was especially ambivalent in the area of civil rights, where his good intentions collided with a pragmatic assessment of his political capital. Kennedy acted when confronted with televised evidence of injustice but looked forward to the 1964 campaign, which he hoped would allow him to alter his strategic calculations. Throughout his time in office, Kennedy avoided pushing too far too fast, making him a source of frustration for those in his party desiring a more aggressive approach. They got their wish, however, when Lyndon Johnson took over following Kennedy's assassination. Putting the New Deal on steroids, Johnson overreached both at home and abroad, paving the way for Richard Nixon in 1968. Kennedy's self-awareness of his constraints proved to be the safer route (Dallek, 2003; Giglio, 2006).

Both Eisenhower and Kennedy were unusually aware of the constraints of their presidencies, of the dynamics of political time, and of the easy temptation to misread election results. Both men remained aware of this dynamic and adjusted accordingly. They did not attempt transformational policy change in the absence of a transformational context. Too, neither could be thought of as particularly polarizing. If more presidents ignored the desire to pursue regime building when it cannot be done, perhaps the political class as a whole would follow along and tamp down the tendency to overpromise.

At the same time, if the electorate became more aware of the constraints of history, perhaps it would adjust its expectations of presidential performance. By itself, an awareness of the constraints of history might not reverse polarization, but lowering the expectations of the electorate and tempering the ambitions of presidents and their parties would be good first steps. At least during his first few months in office, that is exactly what Joe Biden seemed to understand. History, that is, had become his teacher. Only time will tell if Mr. Biden can pass history's test.

Bibliography

Abramowitz, A. I., & Saunders, K. L. (1998, August). Ideological realignment in the U.S. electorate. *Journal of Politics, 60*(3), 634–652.

Baker, P. (2013). *Days of fire: Bush and Cheney in the White House.* New York: Anchor Books.

Campbell, J. E. (2016). *Polarized: Making sense of a divided America.* Princeton, NJ: Princeton University Press.

Crockett, D. A. (2002). *The opposition presidency: Leadership and the constraints of history.* College Station, TX: Texas A&M University Press.

Crockett, D. A. (2012, December). The perils of restoration politics: Nineteenth-century antecedents. *Presidential Studies Quarterly, 42,* 881–902.

Crockett, D. A. (2019, June). The road not taken: Warren G. Harding and the dilemmas of regime restoration. *Presidential Studies Quarterly, 49,* 417–431.

Dallek, R. (2003). *An unfinished life: John F. Kennedy, 1917–1963.* Boston: Little, Brown and Company.

Edwards, G. C., III. (2007). *Governing by campaigning: The politics of the Bush presidency.* New York: Pearson.

Edwards, G. C., III. (2012). *Overreach: Leadership in the Obama presidency.* Princeton, NJ: Princeton University Press.

Giglio, J. N. (2006). *The presidency of John F. Kennedy* (2nd, rev. ed.). Lawrence, KS: University Press of Kansas.

Greenstein, F. I. (1982). *The hidden-hand presidency: Eisenhower as leader.* New York: Basic Books.

Hargrove, E. C., & Nelson, M. (1984). *Presidents, politics, and policy.* New York: Knopf.

Herbert, J., McCrisken, T., & Wroe, A. (2019). *The ordinary presidency of Donald J. Trump.* London: Palgrave Macmillan.

Hetherington, M. J. (2001, September). Resurgent mass partisanship: The role of elite polarization. *American Political Science Review, 95*(3), 619–631.

Hunter, J. D. (1991). *Culture wars: The struggle to define America.* Basic Books.

Jones, C. (1994). *The presidency in a separated system.* Washington, DC: Brookings.

Lowi, T. J. (1985). *The personal president: Power invested, promise unfulfilled.* Ithaca, NY: Cornell University Press.

Shafer, B. E. (2016). *The American political pattern: Stability and change, 1932–2016.* Lawrence, KS: University Press of Kansas.

Skowronek, S. (1993). *The politics presidents make: Leadership from John Adams to George Bush.* Cambridge, MA: Belknap.

Tulis, J. K. (1987). *The rhetorical presidency.* Princeton, NJ: Princeton University Press.

Waterman, R., Silva, C. L., & Jenkins-Smith, H. (2016). *The presidential expectations gap: Public attitudes concerning the presidency.* Ann Arbor, MI: University of Michigan Press.

4 Heed the Prophetic Voice

Theon E. Hill

On March 23, 2017, the *Time* magazine cover story asked readers a simple question: "Is Truth Dead?" (Pine, 2017). President Trump's functional relationship with the truth clearly motivated this question. As *Time* editor Nancy Gibbs (2017) observed, "many would say they believe in Truth, and yet we find ourselves having an intense debate over its role and power in the face of a President who treats it like a toy." Indeed, the 45th president of the United States displayed a remarkable disregard of facts, repeatedly misleading the public about his policies, finances, and legislative victories.

To be sure, politicians normalized political deception long before Donald Trump entered politics. Bill Clinton swore that he did not touch Monica Lewinsky. Ronald Reagan denied exchanging weapons for hostages in the Iran-Contra scandal. Richard Nixon refused to acknowledge US interference in the 1971 Chilean elections (Moyers, 2014). As Hannah Arendt (1967) once observed, "No one has ever doubted that truth and politics are on rather bad terms with each other, and no one, as far as I know, has ever counted truthfulness among the political virtues."

In this chapter, I am not primarily concerned with politicians' loose relationship with the facts or with the advent of what some have called a "post-truth" society.[1] Instead, my focus lies with the impact of these developments on the prospects of prophetic rhetoric within the public sphere. America's democratic experiment lies in a state of crisis, I argue. The disproportionate influence of corporate elites, dominance of neoliberal economics, and commitment to voter suppression testify to its fragility. I also agree with Jeremy Engels's (2015, p. 7) assessment that "contemporary democracy in the United States is on life support."

Fixing American politics requires us to heed the prophetic voices that emerge during moments of crisis and decay and that call society back to values that have been lost, discarded, or forgotten. But what does it mean to articulate a prophetic voice when the very foundation of prophecy has been called into question? That is, the prophetic voice necessarily assumes shared values or community. For example, when Martin Luther

DOI: 10.4324/9781003212515-6

King, Jr. (1986, p. 282) delivered his famous, "I've been to the mountaintop" address, he grounded his rhetorical appeal in just such values:

> If I lived in China or even Russia, or any totalitarian country, maybe I could understand the denial of certain basic First Amendment privileges, because they hadn't committed themselves to that over there. But somewhere I read of the freedom of assembly. Somewhere I read of the freedom of speech. Somewhere I read of the freedom of the press. Somewhere I read that the greatness of America is the right to protest for right.

Shared values, in short, inform prophetic appeals. As rhetorical scholar James Darsey (1999, p. 200) has noted, "radicalism is . . . that which involves the roots of a culture." On what foundation does the prophetic word rest at a moment when "facts" are met with "alternative facts?" What does speaking truth to power look like when society fails to agree on a method for determining truth? If American politics are to be "fixed," then prophetic voices must play an essential role in helping citizens rediscover what it means to live in a genuine community.

To answer these questions, I turn to the experiences of oppressed and marginalized populations because they offer profound insight into the rhetorical challenges of a posttruth society. The lack of shared values and a detachment from community is familiar to African Americans who have consistently found themselves on the receiving end of the vicious legacy of White supremacy. That legacy has forced African Americans to discover ways of articulating a prophetic voice at times when they could not assume shared values with their target audience. For example, in the past, US leaders consistently defended the institution of slavery with false assertions about indentured workers' intellectual inferiority. Frederick Douglass (1852), speaking into this society, exposed the irony of such claims. He questioned why a nation so convinced of a slave's intellectual inferiority felt the need to pass laws forbidding White Americans from teaching slaves to read. He demonstrated the unique ability to speak prophetically at a time when fierce divisions separated people on the question of slavery.

The Black prophetic tradition offers rhetorical lessons in how to articulate a prophetic voice in a moment when shared values cannot be assumed. To spotlight these lessons, I will first detail the rhetorical commitments of the prophetic tradition and then briefly examine three representative historical figures who illustrate how prophetic voices might speak to our current moment. I will conclude by highlighting some of the limitations of prophetic rhetoric as a tool for social change.

The Prophet Speaks Truth to Power

In the face of injustice, prophetic voices like Frederick Douglass, Maria Stewart, Susan B. Anthony, Wong Chin Foo, Ida B. Wells-Barnett, Martin

Luther King, Jr., and Cesar Chavez attempted to shake the nation out of its apathy and steer it toward justice. In a circular fashion, prophecy assumes and depends on the existence of a community capable of receiving the prophetic word. Prophetic voices speak truth to power as a means of evoking an "alternative consciousness" to the status quo (Brueggemann, 2001). In a society riddled with injustice, prophets offer new ways of imagining communal life. As a rhetorical tradition, prophecy owes its inception to the Hebrew prophets of the Old Testament who proclaimed God's word to the people (Darsey, 1999, pp. 15–34). Despite its sacred origins, prophecy is not limited to religious contexts. As historian David Chappell (2005, p. 3) notes, "an atheist might take a prophetic stance more readily and faithfully than a typical twentieth-century Christian."

The prophetic voice comes in both conservative and progressive modes. It is conservative in the sense that it calls people back to a set of shared values (Darsey, 1999, p. 18). However, it also functions in a progressive manner by disrupting and displacing hegemonic interpretations of shared values, with prophets often attempting to awaken a sense of injustice at the status quo (Heschel, 2010, p. 204). In his work on "true believers," Roderick P. Hart (1971, p. 252) argues that their "rhetorical economy is made possible by a shared doctrine." Similarly, shared values serve as the source material from which prophetic rhetoric draws. In the Old Testament, the Mosaic Law provided these shared values, while contemporary prophets rely on civic values like freedom, justice, and equality.[2] The rhetorical power of the prophetic voice lies in its inversion of the Greco-Roman tradition (Darsey, 1999, p. 7). Unlike the audience-centric rhetorical philosophy of that tradition, the prophet focuses on fidelity to their own personal message. This speaker-centered commitment accounts for the unbridled condemnations that often define prophetic rhetoric.

Political polarization erodes community, destabilizing the sense of shared values on which prophetic rhetoric depends. Accordingly, my concern lies not in lost faith but in social fragmentation. The definitions attributed to terms like "justice," "freedom," and "equality" vary widely from community to community. As racial unrest swept throughout the nation during the summer of 2020, for example, divergent responses to the senseless killings of Breonna Taylor, George Floyd, and Ahmaud Arbery revealed the depths of social disunity in the United States. During a #BlackLivesMatter march in New Jersey, for example, a diverse group of protestors was met by White counter-protestors who mockingly reenacted Floyd's death while shouting, "This is what happens when you don't comply with the cops!" (Bella, 2020).

Justice was central to the claims of both groups, but their understandings of what justice meant could not have been further apart. Both groups witnessed the same video footage of Officer Derek Chauvin kneeling on George Floyd's neck for 8 minutes and 46 seconds, yet their assessment of the situation differed drastically. One group saw injustice, while the other celebrated the triumph of law and order. The ideological differences of these groups raise important questions about the role of prophets in a historical moment when the concept of shared values is tenuous at best.

The Prophetic Revelation of Injustice

Prophets look for opportunities to force society to change. As Rabbi Abraham Joshua Heschel (2010, p. 7) argued, "Instead of showing us a way through the elegant mansions of the mind, the prophets take us to the slums." In 1955, Mamie Till-Bradley forced America to consider the horrific nature of Southern racism after the brutal lynching of her 14-year-old son, Emmett Till. White men killed her son after he allegedly made romantic advances toward a White woman at a local convenience store in Mississippi while he was visiting family members. Mamie Till-Bradley, a Chicago resident, brought her son's body back to Chicago for the funeral. City officials pleaded with her to hold a closed-casket service due to the disfigurement of her son's body, including his head, which had swollen to four times its natural size. Till-Bradley steadfastly refused, declaring, "Let the people see what they did to my boy" (Tyson, 2017). Till's brutal murder attracted national attention, with news outlets, including the *Chicago Defender, Pittsburgh Courier, Jet* magazine, and the NAACP's *Crisis*, featuring photos of Till's disfigured body. Mamie Till-Bradley recognized that silence perpetuates injustice and used the tragedy of her son's death to disrupt the normalcy of violence against Black bodies.

Mamie Till-Bradley's decision to hold an open-casket funeral for her son exposed the gap between America's self-image and its racial realties. As part of her antilynching campaign, Ida B. Wells-Barnett documented the tendency of White supremacists to justify acts of domestic terrorism with false assertions of Black criminality, especially interracial rape. Both Mamie Till-Bradley and Ida B. Wells-Barnett illustrate the power that prophetic voices hold to expose pervasive forms of injustice in a manner that pierces through the cultural apathy, apathy that sustains the status quo.

Even as I write, 545 children remain separated from their loved ones in the wake of the Trump administration's disastrous family separation policy on the southern border (Dickerson, 2020, October 21). Countless other children have been deported alone to countries other than their place of origin (Dickerson, 2020, November 3). Undocumented immigrants face the hypocrisy of a country that refuses to offer them a pathway to citizenship even as it designates them as essential workers in the face of a global pandemic (Villa, 2020). In the face of these crimes against humanity, it is the responsibility of prophets, in the words of W. E. B. Du Bois (1986, p. 1158), to raise their voices to "make this world so damned uncomfortable with its nasty burden of evil that it tries to get good and does get better."

The Prophetic Scope of Justice

Prophets challenge a society to expand its concern for justice. Histories of the civil rights movement often obscure or minimize the profound contributions of Bayard Rustin (Morgan, 2018). Ignored by history due to his sexual orientation, Rustin served as a brilliant tactician, organizer, and writer, even introducing Dr. King to the philosophy of nonviolence. As a prophetic voice, Rustin distinguished himself by his commitment to fight injustice wherever and against whomever it occurred. He embodied the Kingian philosophy that "injustice anywhere is a threat to justice everywhere" (King, 1963, p. 290). He fought for the rights of labor unions, colonized peoples, and Japanese Americans imprisoned during World War II. This broad focus enabled Rustin to see the connections between oppressed populations. He also worked with the famous civil rights and labor leader A. Philip Randolph to develop the "Freedom Budget for All," an attempt to respond to the specific forms of injustice in society in a manner that would serve all people (Randolph & Rustin, 1967).

Rustin (1965) believed that the future of American politics as a catalyst for justice depended on people learning to see the interconnectedness of their struggles for equality. Today, when nationalist and isolationist ideologies threaten the fabric of contemporary society, Rustin's career challenges us to expand our concern for justice beyond our social affiliation or conventional markers of identity. The Reverend William Barber (2018) models this universal concern today. As a contemporary prophet, he has spoken out about poverty, anti-Black racism, Native American land rights, organized labor, undocumented immigrants, and anti-Asian racism in the wake of the pandemic.

The Prophetic Imagination and Justice

Prophets push society to reimagine the foundations on which its sense of community is based as a means of permitting a new, more just society to emerge. As theologian Walter Brueggemann (2001, p. 3) wrote, "The task of prophetic ministry is to nurture, nourish, and evoke a consciousness and perception alternative to the consciousness and perception of the dominant culture around us." Imagination helps to concretize the prophet's vision of the desired change.

At the March on Washington in 1963, Dr. King appealed to US citizens based on shared, communal values as located in the Declaration of Independence, the US Constitution, and Judeo-Christian ethics. Yet as he continued fighting for justice, King began to realize that America's understanding of its shared values might be the foundation of its inequality as well. He wrote, "For the vast majority of White Americans, the past decade – the first phase – had been a struggle to treat the Negro with a degree of decency, not of equality. White America was ready to demand that the Negro should be spared the lash of brutality and coarse degradation, but it had never been truly committed to helping him out of poverty, exploitation or all forms of discrimination" (King, 1963, p. 3).

King faced a society in which he could no longer take for granted the existence of shared values. In contrast with earlier appeals, he began to reimagine the formerly taken for granted. For example, he stepped to the lectern at the 1967 meeting of the Southern Christian Leadership Conference to declare, "America, you must be born again." Drawing on religious imagery of conversion, King asserted that the nation needed nothing short of a revolution of values. This rhetorical move is crucial today as well, a moment when the concept of shared values seems to be illusory at best. The United States today desperately needs to reimagine what it means to be just, equal, and free. At a time of deep political polarization, prophets invite society to reconsider what it means to live in community. Such a reconsideration requires abandoning old prejudices even as we citizens reach toward those who are different from ourselves. This is what an *American* view of prophecy especially requires.

Conclusion

Despite their influence, prophetic voices often face steep resistance and rejection, which is why prophets are so often celebrated posthumously. Throughout the Hebrew Bible, prophets like Jeremiah faced public censure, imprisonment, and even death for their disruptive presence. Articulating a prophetic voice is no guarantee that a given public will be receptive to its message. As a result, prophets almost always constitute an existential threat to the status quo.

As I reflect on such matters, I sometimes wonder if American politics is already beyond saving. Still, the goal of the prophetic voice lies in faithfulness to possibility, not in public popularity. The prophet, after all, cannot engage in a cost–benefit analysis when confronting the question of injustice. During such moments, we might find solidarity in the closing words of Cornel West (2005, p. 218) in *Democracy Matters*: "If we lose our precious democratic experiment, let it be said that we went down swinging like Ella Fitzgerald and Muhammad Ali – with style, grace, and a smile that signifies that the seeds of democracy matters will flower and flourish somewhere and somehow and remember our gallant efforts."

Notes

1. See, for example, Enfield (2017), Lakoff (2017), Kavanagh & Rich (2018), and Zeynalov (2016).
2. See Zulick (2003), Darsey (1999), Brueggemann (2001), and Heschel (2010).

Bibliography

Arendt, H. (1967, February 18). Truth and politics. *The New Yorker*. www.newyorker.com/magazine/1967/02/25/truth-and-politics

Barber, W. J., II. (2018, Spring). America's moral malady. *The Atlantic*. www.theatlantic.com/magazine/archive/2018/02/a-new-poor-peoples-campaign/552503/

Bella, T. (2020, June 10). White men mocked George Floyd's death at a protest: Now a corrections officer in the group has been suspended. *The Washington Post*. www.washingtonpost.com/nation/2020/06/10/george-floyd-new-jersey-protest/

Brueggemann, W. (2001). *The prophetic imagination*. Minneapolis: Fortress Press.

Chappell, D. L. (2005). *A stone of hope: Prophetic religion and the death of Jim Crow*. Chapel Hill, NC: University of North Carolina Press.

Darsey, J. (1999). *The prophetic tradition and radical rhetoric in America*. New York: NYU Press.

Dickerson, C. (2020, October 21). Parents of 545 children separated at the border cannot be found. *The New York Times*. www.nytimes.com/2020/10/21/us/migrant-children-separated.html

Dickerson, C. (2020, November 3). U.S. expels migrant children from other countries to Mexico. *The New York Times*. www.nytimes.com/2020/10/30/us/migrant-children-expulsions-mexico.html

Douglass, F. (1852, July 5). Speech at Rochester, New York. In C. G. Woodson (Ed.), *Negro orators and their orations* (pp. 197–223). New York: Russell & Russell.

Du Bois, W. E. B. (1986). A question of policy: The philosophy of Mr. Dole. In *Du Bois: Writings*. New York: The Library of America.

Enfield, N. (2017, November 16). We're in a post-truth world with eroding trust and accountability: It can't end well. *The Guardian*. www.theguardian.com/commentisfree/2017/nov/17/were-in-a-post-truth-world-with-eroding-trust-and-accountability-it-cant-end-well

Engels, J. (2015). *The politics of resentment: A genealogy*. Penn State University Press.

Gibbs, N. (2017, March 23). When a president can't be taken at his word. *Time Magazine*. https://time.com/4710615/donald-trump-truth-falsehoods/

Hart, R. P. (1971). The rhetoric of the true believer. *Communication Monographs*, 38(4), 249–261. https://doi.org/10.1080/03637757109375718

Heschel, A. J. (2010). *The prophets* (3rd ed., vol. 1). Peabody, MA: Hendrickson Publishers.

Kavanagh, J., & Rich, M. D. (2018). *Truth decay: An initial exploration of the diminishing role of facts and analysis in American public life*. RAND Corporation. www.rand.org/pubs/research_reports/RR2314.html

King, M. L., Jr. (1963). Letter from Birmingham Jail. In J. M. Washington (Ed.), *A testament of hope: The essential writings and speeches of Martin Luther King, Jr.* New York: HarperOne.

King, M. L., Jr. (1968). *Where do we go from here: Chaos or community?* Boston: Beacon Press.

King, M. L., Jr. (1986). I see the promised land. In J. M. Washington (Ed.), *A testament of hope: The essential writings and speeches of Martin Luther King, Jr.* New York: HarperCollins.

Lakoff, R. L. (2017, July). The hollow man: Donald Trump, populism, and post-truth politics. *Journal of Language & Politics*, 16(4), 595–606. https://doi.org/10.1075/jlp.17022.lak

Morgan, R. (2018, June 1). Why MLK's right-hand man was nearly written out of history. *History*. www.history.com/news/bayard-rustin-march-on-washington-openly-gay-mlk

Moyers, B. (2014, June 27). 10 big fat lies and the liars who told them. *BillMoyers.com* (blog). https://billmoyers.com/content/10-big-fat-lies-and-the-liars-who-told-them/

Pine, D. W. (2017, March 23). Is truth dead? Behind the TIME cover. *Time Magazine*. https://time.com/4709920/donald-trump-truth-time-cover/

Randolph, A. P., & Rustin, B. (1967). How the civil-rights movement aimed to end poverty. *The Atlantic*. www.theatlantic.com/magazine/archive/2018/02/a-freedom-budget-for-all-americans-annotated/557024/

Rustin, B. (1965, February). From protests to politics: The future of the civil rights movement. *Commentary*. www.commentarymagazine.com/article/from-protest-to-politics-the-future-of-the-civil-rights-movement/

Tyson, T. B. (2017). *The blood of Emmett Till*. New York: Simon & Schuster.

Villa, L. (2020, April 17). Undocumented immigrants are essential but exposed in the coronavirus pandemic. *Time Magazine*. https://time.com/5823491/undocumented-immigrants-essential-coronavirus/

West, C. (2005). *Democracy matters: Winning the fight against imperialism*. New York, NY: Penguin Press.

Zeynalov, M. (2016, September 22). Trump, Erdogan and post-truth politics. *Huffington Post* (blog). www.huffingtonpost.com/mahir-zeynalov/trump-erdogan-and-posttru_b_12090684.html

Zulick, M. D. (2003). Prophecy and providence: The anxiety over prophetic authority. *Journal of Communication & Religion*, 26(2), 195–207.

5 Experiment With Playful Protest

Tiffany Lewis

In 1913, the *Washington Post* announced that British swimmer Lily Smith would "swim to France to win votes for women." The *Post* explained that by braving the treacherous currents of the English Channel, Smith would "prove that woman is man's physical equal" and "put a stop forever to all this twiddle about the weaker sex." She thought that this accomplishment would be of "service towards winning the franchise for her sex" (Swim, 1913, p. MS6). The previous year, Indiana suffragists planned a hot air balloon flight to support women's voting rights. They believed that the balloon trip would "show that woman was capable of entering any sphere of life, even a high one" and "prove that suffragettes are 'game' and able to do and dare as most men" (Suffrage, 1912).

Such histrionics were not uncommon in the 1910s. After decades of giving speeches, holding conventions, and publishing journals in behalf of women's rights, suffragists in England and the United States began using uniquely physical and mobile forms of advocacy – swimming long distances, climbing mountains, and flying airplanes – to protest their disfranchisement (Schultz, 2010). Mountaineers took "Votes for Women" banners to mountaintops. British women walked from Edinburgh to London, organized pilgrimages all over England, and flew hot air balloons for suffrage. New York City activists hiked to Albany and Washington, attempted a 7,000-mile canoe trip, and flew in biplanes for the right to vote. The extensive media attention the stunts received helped circulate their activism widely and won them praise for being savvy publicists. The stunts were essentially embodied arguments to refute the prevalent belief that women were not physically strong enough to vote (Palczewski, 2005, pp. 375–376).[1]

Yet beyond their ability to win attention and enact creative arguments, these activities were also *fun*. The activists later recounted the joy, camaraderie, and liberation their accomplishments provided, and newspapers often reported on the pleasure the women took in such tactics, suggesting that the activists completed the stunts as much for personal satisfaction as for gender equity. Previously, scholars have theorized the rhetorical power of mobile and embodied arguments, and I have written

DOI: 10.4324/9781003212515-7

elsewhere about their persuasiveness for women's rights.[2] Here, I consider the value these feats had for suffragists and how they became a resource for their perseverance, public support, and community building. I argue that playful protest enlivened their movement, won allies, and assisted long-term organizing, connecting members to one another and to those outside their cause.

Scholars generally define play as a voluntary and absorbing activity that seems to have no purpose other than providing pleasure and satisfaction. Play is a slippery concept because it is as much a spirit or an attitude as it is an activity. The same behavior – whether it is hiking, cooking, or dancing – can be playful for one individual, a source of misery for another.[3] Likewise, it can feel like play one day and monotony the next. Sociologist Thomas Henricks (2006) describes play as the human capacity "to hold the world lightly and creatively." Play can be so engrossing that it leads people to lose track of time and become less self-conscious, allowing them to be more improvisational and "in the moment."[4]

Yet play has long been devalued in the United States' puritanical and capitalist culture. The nation's Protestant ethic celebrated devotion to work as a Christian virtue, which positioned play as the enemy of morality. Even secularists circulated the idea that "play is the devil's handiwork" or discussed it as indulgent, morally lax, and unproductive.[5] Capitalism also subordinates enjoyable activities to the race for wealth and control. Today, for example, unorganized and free forms of play are often seen as time wasting. Consumerism can often distort the pleasure of pleasure, requiring that approved forms of play take place in commercial or competitive settings such as televised sports or ticketed theater performances. Too, capitalist culture often conflates play with leisure, restricting it to certain classes and to those more privileged.[6]

Many scholars argue that play can threaten the status quo, disrupting power systems and social structures.[7] Games are a serious matter, Max Weber (1968/1946, p. 1106) has argued, because they are "a counterpole to all economically rational action." Roger Caillois (1979/1961) described play as inherently subversive, a cultural resource tied to power and world making. Part of play's efficacy comes from its ability to subvert hierarchies and challenge power while simultaneously being fun, an expression of personal freedom. For these reasons, social movements including the Yippies, the gay liberation movement, and AIDS activists found play useful in their agitation tactics. These movements communicated social-justice truths and movement goals through ludic activity like street performances and carnivalesque gatherings. Scholars have also illuminated the role of play in the civil rights movement and for the New York Young Lords.[8] Similarly, suffragists used playful protest to create compelling narratives of a more equitable world, helping movement members cope with life along the way to liberation.

Yet for all its subversive power, playful protest is not a panacea. The suffragists examined here, for example, were also well-known for their White supremacy and classism. The elite forms of leisure they adopted required money and time and were most available to White men.[9] The suffragists' racial, class, and ability privileges enabled their participation, making the resulting activities primarily accessible to White, able-bodied activists.

Nevertheless, playful suffragists also faced significant opposition and disapproval. It was still risky and controversial for women to move about freely in the 19th century. Women in Europe and the United States were restricted by laws and other forms of harassment, making their physical safety precarious at times.[10] Unsurprisingly, some of the suffrage histrionics were met with hostility, with suffragists sometimes being pelted with rocks, moldy vegetables, and dead rats (Robinson, 2018, p. 8).

Given these complications, playful suffragists must not be studied uncritically, although their activities certainly helped sustain the movement for many decades. If anything, they teach us that even flawed individuals can make important differences within a supremacist, classist, ableist, and patriarchal culture. Paying close attention to their stunts, therefore, sheds light on the multiple dimensions of social movements.

For one thing, playful protest invites people into social movements. Sociologist and activist Benjamin Shepard argues that, in addition to making organizing more enjoyable, playful protest makes entry easier. People rarely join movements for purely rational reasons; they are usually motivated by a desire to be a "part of the action." Shepard (2011, pp. 17, 22–24, 33) posits that ludic forms of protest can entice citizens to step off the "sidewalk [and] . . . onto the street, into an open-ended, participatory experience in democratic living." This opportunity was offered to British citizens in 1913 when hundreds of suffragists from throughout England set out for London, mostly on foot, as part of their six-week "Great Pilgrimage" for women's voting rights. When marchers reached the village of Braithwaite, resident Gladys Duffield knew very little about the movement, but she became so curious about the smiling marchers that she inquired into their cause. The group's enthusiasm was so contagious and Duffield so taken with the "spirit of the Pilgrimage" and the "general atmosphere of friendliness and good humor" that she became a member of the organization on the spot, subsequently joining the pilgrims on their trek. Duffield felt "an irresistible urge to be part of it all, intoxicated by the noise and colour, the liveliness of the audience and the speakers' heady message" (Robinson, 2018, pp. 167–171).[11] The lighthearted atmosphere caused others to join as well.

Similarly, New York City suffragists' long-distance hikes possessed an allure that attracted people to the movement. After suffragists hiked 170 miles to Albany in December of 1912, for example, their leader, Rosalie Jones, reflected on why their stunt sparked so much interest:

> You know many persons [prior to our hike] had looked upon suffrage as something ponderous and academic. They therefore had no interest in it. I came to the conclusion that it should be made more

> *frolicsome* and *playful* in order to create interest and bring converts to the cause. That is what this walk to Albany has done. We just had a jolly time, and it has created interest among people who had never given suffrage a second thought before.
>
> (Suffragette, 1913)

When planning another hike to Washington, Jones received "letters from women all over the East wanting to join" because when "they heard of the good times we had, they decided they'd like to try it too" (Hikers, 1913). In other words, social movements often embrace Toni Cade Bambara's call to artists and cultural workers of oppressed communities "to make revolution irresistible" (Bonetti, 2012, p. 35).[12]

Play is also a resource that enlivens and sustains social movements and their members. Observers note, for example, that traditional politics can make activism a chore or even a form of alienated labor. In contrast, the life-affirming nature of play sustains and energizes activists, making them feel resilient.[13] As Barbara Ehrenreich (2006, p. 259) argues, "Seasoned organizers know that gratification cannot be deferred until after the 'revolution.'" Play can also release members while they work, making the agitation process easier (Weissman, 1990). This was especially true for Nannie Brown, who, in 1912, joined the women marching 400 miles from Edinburgh to London. Although intending to march for only a few days before returning home, Brown "found herself enjoying the march so much that she decided to carry on" (Robinson, 2018, pp. 144–145). As activist and author Adrienne Maree Brown (2019, pp. 122–123) argues, "What feels good is sustainable. When . . . [I feel good,] I want to keep going, and fight for my right to exist and love and grow and evolve."

Play can be enlivening because it gives rise to the erotic, not in the strictly sexual sense (although that too can be included) but in the more expansive sense that Audre Lorde described as the "internal sense of satisfaction" experienced when one is fully alive and present in their feelings, thereby expanding their capacity for joy.[14] Lorde explained that such feelings replenish the downtrodden, empowering them to resist oppression and giving them "energy to pursue genuine change within our world" (Lorde, 2012/1984). Experiences of power and aliveness, Lorde said, are especially crucial for bodies of historically oppressed people.[15] Since so many social movements are fueled by the labor of those who are marginalized, it is essential they experience what Brown (2019, pp. 122–123) calls the "ease, pleasure, and connection" of "being fully alive."[16]

Play also fosters community among movement members, providing them with another source of strength for sustaining their advocacy. Shepard (2011, p. 20) argues that collective play often results in "social eros – a connection among minds and bodies, tribes and movements."[17] Play encourages people to become attuned to one another, facilitating shared thoughts and emotions. Combined with hard work and a sense of duty, having fun helps to deepen social relationships, turning solidarity into engaged citizenship.[18]

The British suffrage hikers, for example, frequently described the camaraderie they felt on the Great Pilgrimage. Their "shared experiences and achievements exhilarated them; they valued the mutual support which was a hallmark of the Pilgrimage; and it was obviously liberating to have so much fun together" (Robinson, 2018, p. 225). Afterward, pilgrim Alice New wrote in her diary that she "had loved the outdoor life, being on the road from nine in the morning to nine at night; the challenge; the company; the comradeship" (Diary, RL.11080). Reports of the stunts describe how suffragists were able to connect with other activists from a variety of backgrounds. After completing the Great Pilgrimage, Lady Rochdale recalled that "she had been privileged to meet all sorts of women on the road, from duchesses to fishwives. By the end of the march she considered herself indistinguishable from a fishwife herself: 'hot and smelly' and proud to be so" (Robinson, 2018, p. 5). That "fishwife," of course, might well have had a different perspective on these interclass relationships, since even collective play cannot dissipate overriding power differences. Still, play does have the capacity to invert social hierarchies, thereby potentially mitigating the threat of difference.[19]

Although the stunts seemed to allow White suffragists some opportunities to connect across class and gender difference, they did not connect across race. The majority of the stunts were completed by White women and men. While news reports typically focused on women completing the stunts, men were usually involved as well, mountaineering alongside the women or boating near long-distance swimmers to provide them with supplies. Men, of course, were a critical audience for suffrage advocacy because, legally and politically, their support was needed to enfranchise women. As a result, joining together in play sent important signals that men were not monolithic in their opposition to women's suffrage.[20]

On the other hand, White suffragists rarely collaborated with people of color for racial justice. When Jones and the New York City pilgrims were on their hike to Washington, D.C., a group of Black suffragists attempted to join them outside of Baltimore with a banner that read "Votes for Negro Women." Reporters described it as a "negro invasion" and a threat to the movement's success. The White hikers apparently responded with "embarrassed silence," worrying that the Black activists would return again the next day (Army, 1913, p. 6; Recruits, 1913). The papers reported that some innkeepers thereafter refused to lodge the White hikers after hearing about the Black suffragists; unsurprisingly, they did not consider the risk of bodily harm the Black activists themselves suffered when showing their support. Similarly, when Annie Peck placed a "Votes for Women" flag on the top of Mount Coropuna in Peru, she was assisted by the labor of at least five Peruvian guides, whom she publicly derided with racial slurs and complaints about their performance (Triumph,

1912, p. 8; Feat, 1912, p. 7). For all its subversive and democratizing potential, then, play makes no guarantees about racial equity.

Conclusion

When it comes to fixing American politics, playful protest is a complicated solution. As the suffrage stunts illustrate, play is not a cure-all that ensures intersectional allyship. It is also not a novel solution; it has a long history in both conventional movements and marginalized communities. Black activists and writers, including Lorde, Bambara, Adrienne Maree Brown, and Joan Morgan, have long stressed the importance of pleasure.[21] That said, playful protest may be as critical now as ever before, providing vital support for the politics of gender, race, class, sexuality, ability, and the environment.

Recent activism, for example, has theorized about Black pleasure in protest, as Black Lives Matter activists frequently herald the refrain "Black joy is an act of political resistance." When Kleaver Cruz began the Black Joy Project in 2015, he sparked a collective effort to circulate through social media joyous images of Black people laughing, dancing, or having fun at protests and in everyday life. Cruz and his fellow activists explained that Black people must feel collective joy alongside the pain and injustice of living in an anti-Black world, and they must see images of Black joy amid the ceaseless images of violence toward Black people.[22] These concepts have been explored in numerous social media accounts and publications like the *Black Joy Zine*, Adreinne Waheed's *Black Joy and Resistance*, and Gabby Rivera's *Joy Revolution* podcast.

In short, bodies that have been historically oppressed need to feel good, whether protesting or not. As Brown (2019) notes, people who feel good are more likely to have the energy to keep organizing. In a curious way, playful protest can make protest more sustainable, giving activists the joy needed to make connections and get their work done.

Notes

1. See also Edwards (1997), Darwin and Darwin (1896), and Curzon (1912).
2. See Samek (2017), Harris (2018), Palczewski (2016), Cresswell (2006), Lewis (2018), and Lewis (2019).
3. See Brown and Vaughan (2009), Huizinga (2014/1950), and Sicart (2014).
4. See, for example, Huizinga (2014/1950), Caillois (1979/1961), and Brown (2019).
5. See Turner (1982, p. 3) and Shepard (2011, p. 3).
6. See Huizinga (2014/1950, pp. 8, 16, 20, 37), Henricks (2006, p. 39), and Spracklen (2013).
7. Shepard (2011, pp. 3, 8) and Turner (1982, p. 39).
8. See Shepard (2009), Shepard (2011, pp. 9, 20–22, 53–67), and Gould (2009).
9. See Spracklen (2013) and Graham (2018).
10. See Cresswell (2006, p. 213), Harris (2018) and Solnit (2000, p. 238).

11. See also Duffield (DX 33/1).
12. See also Brown and Vaughan (2009, pp. 166–167).
13. See Lorde (2012/1984), Brown (2019) and Shepard (2011).
14. See Ehrenreich (2006, p. 20) and Bronski (1998, p. 20).
15. See also Brown (2019, p. 13) and Morgan (2015).
16. Brown (2019, pp. 122–123).
17. See also Huizinga (2014/1950, p. 13), Brown (2019, p. 20), and Bogad (2005).
18. See Brown (2019, pp. 62–63, 134), Henricks (2006, p. 14), Caillois (1979/1961, p. 158), Shepard (2009, pp. 18–19, 57–60), Brown and Vaughan (2009, p. 166), and Ehrenreich (2006, p. 259).
19. See Lorde (2012/1984, p. 44), Brown (2019), and Shepard (2011, pp. 9, 22–23).
20. Lewis (2018).
21. See Lorde (2012/1984), Bonetti (2012), Bambara (2005/1970), Brown (2019), Morgan (2015), and Camp (2002).
22. For more on these matters, see Waheed (2018), Cruz (2016), Cruz (2017), and Joseph (2020).

Bibliography

Arai, S., & Kivel, D. B. (2009). Critical race theory and social justice perspectives on whiteness, difference(s) and (anti)racism: A fourth wave of race research in leisure studies. *Journal of Leisure Research*, 41(4), 459–470.

Army. (1913, February 28). Army at capital door. *Baltimore Sun*.

Bambara, T. C. (Ed.). (2005/1970). *The Black woman: An anthology*. New York: Washington Square Press.

Bogad, L. M. (2005). *Electoral guerrilla theatre: Radical ridicule and social movements*. Abingdon, UK: Routledge.

Bonetti, K. (2012). An interview with Toni Cade Bambara. In T. Lewis (Ed.), *Conversations with Toni Cade Bambara*. Jackson, MS: University of Mississippi Press.

Bronski, M. (1998). *The pleasure principle: Sex, backlash, and the struggle for gay freedom*. New York: St. Martin's Press.

Brown, A. M. (2019). *Pleasure activism: The politics of feeling good*. Chico, CA: AK Press.

Brown, S., & Vaughan, C. (2009). *Play: How it shapes the brain, opens the imagination, and invigorates the soul*. New York: Penguin.

Caillois, R. (1979/1961). *Man, play, and games*. New York: Shocken Books.

Camp, S. M. H. (2002). The pleasures of resistance: Enslaved women and body politics in the plantation South, 1830–1861. *Journal of Southern History*, 68(3), 533–572.

Cresswell, T. (2006). *On the move: Mobility in the modern western world*. Abingdon, UK: Routledge.

Cruz, K. (2016, September 19). The Black Joy Project: Putting smiles on black faces. *Shoppe Black*.

Cruz, K. (2017, December 28). Black joy is resistance: Why we need a movement to balance Black triumph with trials. *Black Youth Project*.

Curzon, L. (1912). *Fifteen good reasons against the grant of female suffrage*. UK: National League for Opposing Woman Suffrage.

Darwin, C., & Darwin, S. F. (1896). *Charles Darwin's works: The descent of man and selection in relation to sex*. Boston: D. Appleton and Company.

Diary. (RL.11080). Alice New's diary. *New Family Papers*. David M. Rubenstein Rare Book and Manuscript Library, Duke University.

Duffield, G. (DX 33/1). *On the march: A personal story of the Watling Street route*. Cumbria Archive Centre.

Edwards, R. (1997). *Angels in the machinery: Gender in American party politics from the Civil War to the progressive era*. Oxford: Oxford University Press.

Ehrenreich, B. (2006). *Dancing in the streets: A history of collective joy*. New York: Henry Holt and Company.

Feat. (1912, February 16). Miss Peck's latest feat. *York Daily* (PA).

Gould, D. B. (2009). *Moving politics: Emotion and ACT UP's fight against AIDS*. Chicago: University of Chicago Press.

Graham, L. (2018, May 1). We're here: You just don't see us. *Outside Magazine*.

Harris, L. J. (2018). Rhetorical mobilities and the city: The white slavery controversy and racialized protection of women in the U.S. *Quarterly Journal of Speech*, 104(1), 22–46.

Henricks, T. S. (2006). *Play reconsidered*. Champaign, IL: University of Illinois Press.

Hikers. (1913, January 17). Mud daunts no "hikers." *New York Tribune*.

Huizinga, J. (2014/1950). *Homo ludens: A study of the play-element in culture*. Eastford, CT: Martino Publishing.

Joseph, C. (2020, July 29). What Black joy means: And why it's more important than ever. *Vogue*.

Lewis, T. (2018). The mountaineering and wilderness discourses of Washington woman suffragists. *Rhetoric & Public Affairs*, 21(2), 279–315.

Lewis, T. (2019). Mediating political mobility as stunt-girl entertainment: Newspaper coverage of New York's suffrage hike to Albany. *American Journalism*, 36(1), 99–123.

Lorde, A. (2012/1984). *Sister outsider*. Penguin Random House.

Morgan, J. (2015). Why we get off: Moving towards a Black feminist politics of pleasure. *The Black Scholar*, 45(4), 36–46.

Palczewski, C. H. (2005). The male Madonna and the feminine Uncle Sam: Visual argument, icons, and ideographs in 1909 anti-woman suffrage postcards. *Quarterly Journal of Speech*, 91(4), 375–376.

Palczewski, C. H. (2016). The 1919 prison special: Constituting White women's citizenship. *Quarterly Journal of Speech*, 102(2), 107–132.

Prove. (1912). To prove herself "game." *The Star Press* (IN).

Recruits. (1913, February 27). Negro recruits put hikers in quandary. *New York Sun*.

Robinson, J. (2018). *Hearts and minds: The untold story of the Great Pilgrimage and how women won the vote*. New York: Penguin Random House.

Samek, A. A. (2017). Mobility, citizenship, and "American women on the move" in the 1977 international women's year torch relay. *Quarterly Journal of Speech*, 103(3), 1–23.

Schultz, J. (2010). The physical is political: Women's suffrage, pilgrim hikes, and the public sphere. *The International Journal of the History of Sport*, 27(7), 1133–1153.

Shepard, B. (2009). *Queer political performance and protest: Play, pleasure, and social movement*. Abingdon, UK: Routledge.

Shepard, B. (2011). *Play, creativity, and social movements: If I can't dance, it's not my revolution*. Abingdon, UK: Routledge.
Sicart, M. (2014). *Play matters*. Cambridge, MA: MIT Press.
Solnit, R. (2000). *Wanderlust: A history of walking*. New York: Penguin Books.
Spracklen, K. (2013). *Whiteness and leisure*. London: Palgrave Macmillan.
Suffrage. (1912). Suffrage up in the air. *Indianapolis News*.
Suffragette. (1913, January 9). Why I led the suffragette hike from New York to Albany. *World Magazine*.
Swim. (1913, October 26). I'll swim to France to win votes for women! *Washington Post*, MS6.
Triumph. (1912, February 6). Miss Annie Peck's triumph. *Anthony Bulletin* (KS).
Turner, V. (1982). *From ritual to theatre: The human seriousness of play*. Westminster, CO: Performing Arts Publications.
Waheed, A. (2018). *Black joy and resistance*. Brooklyn, NY: Waheedpix LLC.
Weber, M. (1968/1946). *Economy and the society* (G. Roth & C. Wittich, Eds.). Berkeley: University of California Press.
Weissman, H. (1990). *Serious play: Creativity and innovation in social work*. Silver Spring: NASW Press.

Part 2
Exploit Human Capacities

6 Let Consensus Overcome Polarization

Marc C. Hetherington

Trying to work around the hyperpartisanship that grips the United States these days occupies my focus. Fortunately, the best-established theories in the study of public opinion, which help explain why the intense polarization in Washington has infected the public, also provide clues about how to circumvent it. My recommendations in this chapter do not solve what ails the body politic, but they do have the potential to make a nearly unworkable situation a little less catastrophic.

For many Americans, the impact of partisanship now overwhelms most, if not all, other political impulses. When party leaders take a position on an issue or about a group, it is nearly certain that almost all of their co-partisans in the electorate will adopt it. Similarly, it is also nearly certain that partisans of the other party will adopt the opposite stance, largely following the lead of their party leaders. Often, it hardly matters whether these positions are logically inconsistent, bad for the country, or disconnected from reality. Too many partisan voters blindly follow their party's establishment these days, even if said leadership is directing them off a cliff.

Worse still, this party-driven connection between leader and follower seems unbreakable. The psychological costs of following the opposition party are so high that few partisans are willing to pay them. But even when a member of their own party suggests that the party might be wrong about something, as Republican presidential candidate Mitt Romney did on the existence of climate change in 2012, the party's leadership prefers to jettison the heretic outright. Instead of questioning party orthodoxy, the would-be Romneys toe the party line lest they lose their influence.

This state of affairs creates a devastating cycle when it comes to governance. Our political institutions require at least some Republicans and Democrats in Washington to work together to build the majorities and supermajorities needed to enact legislation. If they don't, partisan gridlock ensues, and nothing gets done. Importantly, members of Congress feel no pressure to reach across the aisle to work together unless both Republicans and Democrats in their district demand it. Absent that pressure, legislators' strongest incentives are to pursue narrow partisan interests and to make the other party appear incapable of solving problems.

DOI: 10.4324/9781003212515-9

To change the incentive structure, their constituents, regardless of party affiliation, must agree that a problem needs to be addressed and that legislation needs to be passed. If that happens and legislators fail to heed the call, they run the risk of losing reelection. Unfortunately, because partisans in the electorate almost always follow their partisan leaders in lockstep, that kind of consensus among voters rarely develops these days. As a result, the public rarely gives policymakers the nudge needed to encourage political cooperation.

To change that formula, a substantial number of partisans must eschew party cues and go their own way. The solution I forward in this chapter is to tap the potential persuasive power of nongovernmental and ostensibly apolitical institutions. Parties are not the only actors that can help shape the positions and beliefs of ordinary Americans. If voters like a person or institution and have confidence in them, they, too, can guide public opinion. My research suggests that nonpartisan entities can nudge people away from knee-jerk partisan reactions. That, in turn, creates conditions that encourage political leaders to cooperate rather than fight.

The Nature of Public Opinion

If scholars of public opinion agree on two things, they are these. First, because most Americans do not know much about politics, they lean heavily on one of the few things that is easy for them to deploy – their party identification – to understand the political world. People tend to adopt their party from their parents, much like they choose their religion or their favorite sports team. Such choices then become their political compass.

Second, most Americans look to their partisan leaders to decide who their friends and foes are and what positions they should adopt on the issues of the day. In theory, we would like to think that politics is a "bottom-up" process, in which ordinary Americans come up with strong ideas that then encourage their elected representatives to reflect on the matters in question, but that is not how things work in practice. Instead, politics is a "top-down" process. Typically, leaders in Washington take positions on issues, and ordinary Americans then adopt them as well.

Back in the 1950s and 1960s, when scholars began to develop these theories, they mostly considered a citizen's partisanship a life raft. Because most Americans had little interest in politics, they would sink in a sea of political ignorance without being able to use their party to make sense of the political world. With people rationally more invested in their workaday lives than in politics, parties provided a "shortcut" to help them get by. Following their party leaders allowed people to absorb a political philosophy without needing to develop one on their own.

With America's two parties now so polarized, however, the effect of partisanship is a mixed bag at best. The good news is that party cues can still help inform people about whether a given set of ideas is conservative or liberal. The bad news is that partisanship increasingly produces blind followership as a result. Americans dislike the party they do not belong to with such intensity these days that they'll believe just about anything good about their side and anything bad about the other.

Rarely has the pernicious effect of hyperpartisanship come into clearer focus than in the aftermath of the 2020 presidential election. More than 70 percent of Republicans consistently said they believed that the election had been stolen by the Democrats. Consistent with the scholarly canon, they believed this because Donald Trump and other high-ranking Republicans said that election fraud had been widespread. Of course, there was no actual *evidence* of fraud. In fact, Trump's campaign lost nearly 60 lawsuits, many of which were decided by Republican judges.

Yet an overwhelming majority of Republicans came to believe something that was untrue, following their partisan leaders to that conclusion. We know from hard experience that cues from other *political* entities will not work to counteract partisan cues. Perhaps nonpolitical entities might have better luck.

Breaking the Partisan Cycle

My solution relies on the same theories of public opinion that produce hyperpartisanship. People do not know much about political issues, so they rely on cues from trusted sources of information to help them decide what to believe and where to stand. The key thing to remember is that "party" is just one of many potential cue givers. Parties are influential because they are trusted, credible, and liked by those who identify with the party. But so are other people and institutions.

A few things enjoy near universal affection. Think, for example, of the US military, country music singer Dolly Parton, and actor Tom Hanks. More often, partisans of one party like a group, while those from the other party don't. Democrats, but not Republicans, embrace scientists and environmental groups. Republicans, but not Democrats, feel positively toward organized religion and law enforcement. Here is the key: When the groups that Democrats like take conservative positions or when the groups that Republicans like take liberal positions, it has the potential to persuade partisans away from their party's orthodoxy.

If enough Republicans follow a liberal cue from a conservative nonpartisan source and enough Democrats follow a conservative cue from a liberal nonpartisan source, chances for political cooperation increase. A Republican politician who can easily win reelection, even if only their Republican constituents vote for them, would have to think twice about following the party line in Washington if a substantial number of Republicans in their district are unhappy with them for not supporting their position on an issue. When cross-party consensus develops, it puts pressure on elected representatives to seek compromise rather than to deepen division.

In identifying cue givers who might play this role, consider product advertising that relies on spokespeople with whom people identify to promote credit cards, sell vehicles, or embrace new habits. The most sought-after spokespersons are individuals familiar to most people, individuals who consistently make a favorable impression upon them. Why does Capital One choose Samuel L. Jackson and Jennifer Garner? They are well known and well liked by all who know them.

When it comes to bridging the partisan divide in the electorate, the approach I have in mind is similar but needs to be adapted in important ways. Being well known and well liked is still critical. The target audience need not be the entire country but, rather, only those linked to one of the political parties. Take climate change, for example. Nearly half the country (Democratic identifiers) has followed its party leaders to believe that climate change must be addressed. The problem is that a similar-sized group in the electorate (Republican identifiers) has followed its party leaders to believe that climate change is overhyped. The task, then, is to change the minds of some of those in the latter group.

To build public consensus around the idea that climate change is a pressing problem requires a messenger who is both familiar to and well-liked among Republican partisans. In a study I carried out with Cindy Kam, we had success using the US military to persuade conservatives to take a position that they might not have otherwise. During this past year, a group of my colleagues did the same to encourage North Carolinians to wear masks to fight COVID-19.

Both studies started from the same premise. Year in and year out, the General Social Survey – the gold-standard survey on political and social issues produced by the National Opinion Research Council – shows that Americans love the military. In fact, Americans express more than twice as much confidence in the military as they do in science and religion; they also show much more confidence in the military than in the executive branch and Congress. Better still, Republicans and conservatives – the groups that need to be convinced that spending to protect the environment and mask wearing are important – like the military even more than Democrats and independents do.

The military's endorsement of environmental protection and mask wearing has a surprising quality to it. When it comes to climate change, for example, some Americans might know that the military is the world's biggest polluter, but almost no one is aware of its embrace of climate change mitigation during the last decade. In fact, realizing that a warming planet will produce more instability, the military is a *leader* in deploying electric vehicles, powering planes with alternative fuels, and outfitting bases with solar- and wind-generated electricity. Similarly, when it comes to masks, Americans see soldiers and sailors as tough folks with few physical weaknesses. Seeing them masking up cuts strongly against the public's expectations as a result.

Surprises like these increase the potential for persuasion. When messages are surprising, it is human nature to pay more attention to them. Consider, for example, which of the following is more attention grabbing: (1) the Sierra Club says that the country ought to spend more on climate change mitigation or (2) the US military say the same thing. The first message blends in because people know that the environmental advocate is liberal. When the US military makes a similar statement, however, it stands out from the background, thereby breaking through the noise. Better still, because conservatives like the military, it might persuade them to believe something they might not have believed before.

In addition to being grabbed by the novelty of the information, the fact that the military seems to be on the unexpected side of the issue has the potential to increase its persuasive power even further. Because conservatives like the military, they tend to attribute their ideological leanings to an institution that believes that climate is not a high priority. Social psychology suggests that people ascribe good motives to such messengers. They are not endorsing environmental changes because of institutional pressures but because they think it's smart to do so. "If the military is taking such a counterintuitive stance," people reason, "then it might be time for a conservative like me to give it a chance, too."

We've found encouraging results using this strategy. In the case of environmental protection, we carried out a survey experiment in which one randomly selected group of people was told about the military's expertise on climate change mitigation. Another randomly selected group was told the same information, but, instead of the military, the Environmental Protection Agency – a group Republicans do not like very much – had the expertise. This simple change in cues dramatically decreased party polarization in support of a multibillion-dollar spending program.

The results were similarly heartening when it came to attitudes about wearing masks during a pandemic. In cooperation with a local television station, we produced a public service announcement (PSA) featuring a retired Army general who raised the threat posed by COVID-19 and the importance of wearing masks to combat it. When we surveyed Republicans in the Raleigh DMA after the PSA had run for three weeks, we found that those who reported seeing it had much more positive attitudes about mask wearing and were more likely to have adopted mask wearing themselves compared with those who said they had not seen the PSA.

This strategy should work for Democrats as well. Consider another side of the environment issue. Increased use of nuclear power has the potential to help improve things. Provided that the technology is safe and that waste can be discarded with minimal harm, nuclear power would help combat climate change because it is not carbon based and hence does not emit greenhouse gasses. Although Republicans tend to support increasing reliance on nuclear energy, Democrats largely see it as dangerous.

In this case, the minds of Democrats would need to change to bring about the kind of consensus in the mass public needed to get Democrats in Congress to embrace action. Two messengers would seem especially powerful to persuade Democrats. The first is environmental protection groups. Democrats tend to trust them, and some of the groups are actually coming to see the importance of nuclear power. Although they have traditionally opposed it, their position has begun to evolve as the effects of climate change have worsened. The second group is the scientific community. Democrats tend to trust scientists a great deal, and many of them believe that nuclear power can be generated much more safely than in decades past. Learning the revisionist beliefs of such groups could potentially persuade more Democrats to revise their thinking rather than defaulting to the antinuclear position of their party leaders.

Many other nonpolitical institutions and people can play such a role. For example, many churches support more generous social programs. However, many Republicans who go to church faithfully do not because of the party cues they receive. Encouraging churches to take a more public stance on redistribution of wealth could increase Republican support. Many graduate schools of education have grown weary of the role that some teachers' unions have played to block innovation in public schools. The Democratic Party, however, relies on teachers' unions to help them win elections, so party leaders rarely press these concerns. That means that Democrats in the electorate won't press them either. Amplifying the voices of experts in the field, however, might promote a new consensus on such matters.

Conclusion

We live in politically challenging times. With close partisan margins in both the US House and Senate, majority status is up for grabs every two years. That creates perverse incentives for members of Congress. Because the minority party is always in a position to become the majority party after the next election, it often becomes more important to them to disparage the majority than to solve pressing problems. Because solving problems will make the majority look good, creating division to defeat legislation makes good political sense to the minority party.

Polarized parties not only create gridlock in Washington but also reinforce polarization among ordinary Americans. Because Republicans often obediently follow their party's leaders and Democrats theirs, partisans rarely create the public consensus needed for their leaders to cooperate.

The story might be different if a substantial number of Republicans in the electorate sided with Democrats or a substantial number of Democrats sided with the Republicans on the issues of the day. If genuine consensus develops within the electorate, our elected leaders would see their incentives change instantly. Rather than thinking solely about maintaining their party's majority status, they would calculate whether toeing the party line might undermine their own reelection.

One way to accomplish this kind of recalculation would be to provide partisans in the electorate with cues about where they really stand on political issues, versus the traditional cues provided by party leaders. In addition, well-liked and esteemed *nonpolitical* sources have the potential to help as well. We already know who conservatives like and who and liberals esteem. Getting these kinds of subsidiary opinion leaders more intimately involved in the political process might break the logjams so endemic to the District of Columbia and its environs. Or so one might hope.

7 Use Emotion Wisely

Bethany Albertson

Emotion is central to political life. Without emotion, we would not have seen protests over police brutality in the summer of 2020 or the demonstrations against the 2020 election results and subsequent attack on the US Capitol. Heartbreak and anger, anxiety and disgust, perhaps even hope and pride – the tumultuous events of 2020 brought on all of these and more. Emotion fuels voter-mobilization efforts, and the 2020 election had the highest turnout levels in decades. But emotion influences our politics in less dramatic times as well. Even the simple decision to pick up a newspaper or click on a news story is influenced by emotional states. People engage in politics because they *feel* something.

Politics are messy, and so otherwise smart people imagine that a better politics exists, if only we could take the emotion out of it. This is both impossible and undesirable. In this chapter, I'm going to first establish that this fallacy exists and then explain why it is misguided. I then explain two aspects or truths of emotion I believe we should recognize that could help improve our politics. First, we need to recognize that emotion is a valuable political resource. Second, we must acknowledge that the ability to use emotion is unevenly distributed, with some groups wrongly punished for being emotional. Recognizing these truths can help inform a better politics if we recognize and harness the power of emotion.

The Fallacy of Emotion-Free Politics

While the ubiquity of emotion in our thoughts and behaviors is accepted and obvious for some, emotion has its critiques in politics, specifically American politics, dating back to the founding of the country. The framers of the US Constitution argued that we needed political institutions to constrain the emotional mass public that might act on whim rather than on reason. As Madison (2012) wrote in *Federalist Paper* No. 49, "The Passions ought to be controlled and regulated by the government." Our intricate system of government, with divided power and interests pitted against one another, is thought to encourage debate and compromise – to slow down the machinery of government. A large republic that takes in

DOI: 10.4324/9781003212515-10

competing interests and relies on representation was thought to protect the new country from "mobocracy," where a passionate majority could seize control of government and direct it toward its own, presumably illegitimate, ends.

The idea that politics ought to be insulated from emotion is not restricted to the United States. Pierre Trudeau, Canadian prime minister for most of the period from 1968 to 1984, famously campaigned on a slogan of "Reason over Passion." Trudeau was worried about emotion being used as an instrument of totalitarianism, and some of these concerns have reemerged of late. In the Trump years, there is an emergent understanding of so-called affective polarization between partisans, where people increasingly do not like people of the other party. Partisan differences are rooted in active dislike or even hatred of the other party rather than policy differences. Contemporary polarization is rooted in feelings, not facts (Talisse, 2019), and this heightened animosity is dangerous. Mason and Kalmoe (2021) show across multiple studies that partisans in the United States are increasingly likely to say that using violence to resolve political differences is at least a little bit justified (15% of partisans in 2020 believe this). Further, people who hold this belief are more likely to engage in political violence themselves.

Some people observing these dynamics regard emotions as the enemy. The physicist Neil deGrasse Tyson embraced this naïve view of politics, arguing that politics should be technocratic and data driven, what he called "rationalia" (Atherton, 2016). In the wake of shootings in 2019 in Texas and Ohio, deGrasse Tyson tweeted statistics about medical errors, the flu, and suicide having killed far more people, arguing that, "Often our emotions respond more to spectacle than to data." deGrasse Tyson was roundly criticized for this tone-deaf reaction to the shootings, underscoring the perils of thinking that politics can somehow be emotion free.

Recognizing Two Truths About Emotion and Politics

Emotions are central to political participation. Here, I identify two truths about emotions and politics that can help us understand how to improve governance in the United States. The first recognizes that emotion in politics is inevitable. The second examines why some groups are punished for being emotional in politics.

Truth 1: Emotion is inevitably embedded in our politics.

Justice Charles Evans Hughes once told William O. Douglas that on the Supreme Court level of jurisprudence, "ninety percent of any decision is emotional" and that rationality serves merely a supporting role. This anecdote underscores that emotions and politics are inextricably linked.

In order to use emotion wisely, we have to first acknowledge that emotion is a political resource, that politics is not possible without it. In political psychology, and in the field of psychology more broadly, this is obvious. Research shows "the ubiquity of emotion, with the influence of emotion extending to all aspects of cognition and behavior" (Cacioppo & Gardner, 1999). As Donald Kinder (1994, p. 310) has written, "emotion is, in some respects, an inevitable natural force." Emotion may directly cause behavior (for example, a startle response), but more commonly, emotions exert effects on our behavior through cognitive processes (Baumeister et al., 2007). If people feel anxious about an accelerating pandemic, for example, they put their trust in medical experts and support protective policies (Albertson & Gadarian, 2015). When we are angry about the state of the economy and about mismanagement in government, we become resolved to vote in the next election (Valentino et al., 2011).

Emotions tell our bodies to do something, but what? Say, for example, that you read a story about children being separated from their families by border control or about lines of people hoping for food because of economic problems brought on by the pandemic. Perhaps you feel sad or angry – but what can you do about these things? Quite often, we feel things in response to the news we read about or experience firsthand but feel ill equipped to take action. That disconnection itself can be upsetting.

Anxiety might shake us out of our inattentiveness and turn us into newshounds, anger might take us to the polls. Each of us can remind friends and family members of our ability to be engaged members of our communities. We can call our representatives, participate in city council meetings, or join a local volunteer effort. Hersch (2020) argues that many of us are political hobbyists – we see ourselves as politically engaged because we obsessively read the news (doomscrolling, in 2020 parlance) and perhaps offer our takes on social media. He argues that real political change requires that people get involved in their communities. Emotion can help in that regard.

So far, I've offered a fairly positive picture of emotion in politics, but that is not a complete picture. Angry people might vote, but angry people might also storm the US Capitol. Anxiety triggers political attention and learning (Marcus & MacKuen, 1993), but it also biases our attention toward threatening information and away from more balanced portrayals (Gadarian & Albertson, 2013). For example, certain political advertisements can use emotion to push a disgusting narrative to promote anti-LGBTQ legislation. Emotion is not inherently good or bad for politics – as Kinder noted, nothing so ubiquitous could be all good or all bad. But as political consultants know all too well, successful campaigns use emotional appeals to win (Brader, 2006).

Truth 2: The ability to use emotion in politics is unequally distributed; some groups are punished for being too emotional.

I've argued that emotion is a political resource. The next step is to recognize that, like most political resources in this country, there are haves and have nots when it comes to emotion. The usefulness of emotion in politics is not evenly distributed, either in terms of how it is expressed or how emotional citizens map onto our two-party system.

In year after year of survey data, Davin Phoenix (2019) shows that African Americans are more disappointed in politics than are Whites, while at the same time, Whites consistently show higher levels of anger. Black Americans not only exhibit lower levels of anger, but their anger has weaker consequences for political activity. Why are African Americans less angry than Whites, and why is their anger less consequential when it comes to electoral politics?

Phoenix (2019) argues that White grievance has long had a legitimate space in American politics. Anger from such ideologically diverse sources as Tea Party enthusiasts and Bernie Sanders is broadly understood as compatible within the two-party system. On the other hand, Black anger tends to exist on the periphery of major party politics. White anger is often welcomed and courted in American politics, while Black anger is more often feared, perhaps because it is so often packaged for negative advertisements.

The emotional bandwidth afforded members of racial minority communities in politics is narrower – a phenomenon so commonly understood that comedians assigned President Obama an 'anger translator.' As Garber (2017) wrote in *The Atlantic*, the comedy duo Key & Peele's sketches were "as much about the country Obama governed as they were about the president himself." Black candidates who sponsor attack advertisements are disproportionately punished, suggesting that Obama's reserved tone was politically useful (Krupnikov & Piston, 2015). Other identities further complicate the place of emotion in politics. Traister (2018) argued that women's anger has changed US politics at key historical junctures in ways that are misremembered in history. For example, Rosa Parks is portrayed as tired and docile rather than as a committed and quite angry political activist. Social and historical contexts shape how people's emotional experiences are expressed and understood.

There are other emotions that certain groups express and for which they sometimes face political penalties. Women, for example, face challenges of being perceived as too emotional, so public manifestations of emotion such as crying can undermine female politicians' reputations. As Alice Eagly and Linda Carli argued in their book *Through the Labyrinth: The Truth About How Women Become Leaders*, "People scrutinize women's behavior in very masculine environments, searching for any weakness . . . Given the demands of masculine environments, emotional displays can suggest weakness, and women are advised to avoid crying when upset" (Nelson, 2011).

Examples like these harken back to negative and damaging stereotypes of women as being less rational individuals. These stereotypes have precluded women from full participation in governance. Former Colorado Representative Pat Schroeder famously cried in 1987 when announcing that she would not run for president, and she was roundly criticized for doing so. As reported in Hu (2011), *The Chicago Tribune* wrote that "women across the country reacted with embarrassment, sympathy and disgust."

That may overstate the degree to which tears are an impediment to female politicians' progress. Hillary Clinton famously cried on the eve of the New Hampshire primary in 2008, and this may have helped humanize her to voters, who had tended to see her as a more austere figure. Clinton's primary opponent, Barack Obama, told her that she was "likable enough." Clinton's experience may be something of an anomaly for female politicians, who may tear up at their peril.

In 2021, Congresswoman Pramila Jayapal from Washington State was being interviewed after the January 6 attack on the US Capitol. She apparently cried during the interview, and the interviewer asked her if she could mention her doing so in the story. Jayapal, aware of the relevant stereotypes, said the reporter would do so only if the story acknowledged that she was able to control herself quickly. Jayapal elaborated: "I like to say that it's a good thing when we cry because policy-making is better when you have emotion about it. I think this whole myth that you have to be dispassionate, that you can't feel things, was constructed by men in power and is an excuse for why we have bad policies" (Traister, 2021). It is striking that just days after the congresswoman faced an attack while at work, she felt conflicted about the fact she had cried; the reporter, recognizing the potential downside, wisely asked permission. Clearly, the challenges that certain groups face when displaying emotion is yet another source of inequality in US society.

Conclusion

Recognizing these emotional truths can potentially improve our politics. Acknowledging that emotions are essential in governance but, at the same time, subject to excess and abuse leads us to ask how emotion can be used wisely.

I mentioned earlier that we need to move beyond being mere spectators in politics and encourage greater civic engagement. As I noted, each of us could be telling friends and family about ways to get involved in the community, drawing on emotional appeals to encourage their participation and channeling it for public purposes.

Last fall, I was asked to write a piece on voter suppression for the University of Texas student newspaper *The Daily Texan*, a topic that makes me angry. I didn't want to write a piece that just recited a litany of problems that dampened the ability of people to vote, including restrictions that made it hard for our students to cast a ballot. I feared that a story on voter suppression itself might dampen students' enthusiasm to vote if they thought it would be time consuming or difficult to do so. That piece (Albertson et al., 2020), which I co-authored with two students, highlighted the problems of voter suppression (which often makes people angry), but it also included reflections on how to overcome the problem (like bringing your ID, voting early if you can, knowing your right to vote if you are already in line when the polls begin to close). These steps don't deny emotion in our politics, but they do encourage us to use it for good and to avoid fatalism and disengagement.

What to do about displays of emotion that go beyond the bounds of acceptable behavior? Here, I am thinking about the January 6 insurrection, in which angry people stormed the US Capitol in search of lawmakers to punish for having affirmed that Joe Biden won the 2020 election. Here, I admit that I have struggled to come up with recommendations. Recognizing that emotions are an essential part of politics and an important motivation for political participation does not mean that all emotional expressions are equally valid responses. That is, emotions don't get you out of culpability for having broken the law. Emotions are central to politics, and politicians have a special obligation not to instrumentalize emotional appeals to encourage violence or other actions contrary to democratic norms.

Finally, how can we combat the problem that some groups (like people of color or women) cannot really avail themselves of this political resource without coming across as angry or irresponsibly emotional? Emotions are valuable in politics, and people from all backgrounds should have access to them. Part of the solution is for politicians from such groups to reclaim the power of emotion and embrace it, which may help diminish the backlash from having used them. New York Congresswoman Alexandria Ocasio-Cortez (2019) captured this ethos in a Twitter thread when she said: "Both rationality & emotion are inextricable to good leadership, which balances the two. If a person doesn't feel urgency in their gut when communities are poisoned or when a young man dies bc (sic) he couldn't afford price-gouged insulin, they shouldn't be in politics. At all." Ordinary people working in their communities can benefit, too, from finding projects that connect to their passions and persuading others to join them. Making emotion work means sharing our ideas for community improvement with our neighbors and letting them know how we feel. Politics cannot function, that is, without sustaining people's interest and engagement in the issues of the day, and that is exactly what makes emotion central to any form of enlightened politics.

Bibliography

Albertson, B., & Gadarian, S. K. (2015). *Anxious politics: Democratic citizenship in a threatening world.* Cambridge: Cambridge University Press.

Albertson, B., Maedgen, J., & O'Toole, E. (2020). As you prepare to vote this November, here is what you need to know. *The Daily Texan.* https://thedailytexan.com/2020/09/17/as-you-prepare-to-vote-this-november-here%E2%80%99s-what-you-need-to-know (accessed January 30, 2021).

Atherton, K. D. (2016, June 29). Neil deGrasse Tyson's proposed "rationalia" government won't work. *Popular Science.* www.popsci.com/neil-degrasse-tyson-just-proposed-government-that-doesnt-work/ (accessed January 30, 2021).

Baumeister, R. F., Vohs, K. D., DeWall, C. N., & Zhang, L. (2007). How emotion shapes behavior: Feedback, anticipation, and reflection, rather than direct causation. *Personality and Social Psychology Review, 11*(2), 167–203.

Brader, T. (2006). *Campaigning for hearts and minds: How emotional appeals in political ads work.* Chicago: University of Chicago Press.

Cacioppo, J. T., & Gardner, W. (1999). Emotion. *Annual Review of Psychology, 50,* 191–214.

Gadarian, A. K., & Albertson, B. (2013). Anxiety, immigration, and the search for information. *Political Psychology, 35*(2), 133–164.

Garber, M. (2017, January 6). Obama's anger translator takes a final bow. *The Atlantic.*

Hersch, E. (2020). *Politics is for power: How to move beyond political hobbyism, take action, and make real change.* New York: Scribner Press.

Hu, E. (2011, November 25). Campaign trail tears: The changing politics of crying. *National Public Radio.* www.npr.org/2011/11/25/142599676/campaign-trail-tears-the-changing-politics-of-crying (accessed January 30, 2021).

Kinder, D. R. (1994). Reason and emotion in American political life. In R. C. Schank & E. Langer (Eds.), *Beliefs, reasoning, and decision-making: Psychologic in honor of Bob Abelson* (pp. 277–311). New York: Psychology Press.

Krupnikov, Y., & Piston, S. (2015). Accentuating the negative: Candidate race and campaign strategy. *Political Communication, 32*(1), 152–173.

Madison, J. (2012). *The federalist papers.* New York, NY: Dutton/Signet.

Marcus, G. E., & MacKuen, M. B. (1993). Anxiety, enthusiasm, and the vote: The emotional underpinnings of learning and involvement during presidential campaigns. *American Political Science Review, 87*(3), 672–685.

Mason, L., & Kalmoe, N. (2021, January 11). What you need to know about how many Americans condone political violence: And why. *Washington Post,* The MonkeyCage.www.washingtonpost.com/politics/2021/01/11/what-you-need-know-about-how-many-americans-condone-political-violence-why/ (accessed January 30, 2021).

Nelson, A. (2011, January 2). The crying game. *Psychology Today.* www.psychologytoday.com/us/blog/he-speaks-she-speaks/201101/the-crying-game (accessed January 30, 2021).

Ocasio-Cortez, A. (@AOC). (2019, October 15). Both rationality & emotion are inextricable to good leadership, which balances the two: If a person doesn't feel urgency. *Twitter.* https://twitter.com/aoc/status/1184128201913720832?s=10

Phoenix, D. L. (2019). *The anger gap: How race shapes emotion in politics*. Cambridge: Cambridge University Press.

Talisse, R. (2019). Political polarization is about feelings, not facts. *The Conversation*. https://theconversation.com/political-polarization-is-about-feelings-not-facts-120397 (accessed January 30, 2021).

Traister, R. (2018). *Good and mad: The revolutionary power of women's anger*. Simon & Schuster.

Traister, R. (2021, January 8). It was no accident. *New York Magazine*. www.thecut.com/2021/01/pramila-jayapal-surviving-capitol-riots.html (accessed January 30, 2021).

Valentino, N. A., Brader, T., Groenendyk, E. W., Gregorowicz, K., & Hutchings, V. L. (2011). Election night's alright for fighting: The role of emotions in political participation. *Journal of Politics*, 73(1), 156–170.

8 Explore the Reasons for Incivility

Emily Sydnor

As an academic who studies civility, I have a Google News alert set up for any mention of the word "civility" in local and national news sources, and I get at least one hit almost every day. Many of these stories decry the state of civility in American politics today. "Respect, Manners, and Civility in America Need Some Work," claimed one opinion writer for the *Sioux City Journal* in Iowa (Yanney, 2020). Another writer, for the *Lincoln Courier* in Illinois, noted that the first presidential debate in 2020 marked "The Tragic Death of Civility in American Politics" (Tackett, 2020). Americans – whether op-ed writers or participants in national surveys – think that the United States has gotten less civil, and they see this as a central problem for contemporary politics.

But the problem is not that our political discourse has grown coarse and vitriolic – incivility has always been present in American politics and has even risen to greater levels at times of great polarization (Shea & Sproveri, 2012). Instead, the problem is that what we perceive as uncivil varies with our own identities and experiences. Indeed, the very act of labeling particular acts or language as uncivil has its roots in racist, classist, and gendered power structures. To fix American politics, we need a more nuanced understanding of the strategic use of incivility. We need to know when it can help achieve democratic ends, and we need an awareness of our own limitations in processing and reacting to name-calling, insults, and disagreement.

Problem: Incivility Is in the Eye of the Beholder

We tend to think that Americans have a shared understanding of what counts as civil or uncivil, that – just like Supreme Court Justice Potter remarked about pornography – we'll "know it when [we] see it" (Gewirtz, 1996). Academics tend to agree that incivility requires a violation of cultural norms (Mutz, 2015; Jamieson & Hardy, 2012). Some forms of incivility are tied to politeness and "features of discussion that convey an unnecessarily disrespectful tone" (Coe et al., 2014, p. 660), while others are rooted in deliberative theory and what Ashley Muddiman (2017)

DOI: 10.4324/9781003212515-11

calls "public-level incivility" – argumentation based in reciprocity, factual reasoning, and comity. But survey data from the last two decades suggests that while there are some uses of language that we all agree are uncivil, other dimensions are less clear or change over time. For example, Allegheny College sponsored two nationally representative surveys about civility in US politics in 2010 and 2016. In 2010, 89 percent of respondents said belittling or insulting someone was uncivil, and 73 percent of the participants reported that questioning someone's patriotism because they have a different opinion was also uncivil. By 2016, the percent of respondents who believed these acts were uncivil had declined, to 74 percent for belittling or insulting someone and 52 percent for questioning someone's patriotism (Allegheny College, 2016). As we find ourselves in an increasingly polarized and fractured political sphere, the gaps in our agreement on what types of language are civil or uncivil are widening as well. So why do some people see insults as uncivil, while others find them to be an acceptable part of political discourse? As with any personal opinion, a wide range of factors explains differences across people, but we'll focus on two here: partisanship and gender.

In order to understand how our partisan and gender identities shape our judgment of rhetoric as civil or uncivil, we first need to understand two psychological concepts: motivated reasoning and affective polarization. The human brain is naturally predisposed to process information in a biased manner; we are motivated to "arrive at a particular directional conclusion" when presented with information that aligns with or diverges from our preexisting beliefs (Kunda, 1990, p. 480). In politics, this manifests as a motivation to focus on and accept information that supports our partisan beliefs while rejecting information that seems to advantage the other side (Lord et al., 1979). Combined with an increased tendency toward affective polarization – strong positive feelings for one's own party and animosity towards the out-party (Iyengar et al., 2012) – it seems plausible that Americans will view the same rhetoric from the same political figure through a partisan lens, making judgments about the civility of language determined by the match between their own preferences and the party of the speaker (Muddiman, 2017, 2019).

Indeed, the scholarly evidence bears this out. People perceive politicians from their own political party to be significantly less uncivil than members of the opposing party. When asked to provide examples of incivility, about 17 percent of participants in one experiment specifically mentioned partisan political figures or events (Muddiman, 2017). Reactions to incivility are also dictated by partisanship; when incivility is used to attack our own party, we're more likely to retaliate with incivility ourselves and to take more extreme views (Gervais, 2015; Druckman et al., 2019). And when comments posted to *The New York Times* website contain uncivil and partisan language, they are more likely to be boosted or recommended by other readers than when they contain either uncivil or partisan rhetoric alone (Muddiman & Stroud, 2017). While Americans support civility in the abstract, they prefer that politicians – particularly those who share their partisan beliefs – stand firm in support of principles (Wolf et al., 2012). When you consider the partisan diversity in assessments of and reactions to incivility, it's clear that a blanket understanding of what qualifies as "uncivil" is impossible.

This sense is reinforced when we consider the role gender and personality play in the interpretation of incivility. Theories of the role of gender in political discussion argue that women are socialized to be consensus builders and to avoid confrontation (Tannen, 1998); therefore, we should expect women to be more sensitive to uncivil rhetoric than men might be. Several studies find this to be the case: women are more likely to perceive speech acts as uncivil, while men tend to enjoy arguments and disagreement, regardless of whether they are civil (Kenski et al., 2019, 2020; Wolak, 2020). This desire to lean in to conflict (or conversely, to avoid conflict) also shapes reactions to incivility among both men and women (Sydnor, 2019). While men are more likely to enjoy engaging in political debate that turns contentious or even nasty and rude, women are more sensitive to uncivil language and are more likely to identify it in political rhetoric than men who are exposed to the same language.

Clearly, we can't declare incivility "bad for democracy" if we can't even agree on what is civil or uncivil, and the research suggests we are far from a consensus on such matters. Our perceptions of political rhetoric as civil or uncivil depend fundamentally on our own perspectives and the identities we share (or don't) with others who are a part of the conversation. But this isn't the only problem that comes with the rise of incivility in American politics. Political elites and activists use incivility strategically, both to extend democratic values and to maintain unequal and discriminatory institutions.

Problem: Norms of Civility Maintain Existing Racial and Gendered Power Structures

What counts as civil or uncivil varies across individuals. As a result, political elites, activists, and news organizations take advantage of this uncertainty to strategically and intentionally deploy incivility to achieve their political goals. In her 2010 book, *Rude Democracy*, Susan Herbst offers examples from both sides of the aisle of the strategic use of civility and incivility. She points to Sarah Palin's 2008 vice-presidential run, during which Palin simultaneously praised crowds for their clever signs and chants and opened up about her personal life, while also demeaning Democratic presidential candidate Barack Obama by calling him un-American, a socialist, and linked to terrorist activity. This rhetoric effectively rallied the Republican base and ingratiated Palin with those who attended her campaign events.

The rise of "outrage programming" on cable news offers another example of the strategic use of incivility to boost popular support and reinforce group identities. Berry and Sobieraj distinguish outrage from incivility, saying that the "discourteous gestures implied by incivility . . . are considerably less dramatic and demeaning than the remarks and behaviors we define as outrageous" (2014, p. 32). And yet there is substantial overlap – name-calling, insults, character assassination, and obscenities are widely accepted as examples of incivility and outrage. Outrage has increased with the growth of cable news programming, particularly on the Right, and Berry and Sobieraj find that these shows are particularly appealing to viewers because they connect fans to like-minded others in an imagined community. By using outrage rhetoric appealing to viewers' partisan sensitivities, cable news programs reduce viewers' anxieties about abetting social conflict or appearing to be uninformed, and as a result, see their ratings and viewership climb. While incivility was deployed by Palin on the campaign trail in hopes of turning out more voters, outrage is used by cable news programs to effectively increase viewership and distribution of outlets' content.

The rhetoric of civility and the ways in which calls for civility are deployed not only offer political advantages to one "side" over the other, but also frequently serve to reinforce traditional power structures and hierarchies. As Strachan and Wolf write, "Norms of appropriate behavior almost always reflect differences in power and authority. Groups of people who lack access to power are often expected to defer politely – and without question – to those who wield authority over them . . . in some cases, then, calls for civility are really a mechanism of political control" (2013, pp. 42–43). We see these "civility contests" being manifested in the debates around racial justice and immigrant rights over the past century (Braunstein, 2018). In the South during the civil rights era, for example, an emphasis on Southern gentility and consensus perpetuated structures that ensured White success over racial equality. Nonviolent sit-ins, protests, and challenges to the notion of "separate but equal" were quickly labeled as uncivil in an attempt to delegitimize the protestors' underlying arguments (Chafe, 1980).

Today, we see a similar pattern in the advocacy work of undocumented immigrants. Denied the right to vote or participate in traditional political processes, DREAMers – undocumented immigrants brought to the United States as children – advocated for immigrant rights and citizenship through protest marches and demonstrations. In doing so, they were quickly labeled uncivil, rude, and inappropriate, even as their activism sought to extend democratic values and equality to a broader swath of the American population (Volpp, 2014). In both the civil rights–era South and contemporary immigration debates, expectations of civility are based on social hierarchies that privilege Whiteness and traditional conceptions of citizenship. In these cases, it is not the use of insults, name-calling, shouting, or protest activity – the use of incivility – that is the problem with American politics. It is the continued inequality and anti-democratic policy inherent in the political system.

While the previous examples suggest that there are times when incivility can be deployed for democratic aims and to break down existing hierarchies, we also see it used to reinforce power structures, particularly those built around traditional gender relations. On the Internet, these strategies are manifested as gendered harassment; women in journalism, for example, are frequently subjected to comments that criticize, attack, marginalize, stereotype, or threaten them based on their gender or sexuality when they attempt to engage with their audiences online (Chen et al., 2020). As Sarah Sobieraj writes, "this abuse is structural, rooted in hostility toward the voice and visibility of individual speakers as *representatives* of specific groups of people . . . this phenomenon is a patterned, visceral response to the threat of equality in valued digital conversations and arenas" (2018, p. 5). In other words, digital sexism is yet another example of the strategic employment of incivility for political ends. Gendered incivility and harassment inhibit women's use of public space; even when no harassment has occurred, women are wary of making political statements or engaging online for fear of intimidation and threats (Gardner, 1995; Sobieraj, 2018). In this case, incivility has a detrimental effect on democratic values, systematically silencing voices and rendering members of the public invisible on issues that matter to them.

Conclusion

Americans are turned off by the nastiness of contemporary politics. Almost half of those surveyed as part of Weber Shandwick's "Civility in America 2019" poll reported that they avoid discussing politics or President Trump because they fear the conversation will lead to incivility (Weber Shandwick et al., 2019). And yet discussion of political issues, opinions, and feelings is one of the fundamental ways in which we can ensure democratic representation and legitimacy (Carey, 1997; Habermas, 1974; Mill, 1989). Nasty politics aren't going away anytime soon, so what can we do to more effectively navigate the public sphere and encourage productive political discussion?

First, we must be aware of and reflect on the strategic use of incivility rather than simply dismissing it as bad for democracy, governance, and representation. The next time you encounter protestors calling the president names or engaging in an insult war on Twitter, think about why the speaker might be using that language. When incivility results from a failure of mutual respect or an attempt to call attention to injustice, it can have positive democratic effects – greater inclusivity and awareness of diverse political voices. As an example, consider the graffitied messages that now cover the statue of Confederate General Robert E. Lee in Richmond, Virginia. Mixed in with the calls of "No Justice, No Peace" and to "Say His Name" are messages like "Fuck 12" and "All Cops are Bastards" (or ACAB). The latter comments qualify as uncivil under most definitions of the word, and yet I would caution against writing them off as inappropriate democratic discourse. In the wake of Black Lives Matter protests, both in 2014 and in 2020, Whites' racial attitudes shifted in a more progressive direction as the spotlight was pointed on widespread police brutality against Blacks (Tesler, 2020). Even if we don't like to see obscenities painted on a historic statue, that incivility, in conjunction with the efforts of activists and protestors, is shifting American public opinion in the direction of greater racial equality.

In contrast, consider the reaction of President Donald Trump when vehicles with Trump signs and flags surrounded a Biden-Harris bus on the highway outside of Austin, Texas, and tried to use their vehicles to slow down the bus or run it off the road. The next day, the President tweeted "I LOVE TEXAS!" with a video of the altercation between vehicles (Tilove, 2020). While not engaging in name-calling or insults, the president's tweet qualifies as uncivil under typical academic understandings – it is encouraging violence (or at minimum, the threat of violence), engaging in an emotional display through the use of capitalization (usually used online to denote shouting), and displaying a lack of respect for the other side. Here, incivility serves to undermine a key component of legitimate political competition between parties and is harmful to democratic values. As I discussed earlier and will return to shortly, our tendency toward motivated reasoning and our willingness to accept arguments that support our "team" are strong. Trump's incivility was strategic – it likely generated enthusiasm or engagement among his supporters during the final days of a campaign in which both parties were seeking to maximize turnout among their members. But it also damages the democratic fabric of American life.

The second prong of our approach to navigating an uncivil political environment requires some self-assessment. Politics is always going to be about disagreement, confrontation, and intractable conflict. How we handle that conflict, confrontation, and disagreement is important for our ability to engage in the public sphere. As I show in my recent book, people who are more accepting of conflict in their personal and professional relationships are also more likely to engage in certain types of political activity and to share their opinions about politics – even if they face incivility when doing so (Sydnor, 2019). What the research is less clear on, however, is how we can deal with the conflict we see, especially when we want to crawl under a rock every time political pundits start shouting at each other on television. One place to start might be to practice having difficult political conversations, in much the same way we practice public speaking. Just as the typical person can become more comfortable the more often he or she is asked to speak in front of groups, so, too, might we expect people who would prefer to shy away from controversy to better handle it as they practice dealing with it more and more often.

Finally, we must also be thoughtful in our own engagement with information and when communicating our own beliefs. Every time we read a news story, scroll through Twitter, or listen to a podcast, we should be thinking about how our own predispositions lead us to interpret the facts and opinions being shared. If you're a Democrat, it's not enough to turn on Fox News, only to start shouting at the pundits on the screen about misinformation and Republican stupidity. Instead of writing off the arguments, reflect on them: Why do you feel they are stupid? Where do those arguments come from, and can you understand why they are appealing to others? Are the claims based on factual evidence, even if you ultimately disagree with the overall claim being made? The same exercise must be completed by Republicans who dismiss the mainstream media as having a liberal bias. There are real structural critiques to be made of the American media, and we should not dismiss concerns about the ways in which contemporary news is shared with the public. But confronting and reflecting on our own biases can be an effective initial step toward increasing mutual respect and understanding.

In her book on gendered harassment online, Sobieraj notes that "it's not illegal to be an asshole" and that, in spite of the harm done by attacks on women, we must preserve the right to free expression. "As uncomfortable and counterintuitive as it seems," she writes, "this means that those hell bent on silencing others need to find something else to say. They should argue with ideas, challenge assumptions, and by all means question facts, but they need to take the rape threats and pornographic gifs off the table" (2020, p. 152). Structural and institutional rules can encourage this sort of reoriented conversation, but we can also take a huge first step in fixing American politics by making the personal decision not to engage in rhetoric designed to undermine, silence, and marginalize other people and to refuse to be persuaded by those who resort to such tactics. An enlightened democracy, after all, hangs in the balance.

Bibliography

Allegheny College. (2016). Allegheny survey: 2016 presidential campaign reveals chilling trend lines for civility in U.S. politics. *Allegheny.edu.* https://sites.allegheny.edu/news/2016/10/17/allegheny-survey-2016-presidential-campaign-reveals-chilling-trend-lines-for-civility-in-u-s-politics/ (accessed October 23, 2020).

Berry, J. M., & Sobieraj, S. (2014). *The outrage industry: Political opinion media and the new incivility.* Oxford & New York: Oxford University Press.

Braunstein, R. (2018). Boundary-work and the demarcation of civil from uncivil protest in the United States: Control, legitimacy, and political inequality. *Theory and Society, 47*(5), 603–633.

Carey, J. (1997). The press, public opinion, and public discourse: On the edge of the postmodern. In E. S. Munson & C. A. Warren (Eds.), *James Carey: A critical reader* (pp. 228–258). University of Minnesota Press. www.jstor.org/stable/10.5749/j.ctttsvzt.17 (accessed October 23, 2020).

Chafe, W. H. (1980). *Civilities and civil rights: Greensboro, North Carolina, and the black struggle for freedom.* New York: Oxford University Press.

Chen, G. M. et al. (2020). "You really have to have a thick skin": A cross-cultural perspective on how online harassment influences female journalists. *Journalism, 21*(7), 877–895.

Coe, K., Kenski, K., & Rains, S. A. (2014). Online and uncivil? Patterns and determinants of incivility in newspaper website comments. *Journal of Communication, 64*(4), 658–679.

Druckman, J. N., Gubitz, S. R., Levendusky, M. S., & Lloyd, A. M. (2019). How incivility on partisan media (De)Polarizes the electorate. *The Journal of Politics, 81*(1), 291–295.

Gardner, C. B. (1995). *Passing by: Gender and public harassment.* Berkeley, CA: University of California Press. www.ucpress.edu/book/9780520202153/passing-by (accessed November 1, 2020).

Gervais, B. T. (2015). Incivility online: Affective and behavioral reactions to uncivil political posts in a web-based experiment. *Journal of Information Technology & Politics, 12*(2), 167–185.

Gewirtz, P. (1996). On "I know it when I see it". *Yale Law Journal, 105*, 1023–1047.

Habermas, J. (1974). The public sphere: An encyclopedia article. *New German Critique,* (3), 49–55.

Iyengar, S., Gaurav, S., & Yphtach, L. (2012). Affect, not ideology a social identity perspective on polarization. *Public Opinion Quarterly, 76*(3), 405–431.

Jamieson, K. H., & Hardy, B. (2012). What is civil engaged argument and why does aspiring to it matter? *PS: Political Science and Politics, 45*(3), 412–415.

Kenski, K., Coe, K., & Rains, S. A. (2019). Perceptions of incivility in public discourse. In R. G. Boatright, T. J. Shaffer, S. Sobieraj, & Young, D. G. (Eds.), *A crisis of civility? Political discourse and its discontents* (pp. 45–60). New York: Routledge.

Kenski, K., Coe, K., & Rains, S. A. (2020). Perceptions of uncivil discourse online: An examination of types and predictors. *Communication Research, 47*(6), 795–814.

Kunda, Z. (1990). The case for motivated reasoning. *Psychological Bulletin, 108*(3), 480–498.

Lord, C., Ross, L., & Lepper, M. R. (1979). Biased assimilation and attitude polarization: The effects of prior theories on subsequently considered evidence. *Journal of Personality and Social Psychology, 37*(11), 2098–2109.

Mill, J. S. (1989). *J. S. Mill: "On liberty" and other writings.* Cambridge: Cambridge University Press.

Muddiman, A. (2017). Personal and public levels of political incivility. *International Journal of Communication, 11*(0), 21.

Muddiman, A. (2019). How people perceive incivility. In R. G. Boatright, T. J. Shaffer, S. Sobieraj, & Young, D. G. (Eds.), *A crisis of civility? Political discourse and its discontents* (pp. 31–44). New York: Routledge.

Muddiman, A., & Stroud, N. J. (2017). News values, cognitive biases, and partisan incivility in comment sections. *Journal of Communication, 67*(4), 586–609.

Mutz, D. C. (2015). *In-your-face politics: The consequences of uncivil media.* Princeton, NJ: Princeton University Press.

Shea, D. M., & Sproveri, A. (2012). The rise and fall of nasty politics in America. *PS: Political Science and Politics, 45*(3), 416–421.

Sobieraj, S. (2018). Bitch, slut, skank, cunt: Patterned resistance to women's visibility in digital publics. *Information, Communication & Society, 21*(11), 1700–1714.

Sobieraj, S. (2020). *Credible threat: Attacks against women online and the future of democracy.* New York, NY: Oxford University Press.

Strachan, J. C., & Wolf, M. R. (2013). Calls for civility: An invitation to deliberate or a means of political control? In D. M. Shea & M. P. Fiorina (Eds.), *Can we talk? The rise of rude, nasty, stubborn politics* (pp. 41–52). New York, NY: Pearson Education.

Sydnor, E. (2019). *Disrespectful democracy: The psychology of political incivility.* New York: Columbia University Press.

Tackett, D. (2020). The tragic death of civility in American politics. *Lincoln Courier.* www.lincolncourier.com/opinion/20201002/tragic-death-of-civility-in-american-politics (accessed October 7, 2020).

Tannen, D. (1998). *The argument culture: Stopping America's war of words.* New York: Ballantine Books.

Tesler, M. (2020). Analysis | the Floyd protests have changed public opinion about race and policing: Here's the data. *Washington Post.* www.washingtonpost.com/politics/2020/06/09/floyd-protests-have-changed-public-opinion-about-race-policing-heres-data/ (accessed November 1, 2020).

Tilove, J. (2020). Trump train swarms Biden bus on 1–35, and Trump is delighted. *Austin American-Statesman.* www.statesman.com/news/20201031/trump-train-swarms-biden-bus-on-1-35-and-trump-is-delighted (accessed November 1, 2020).

Volpp, L. (2014). Civility and the undocumented alien. In *Civility, legality, and justice in America.* New York: Cambridge University Press.

Weber-Shandwick, Powell-Tate, & KRC Research. (2019). *Civility in America 2019: Solutions for tomorrow.* Washington, DC. www.webershandwick.com/wp-content/uploads/2019/06/CivilityInAmerica2019SolutionsforTomorrow.pdf (accessed October 23, 2020).

Wolak, J. (2020). Conflict avoidance and gender gaps in political engagement. *Political Behavior.* https://doi.org/10.1007/s11109-020-09614-5 (accessed February 18, 2021).

Wolf, M. R., Strachan, J. C., & Shea, D. M. (2012). Incivility and standing firm: A second layer of partisan division. *PS: Political Science & Politics, 45*(3), 428–434.

Yanney, C. (2020). The regulars: Respect, manners and civility in America need some work. *Sioux City Journal.* https://siouxcityjournal.com/opinion/columnists/the-regulars-respect-manners-and-civility-in-america-need-some-work/article_34654b97-9687-5b59-8a25-d0e56c5640ad.html (accessed October 7, 2020).

9 Tell the Story of Poverty[1]

Eunji Kim

The United States is now experiencing an apocalyptic level of economic inequality, and the global pandemic has only exacerbated that trend. With the daily death toll reaching up to 4,000 and the number of jobs plummeting, the stock market and the prices of cryptocurrencies nonetheless soared through the roof. The wealth of CEOs like Jeff Bezos and Elon Musk more than tripled, while Main Street Americans cried over their loss of loved ones.

If the trends of the last 20 years continue, it seems unlikely that there will be a meaningful shift in public demand for more progressive redistribution of wealth. Defying the predictions of standard political economy models (Meltzer & Richard, 1983), Americans have generally moved away from more egalitarian policy preferences as the income gap has widened (Ashok et al., 2015; Kelly & Enns, 2010; Kenworthy & McCall, 2008). In other words, Americans, on average, have become more economically conservative and the top 1 percent has accumulated a jaw-dropping amount of wealth. This has led some to conclude that "the current consensus seems to be that inequality does not matter for the politics of redistribution" (Lupu & Pontusson, 2011, p. 316).

A burgeoning amount of social science research has tried to answer how all this has happened. Explanations range from increased tolerance of income inequality (Trump, 2018) to increasing opposition to redistribution among higher-income voters (Kelly & Enns, 2010). Yet scholars of inequality are missing an essential piece of the puzzle. Public economic perceptions are shaped by informational ecosystems, which create the context in which policy demands are made. Hence, a careful and candid look at the types of information available and, more importantly, the information actually consumed by the public is urgently needed.

Here is an uncomfortable truth that too many social scientists have overlooked. Once upon a time, an evening news program was a daily ritual for most American families. It is unthinkable now, but the nation's most-watched TV program used to be CBS's *60 Minutes*,[2] an hour-long newsmagazine broadcast. Not anymore. With an astonishing number of media choices – ranging from Netflix and Amazon Prime to Hulu and

DOI: 10.4324/9781003212515-12

YouTube – Americans are consuming an astounding amount of entertainment media. Watching the news is more like a niche hobby for a small subpopulation.

Consider for example that Fox News – the most-watched cable news channel – attracts only 3 million viewers during an average primetime hour. Although news headlines based on a self-reported survey create the misleading impression that many Americans are getting political news, a study of web-browsing activities during an election year as highly contentious as 2016 found that only 1.9 percent of web traffic went to news sites. In stark contrast, *American Idol's* peak ratings were 36.5 million viewers (for the Season 5 finale). Approximately 96.4 million viewers watched the 2021 Super Bowl victory by the Tampa Bay Buccaneers. An estimated 130 million people used Instagram as of July 2020.

The glaring fact that the American media diet is primarily composed of entertainment media can be a key to understanding the politics of inequality and public preferences for redistribution. In this chapter, I outline three ways in which the current media environment can propagate ideas that fuel economic conservatism during this age of inequality.[3] I then propose how redirecting our policy discussion to poverty instead of inequality offers a solution.

The American Dream, Alive and Well in Reality TV Shows

While researchers in the ivory tower might watch Noam Chomsky's documentary, *Requiem for the American Dream*, in their leisure time, ordinary Americans expose themselves to entirely different stimuli. Reality TV shows, like *American Idol* and *Shark Tank*, featuring ordinary Americans have been attracting millions of eyeballs for the last two decades. The number of reality TV shows surged in early 2000. By 2008, 1 in 5 newly released programs was a reality TV show (Kim, 2020). In this golden age of reality TV, all but one such show among the top 10 most-watched programs from 2000 to 2017 had a competitive format featuring the American Dream (see also Kim, 2019).[4] These TV shows envisioned an America where anyone – from budding entrepreneurs to amateur singers – could charm the audience and the judges and then climb the economic ladder.

These narratives of economic mobility could not be more different from those seen in the news media. With its well-known bias for negativity, the press typically focuses on stories of downward economic mobility, tales of those who lost jobs, had soaring debts, or missed payday loan deadlines, to name just a few. In tandem with the worsening economic realities of this new Gilded Age, computational text analysis confirms that *The New York Times*'s coverage of economic mobility from 1980 to 2020 consistently displayed negative sentiments (see Kim, 2020, Appendix C). Most importantly, by using an array of observational and experimental data, Kim (2020) demonstrated that shows offering powerful exemplars of upward mobility promote people's beliefs in the American Dream and the internal attributions of wealth. Beliefs in economic mobility are known to legitimize economic disparity and diminish support for wealth redistribution (Piketty, 1995). In other words, this prevalent and popular genre of TV programming has exerted a conservative influence over American politics in this era of massive class stratification.

Sports and Winner-Takes-All Society

In this high-choice media market, no single TV show – however popular – attracts the kind of audience share seen before. In the 1980s, for example, one of the most popular entertainment shows, *The Cosby Show*, attracted more than 60 million Americans at its peak popularity. But in 2019, even *Game of Thrones*, which drew a record viewership on HBO and had an active fan base, attracted only 19.3 million viewers.

Within this fragmented audience, a major strand of today's media environment consists of sports broadcasts. Since 1970, viewership for the Super Bowl has been on the rise: 46.9 million Americans tuned in to the show in 1970, yet around 100 million people have watched it in each of the last 11 years, making it easily the most-watched television event of each TV season.[5]

Although scholars of American politics typically pay attention to sports only when it is highly politicized – for example, when players drop to one knee to protest racial injustice – it is worth noting that sports broadcasts have ample potential for influencing Americans' beliefs about meritocracy.

In the world of sports, nothing matters more than raw talent. The tone of someone's skin or their family background is immaterial, and famous sports stars – from Babe Ruth to Tom Brady – serve as the exemplars of those who have achieved the American Dream. In addition to their own rags-to-riches stories, the level playing field of sports typically evokes Darwin's survival of the fittest. These messages are especially good at conveying subtle conservative messages (Sage, 1990; Whannel, 2005).

Indeed, in one of the few studies that has examined the impact of sports on political attitudes, Emily Thorson and Michael Serazio (2018) hypothesized that sports media might reify a narrative of economic individualism and lead Americans to attribute economic success to internal factors. Using a nationally representative survey, the study found that sports fans are more likely to believe that economic success results from a meritocratic process and that internal factors, such as individual ambitions and perseverance, matter more for getting ahead than do structural factors. Here again, an important pillar of today's media environment – sports, like reality TV shows – promotes beliefs in meritocracy and the legitimacy of the winner-take-all system.

Social Media and Envy for the Better-Offs

People tend to assess their self-worth by comparing themselves to others, envying those who are better off and who desire power and status within their reference group (Tesser, 2000). As central as it is to our everyday life, social comparison is also a powerful driver of our political life. Why? Because our political preferences and behaviors change depending on our social reference group (Condon & Wichowsky, 2020; McClendon, 2018).

Who becomes part of our reference group? Before the advent of social media, we primarily compared ourselves to those with whom we directly interacted. Now, it is hard not to miss the ample opportunity social media offers us to compare our lives to those of complete strangers. In the world of Facebook, Instagram, and YouTube, many unknown others boast of their exotic trips abroad or their giant mansion with a pool. In this carefully curated online world, we rarely encounter the stories of those who are poor. One computational social science study that examined 7.5 million geotagged photos taken in Manhattan (and publicly shared on Instagram) confirmed the pattern we have already observed: the underprivileged portions of Manhattan are poorly represented in the world of Instagram. Just as we are economically segregated in physical space, we rarely see the lives of those who have less than us in cyberspace.

What are the economic consequences of the social comparisons enabled by social media? What important implications do they carry for the politics of inequality? First, by fueling envy and social status concerns, social media lead affluent Americans to support conservative economic policies that benefit themselves, such as decreasing taxes on affluent households or capital gains (Thal, 2020). To the extent that wealthy Americans have disproportionate influence in American politics, social media have the potential to facilitate this peer comparison, provoke social status concerns, and ultimately encourage them to pursue conservative economic policies fostering economic inequality.

Second, even though seeing the advantaged makes us more accurate about our own status and more supportive of welfare and social spending, this experience is not true in the world of social media. In these newer platforms, mediated contacts with the rich are crafted to deter people from rethinking redistribution or from questioning how wealthy individuals got their wealth. Meghan Condon and Amber Wichowsky (2020), for instance, wrote that social media allow "audiences to consume celebrity culture without feeling less-than" and that this "equalizing" communication creates a parasocial relationship for the audience. "The class contact fantasyland in the media landscape disguises a deeper truth of growing class difference and separation," they conclude.

Either way, whether through peer comparison that evokes status concerns or through pleasant encounters with the advantaged, the economic implications of social media remain the same, making us more favorable toward economic conservatism and less likely to address growing income inequality.

Conclusion

So far, I have covered how three major strands of today's media environment – reality TV programs, sports broadcasts, and social media – might function to legitimize economic inequality. Yet solutions are, as always, not simple. I am wary of addressing complex social problems only to suggest feel-good conclusions at the end. Ultimately, in a society that values free speech and individual choice, we can control neither the types of media programs that TV producers create nor the contents Americans consume in their leisure. The fragmented nature of today's media environment will push networks to keep producing low-cost reality TV shows featuring ordinary Americans. Our cultural obsession with the Super Bowl – or its commercials – will not end anytime soon. Too, the number of social media users is projected to only increase, and newer platforms, like TikTok and Clubhouse, are popping up constantly.

So how can economic inequality be fixed when support for redistributive policies that could address this wealth inequity is clearly lacking? One solution would be to reframe our public discourse – particularly media and elite discourse – to center on poverty instead of economic inequality. It is worth noting that the current level of economic disparity in America is primarily top driven; that is, the problem arises not because the poor have become poorer but because the richest Americans have become wealthier (see also Kim et al., 2019). Most Americans have not been supportive of policies that take money from the rich because of people's deeply rooted beliefs in economic individualism. We must remember that in the current media environment, economic success is increasingly framed around individual talents. During an age in which the highest-paid YouTubers are now millionaires, it is hard to disparage wealth accumulation. The American dream, that is, still persists.

In light of this firmly entrenched, highly individualistic ideology, it would be easier to attract public support for policies that address poverty instead of inequality. In many ways, "inequality" has become a buzzword that pops up in many news headlines, but it might have come at the expense of covering the poor (Froomkin, 2013). Although poverty and inequality are different problems, elites tend to feature the latter rather than the former when discussing the same underlying concern. People's willingness to help the poor far surpasses their desire to lower the incomes of the rich. That is especially true in the current media environment.

Some pundits have predicted that only disasters of an apocalyptic scale might fix economic inequality in the United States. But the COVID-19 pandemic only exacerbated economic inequality. It might be time to stop focusing on how much money Elon Musk makes (since media coverage of his wealth only seems to have strengthened his loyal fan base) in an attempt to provoke broad resentment. It is time, instead, for us to talk about how millions of hungry people are turning to food banks in the world's most powerful economy.

Media coverage of poverty, of course, has a long history of racial stereotyping (Gilens, 1996). Yet when there is a clear and broadly shared understanding that poverty results not from a lack of individual effort but from forces beyond human control – such as pandemic-triggered unemployment – broader policy support might well be mobilized. Even though Republican elites were not sympathetic to President Joe Biden's pandemic stimulus bill, poll after poll showed that most Republican *voters* supported his $1,400 direct stimulus payments.

Speaking of unity seems almost delusional in American politics these days, a time when the mere act of wearing a mask has become politicized. But Americans of all stripes now have an intense longing for the little joys of ordinary life, whether it is watching sports in a packed bar with strangers or hugging a grandmother. If restoring those days requires government redistribution, a shared longing for normalcy might stave off the pandemic's lasting scars on American poverty. That, at least, is my hope.

Notes

1. This chapter contains ideas and evidence that have been empirically demonstrated or articulated in Kim (2019).
2. *60 Minutes* (CBS) was a top-10 show for 23 seasons in a row from 1977 to 2000.
3. These ideas have been outlined in Kim (2019).
4. The exception was *Desperate Housewives* in the 2004–2006 and 2007–2008 TV seasons.
5. It comes as no surprise, then, that even the president wants to exploit this moment to deliver political messages to otherwise inattentive public. Just before the 2021 Super Bowl kickoff, President Joe Biden and First Lady Jill Biden made a video appearance to express their gratitude to front-line workers who served Americans during the pandemic.

Bibliography

Ashok, V., Kuziemko, I., & Washington, E. (2015). *Support for redistribution in an age of rising inequality: New stylized facts and some tentative explanations* (No. w21529). Cambridge, MA: National Bureau of Economic Research.

Condon, M., & Wichowsky, A. (2020). *The economic other: Inequality in the American political imagination*. Chicago: University of Chicago Press.

Froomkin, D. (2013). It can't happen here: Why is there so little coverage of Americans who are struggling with poverty? *Nieman Reports*, 66(4), 40–43.

Gilens, M. (1996). Race and poverty in America: Public misperceptions and the American news media. *Public Opinion Quarterly*, 60(4), 515–541.

Kelly, N. J., & Enns, P. K. (2010). Inequality and the dynamics of public opinion: The self-reinforcing link between economic inequality and mass preferences. *American Journal of Political Science*, 54(4), 855–870.

Kenworthy, L., & McCall, L. (2008). Inequality, public opinion, and redistribution. *Socio-Economic Review*, 6, 35–68.

Kim, E. (2019). *Entertaining beliefs in economic mobility* (Doctoral dissertation), University of Pennsylvania.

Kim, E. (2020). *Entertaining beliefs in economic mobility*. Working paper.

Kim, E., Pedersen, R. T., & Mutz, D. C. (2019). *Misunderstanding income inequality*. Working paper.

Lupu, N., & Pontusson, J. (2011). The structure of inequality and the politics of redistribution. *American Political Science Review*, 105(2), 316–336.

McClendon, G. H. (2018). *Envy in politics*. Princeton, NJ: Princeton University Press.

Meltzer, A. H., & Richard, S. F. (1983). Tests of a rational theory of the size of government. *Public Choice*, 41(3), 403–418.

Piketty, T. (1995). Social mobility and redistributive politics. *The Quarterly Journal of Economics*, 110(3), 551–584.

Sage, G. H. (1990). *Power and ideology in American sport: A critical perspective*. Champaign, IL: Human Kinetics Publishers.

Tesser, A. (2000). On the confluence of self-esteem maintenance mechanisms. *Personality and Social Psychology Review*, 4(4), 290–299.

Thal, A. (2020). The desire for social status and economic conservatism among affluent Americans. *American Political Science Review*, 114(2), 426–442.

Thorson, E. A., & Serazio, M. (2018). Sports fandom and political attitudes. *Public Opinion Quarterly*, 82(2), 391–403.

Trump, K. S. (2018). Income inequality influences perceptions of legitimate income differences. *British Journal of Political Science*, 48(4), 929–952.

Whannel, G. (2005). *Fields in vision: Television sport and cultural transformation*. Abingdon, UK: Routledge.

10 Imagine New Political Coalitions

Vincent N. Pham

Prior to becoming a somewhat popular actor, writer, and comedian, Hari Kondabolu worked as an immigrant rights community organizer in Seattle. In his 2014 debut comedy album, *Waiting for 2042*, he offered a bit about people critiquing his "obsession" with race as part of his stand-up routine (Kondabolu, 2014). He then disarmed this accusation by likening it to "being obsessed with swimming when I'm drowning." He then quickly pivoted to saying, "I'm not the one (who is obsessed). I'm not the one bringing up 2042." Noting this as the moment when Census figures mark the beginning of the White minority, his punchline comes as a sardonic explanation; "49% white doesn't make you a minority; that's not how math works.... (it's) only a minority if you think the other 51% is *exactly* the same."

In this snippet, Kondabolu highlights two key things. First, he draws attention to how the public discourse about race views it primarily in quantitative terms, how race most commonly makes itself evident and legible for White audiences. Second, he implies that it is White people who are obsessed with race, not people of color, who simply talk about race as it springs from their daily lives and lived experiences.

Much has been said about the 2042 demographic shift that will produce a "White minority," especially as the last five congressional elections have increasingly ushered in the "most ethnically and racially diverse Congress" (Bialik, 2019). Yet these instances highlight the public's adherence to representation as the end goal of political involvement and cultural relevance while also sounding alarms to the White status quo about its impending loss. Such assumptions hinder a politics drawn from but not essentialized in identity, a politics that would serve us well in a multiethnic democracy. In fact, racial identity is but one of many identities that become articulated, that provide a means of linkage, but that also become essentialized for political purposes. In this chapter, I address notions of racialized representations that hinder our ability to imagine new coalitions drawing on a range of human identities. And for the future, we must imagine far more for ourselves as a nation than we have imagined in the past.

DOI: 10.4324/9781003212515-13

Beyond Representation

The obsessive regard for the shifting demographics leading to 2042 relies on a couple of assumptions mentioned earlier: one about quantitative representation and the other about the essentialization of race. Some people assume that representation is automatically commensurate with power or having access to it. This is especially true in the representation industries in Hollywood. If politics is downstream from culture, that is, Hollywood provides unique insight into the limits of representation.

In 2015, the Academy of Motion Pictures Arts and Sciences and its most well-known event, the Oscars, were publicly critiqued with the twitter hashtag #OscarsSoWhite, calling attention to the historical Whiteness of Hollywood and its award structure, a structure that overwhelmingly overlooked the accomplishments of (most notably) Black people but other people of color as well. To reconcile the issues brought on by #OscarsSoWhite, the Academy inserted people of color into the programming of the 2016 Oscars show, with Kevin Hart providing a monologue and Chris Rock serving as host. While Chris Rock shined the light on the overwhelming Whiteness of the Best Actor and Best Picture nominees, he was also remembered for bringing three adorable Asian children dressed in suits onto the stage, mentioning that they were "dedicated, accurate, and hard-working" accountants and then joking about Chinese kids making phones in sweatshops (Abad-Santos, 2016).

This vignette illustrates that inclusion and representation do not inherently change the system that produces said exclusion. Instead, the mere insertion of people of color into an already existing structured framework can still maintain the "OscarsSoWhite" dynamic and do little to change an exclusionary system. In other words, the notion that representation in the quantitative sense will inevitably lead to widespread change is highly questionable. That is not to say that "representation" doesn't matter; rather, I want to emphasize that while representation is a worthy objective, it *should not* be the end goal, even though it is often treated as such. Instead, the goal must be a wholescale shift in what kinds of stories are being told and what concerns are being brought up, many of which might be tied to race but that do not exclusively focus on people's racial backgrounds.

This leads to a second assumption about racialized representation – that race is the only component of one's practiced politics. Racial identity is but one identity with which we are born and within which we are situated, but race does not constitute our sole identity nor does it encapsulate our political and moral valence. Essentialization is occasionally necessary, as Gayatri Spivak argues, for its strategic purposes (Danius et al., 1993). But all too often, essentializing racial identity leads to such things as discussions of the "Latino vote" or the "Asian vote." Here, race becomes a constraining category, a kind of political punditry that encapsulates a diverse community into legible categories but that limits our understanding of the varied, lived experiences of the people within that community.

For example, a phrase like "the Latino vote" clumps Cubans and Mexicans into the same group despite their sharply different lived experiences. The "Asian American vote" also aggregates multigenerational Japanese Americans with Vietnamese Americans whose families have immigrated from Communist countries. In these cases, their recognized "representation" conflicts with the real-life experiences of people within these racialized groups.

Kamala Harris, the first woman and woman of color as vice president, serves as a useful case for thinking through some of these issues. The labeling of her within particular categories – i.e., woman, Black woman, Asian woman, woman of color, etc. – serves to make her legible within the framework of representation, particularly that she is a "first" and hence is breaking barriers. Whether "woman," "Black," or "Asian" becomes the dominant motif for describing Harris often depends on the audience being addressed. The primary emphasis might be placed on her being the "first Black woman," with an emphasis on "Black" and "woman," whereas her "Asian," or "South Asian" characteristics only come into play afterward. Sometimes, the reporting about Harris becomes ethnically specific, with references to her "Jamaican father" or "Indian mother." All of this draws our attention to the many ways Harris's identity can be articulated. Throughout, though, the emphasis on her *identity* (versus her politics) served to unite the diverse coalition of voters hoping to shape the future via Kamala Harris's ascension to the vice presidency.

In any event, Harris's accomplishments paid tribute to her importance for the groups mentioned (and for overall societal acceptance as well). The representation of Harris as a Black and Asian or "Blasian" mixed-race woman vice president was itself groundbreaking.[1] Harris's story is partly about reconciling the past – she was able to transcend the barriers of racism – but it is also about a future embracing a linear narrative of progress. The strategic deployment of Harris's intersectional identity speaks to the possibilities lying ahead for the United States and, particularly, to the possibilities of coalitional politics. Instead of treating racial identity in an essentialized manner, then, we must recognize how it is activated and articulated in coalitional ways as well, something that will become truly pressing as more diverse, interactive, or niche-oriented politics arrive on the scene. That is, our present modes of understanding race are not adequate for grasping the possibilities that will come about in a nation becoming more and more diverse by the day. So what we need at this point is a way of thinking about the future that imagines a new and more vigorous brand of coalitional politics.

Unexceptional Coalitions

Barack Obama and Kamala Harris seem to embody the possibilities of racial coalitions through the common narrative of mixed-race people as precursors to a postracial society. Yet their mixed-race identities do not prevent them from mortgaging Black and Brown lives for the sake of political expediency (examples include Obama's deportation record with immigrants and Harris's criminal justice history when serving as attorney general of California). Their presence spurred what Emily Apter (2018) describes as "unexceptional politics," politics below the radar that features the messiness of everyday life. This sort of politics – of impasse, obstruction, and obstinacy – has inspired many social movements. Political groups like the Tea Party and Occupy Wall Street, for example, made their presence known in the early 2010s. Groups like these are born out of formerly "essentialized" cadres that become more variegated and more united when political circumstances suddenly become open to new coalitions.

Such coalitions present the possibility of working across differences by uniting in a common cause, even though the desire for unity can obscure the very real differences that inspired the coalition in the first place. Karma Chávez's (2013) important work on "queer migration politics" dives into the uncertainties of such coalitions, showing that they operate in tense precarity, one that is present and relationship affirming but that cannot be taken for granted because of "new rearticulations, changing identities, and future political relationships" (8). Here, queerness invokes future, utopian potentialities even as it engages with the urgency of now. As Chávez says, such coalition must still confront the "identity, subjectivity, power, and politics located on the dirt and concrete where people live, work, and play" (7).

If we are to think of issues that have been historically generated but that have overriding importance for our future, arguably the most pressing ones are the racial justice movement regarding Black lives and the worldwide climate crisis. At the forefront of these movements are the Black Lives Matter Global Network Foundation, Inc. and the Sunrise Movement. While their opponents critique both groups for what they seek to change and to miscast their politics as misguided or impractical, I want to focus on what they *envision* for a future in which all may benefit.

BLM is often seen as an antipolice and racist organization by some and a terrorist organization by others. Yet BLM was founded out of love – Alicia Garza's love letter to Black people in the aftermath of George Zimmerman's acquittal after the shooting of Trayvon Martin, an unjust and tragic event transformed into a hashtag that then resonated across the Black diaspora. Importantly, BLM was always about the future, "moving forward towards justice, towards visions, towards a world where our families and communities are no longer the sacrifice for a better America, for a better world." Central to this mantra was an inclusive vision, regardless of political party, of those who "share a vision that is radical and intersectional," (*About*, n.d.).

Starting in 2013, antipolice sentiment was simmering in the United States under the eyes of mainstream politics, ready and organizing on local levels and operating in a decentralized fashion even as its founders and leaders were giving talks across the country. Yet it was in the summer of 2020, upon the release of a video documenting Ahmaud Arbery's murder by White vigilantes, George Floyd's murder by police officer Derek Chauvin (with three other officers aiding and abetting), and news of Breonna Taylor's death in her own home by police officers entering via no-knock warrants, that Black Lives Matter rebellions, protests, and marches overtook the country.[2]

Naturally, these marches featured Black people, but they were now filled with White people as well – men and women, little children, teenagers, and the elderly alike. Even in small rural areas like Prineville, Oregon, local community members had a Black Lives Matter march, despite the resistance of Proud Boys and other right-wing militia (Cureton, 2020). Invoking and incorporating Crenshaw's (1991) and the Combahee River Collective's (2017) notion of intersectionality, which included identity's multiple axes but without overly essentializing them, BLM set forth a vision that included all who cared for Black lives along with the recognition that all lives cannot matter until Black lives matter as well.

It is within the BLM movement and its temporal reach from past to future that allowed for a transcendent brand of coalitional politics to emerge, one that reached across time and place to allow for the articulation of identities beyond racial essentialism. While all groups were "represented" in such coalitions, their representation alone did not account for the group's power. Instead, it was the common dedication to "combatting and countering acts of violence, creating space for Black imagination and innovation, and centering Black joy" that brought such diverse representation together (*About*, n.d.).

While the BLM movement is responding to centuries-long, recurring violence against Black bodies combined, the Sunrise Movement confronts the impending climate disasters. Akin to turning around a cruise ship as it heads into a glacier, the Sunrise Movement's goal is "to reorient the entire project of government around climate change" (Grandoni, 2020). Combining policy orientations (i.e., the Green New Deal) with social movement tactics (i.e., "wake-ups"), the Sunrise Movement stresses that while the environment and climate change affect everyone, they do not affect everyone equally. As a result, the movement goes beyond the racially neutral politics of early environmental activism to proclaim environmental and climate *justice*. As Mattias Lehman (2020), Sunrise Movement Digital Director, states, "We *cannot* achieve climate justice without moving away from police and prisons." The Sunrise Movement and its intersectional focus recognizes the value of articulating identities, but it also realizes how these articulations and coalitions are necessarily contingent. In their political endorsements, for example, Sunrise admits to "no permanent friends, no permanent enemies," signaling that coalitions and alignments are always possible but that they must not be assumed or taken for granted ("Political Endorsements").

BLM and the Sunrise Movement epitomize the ability of contemporary coalitions to attract different types of identities, identities that aren't essentialized but instead connected and articulated in a fast-moving and contingent political universe. Such contingency requires that those involved witness, listen, and act in ways that reinforce the coalition's overall political stance and go beyond essentialized notions of identity. In doing so, these coalitions make themselves politically viable – simultaneously predictable in their desires but unpredictable in their alignments. Equally important, they remain future focused even as they reconcile the past with an ever-changing present.

Conclusion

Although this chapter focuses on how coalitional possibilities deal with the contingencies of the future, it is also concerned with how we might "fix politics." While the idea is to repair what is broken, the notion of "fixing" politics takes on a double meaning. "Fixing" is an act of restoration or repair, an attempt to move toward a previous state of unbrokenness. A secondary meaning of "fixing" is to make things stable, to keep in place that which already exists. Yet US politics has always been broken in one sense, sublimating the voices and concerns of Black, Brown, Asian, and indigenous peoples, so there is still a great deal of *reenvisioning and building* left to do.

As mentioned earlier, the strictly quantitative representation of bodies can lead to the possibility of power, both the power to maintain the status quo and the power to change things outside the boundaries of what is currently deemed possible. However, the shifting demographic and collective discomfort with racial categorizing reveal the flaws of common assumptions about racial representation within political discussions. Essentializing people without purpose or strategy (except to constrain those very communities) is neither progressive nor practical. Doing so often misrepresents their concerns and frustrates their common interests. Putting people into simple (noncoalitional) categories reinforces White positionality and epistemology when making sense of our contemporary moment. Doing so also maintains the status quo while arguing for incremental change in a dynamically changing demographic landscape.

The changing face of America assumes that traditional voting blocs (e.g., the "Latino vote" or the "Asian vote") will vote in partisan ways (e.g. Black voters for Democrats) despite their varied histories and differences. But in fact, things are now considerably more complicated. Ours is a nation with an increasingly multiethnic demographic operating within a multiracial democracy that *numerically* displaces Whiteness but that still preserves its political power and epistemological orientation. Thus, "inclusion" alone is not the issue here but what such groups' *joint* voting power might achieve.

If our future is one filled with racial, sexual, gender, intellectual, and bodily diversity, will we finally learn to take these voices seriously instead of sidelining them because their "numbers" are not plentiful enough to consider? Political philosopher Daniel Innerarity (2012) orients us toward a theory of intergenerational justice in which he asks us to take the future seriously. To pivot toward such a future, I ask the simple question: What do we want that future to look like? One in which people remain placed in their own categories, essentialized without care, and treated singularly? Or do we want a future of vibrant coalitions, which are often messy and confusing but which bring diverse people together?

Clearly, we must imagine the presence of new political actors and new coalitional politics when reconfiguring the future. We must also deal with its enemies – essentialists who can only think in terms of left or right, Democratic or Republican, White or non-White. Instead, we need to ask who will become the "friends of our future?" Who will build the needed possibilities and coalitions? What I posit here is a different way of approaching our broken politics to envision one that foregrounds cross-racial coalitions that span space, time, and identity by placing our intersectional identities at the very center. Such a future would feature shifting demographics as tailwinds, a politics that would allow for a multiplicity of political actors to become involved. Organizations and movements like the Black Lives Matter Global Network and the Sunrise Movement imagine just such a future, one that can imagine children playing outside in clean air and with hospitable temperatures, communities featuring good health care and well-being for all, and, especially, a time when Black Lives Matter is a lived reality.

Notes

1. See Washington's (2017) work on mixed race Black and Asian (i.e., "Blasians") in celebrity culture.
2. I want to note here that these are not passive deaths but people's lives taken far too early. I also want to emphasize precisely who they were, much in line with the "Say Their Names" list that draws attention to Black lives that have been taken unjustly.

Bibliography

Abad-Santos, A. (2016, March 1). What Chris Rock's lazy Asian joke revealed about "diversity" in Hollywood. *Vox*. www.vox.com/2016/3/1/11142390/chris-rock-asian-joke-oscars

About. (n.d.). *Black lives matter.* https://blacklivesmatter.com/about/ (accessed December 18, 2020).

Apter, E. (2018). *Unexceptional politics: On obstruction, impasse, and the impolitic.* London: Verso.

Bialik, K. (2019, February 8). 116th congress is most racially, ethnically diverse ever. *Fact Tank: News in Numbers by The Pew Research Center.* www.pewresearch.org/fact-tank/2019/02/08/for-the-fifth-time-in-a-row-the-new-congress-is-the-most-racially-and-ethnically-diverse-ever/

Chávez, K. R. (2013). *Queer migration politics: Activist rhetoric and coalitional possibilities.* Champaign, IL: University of Illinois Press.

Combahee River Collective. (2017). The Combahee River Collective statement. In K.-Y. Taylor (Ed.), *How we get free: Black feminism and the Combahee River Collective* (pp. 15–27). Chicago: Haymarket Books.

Crenshaw, K. (1991). Mapping the margins: Intersectionality, identity politics, and violence against women of color. *Stanford Law Review, 43*(6), 1241–1299. https://doi.org/10.2307/1229039

Cureton, E. (2020, September 3). In rural Oregon, threats and backlash follow racial justice protests. *NPR.Org.* www.npr.org/2020/09/03/906809148/in-rural-oregon-threats-and-backlash-follow-racial-justice-protests

Danius, S., Jonsson, S., & Spivak, G. (1993). An interview with Gayatri Chakravorty Spivak. *Boundary 2, 20*(2), 24–50.

Grandoni, D. (2020, October 30). A youth-led climate group is campaigning for Biden. If he wins, the honeymoon will be short. *Washington Post.* www.washingtonpost.com/politics/2020/10/30/youth-led-climate-group-is-campaigning-biden-if-he-wins-honeymoon-will-be-short/

Innerarity, D. (2012). *The future and its enemies: In defense of political hope* (S. Kingery, Trans.). Stanford, CA: Stanford University Press.

Kondabolu, H. (2014, February 5). *Hari Kondabolu-2042 & the white minority.* www.youtube.com/watch?v=85fr6nbiMT4

Lehmann, M. (2020, May 29). The climate justice movement must oppose white supremacy everywhere: By supporting M4BL. *Sunrise Movement.* www.sunrisemovement.org/movement-updates/the-climate-justice-movement-must-oppose-white-supremacy-everywhere-by-supporting m4bl-4e338cf91b19/

Washington, M. S. (2017). *Blasian invasion: Racial mixing in the celebrity industrial complex.* Jackson, MS: University Press of Mississippi.

Part 3
Open Your Mind

11 Listen to the First Amendment

Lisbeth A. Lipari

It was not until I began writing this chapter that I realized how my now-24-year-old doctoral dissertation about the rhetorical and ethical problems of public opinion polling was, at heart, about the problems of political listening – as in what happens when the vox populi, the voice of the people, is hijacked by politicians such that the policies of democracy emerge not from the roots but from the crown. After spending the past ten years as a scholar of listening, I now understand that this problem with polling is merely one of a proliferation of problems we face that stem, at heart, from our utter failure, intransigence, and inability to take the study and practice of political listening seriously.

Today, when political opinions and speech have seemingly lost all credibility, when news with which one disagrees is considered fake, and when the science one dislikes gets labeled a hoax, the lapse in our listening seems even more profound. But the problem goes even deeper. In nearly every area of US culture – in education, politics, law, or religion – we seem to focus on speaking at the expense of listening. High schools have debate teams, and colleges teach courses in public speaking, persuasion, and argumentation. From legislatures to Twitter and nearly everything in between, verbal wrestling matches masquerade as dialogue, and listening occurs only, if at all, as a means of preparing one's next move in the game. And even when listening is addressed in classrooms, courtrooms, or television studios, it is done primarily with the aim of conquest and control. We either listen to our adversary's arguments so we may defeat them, or we listen in order to master some material, facts, or theories. And when it comes to the First Amendment, it is no surprise that listening gets ignored; we imagine freedom of expression as the act of speaking and forget all about the freedom of listening and the right to hear. But just ask any librarian, those faithful and understated keepers of democracy, whether freedom of speech is possible without the right to listen and read.[1]

In this chapter, I examine the political implications of the US First Amendment (constitutional protection for the freedom of speech, press, religion, and assembly to be free from government constraint) through a listening lens. I do so to better understand our current moment of

DOI: 10.4324/9781003212515-15

political polarization and the resultant upside-down world of politics in which we find ourselves. With nearly half the country currently arrayed against the other half, like the ancient Pandavas and Kauravas, there is little actual listening taking place, let alone an underlying sense of community that both etymologically and practically constitutes communication and, by extension, democracy. How did we get here, and what might we accomplish if we took the freedom to listen as seriously as we take the freedom to speak?

The First Amendment and the Right to Listen

The First Amendment, written by James Madison and added to the Bill of Rights in 1791, sanctifies both freedom of expression and freedom of the press as the prerequisite and preeminent virtues of democracy. The spirit of this amendment stems from the founders' dedication to contentious public debate and deliberation as core elements of democratic politics. Lawmakers, historians, jurists, and political theorists have long cherished this virtue by repeatedly emphasizing the importance of free speech, rendered as truly robust public discourse and political deliberation, to the ascertainment and achievement of a democratically founded common good. In his most recent book, Michael Sandel (2020, p. 31) recapitulates this long-lived theme, stating that "to reinvigorate democratic politics, we need to find our way to a morally more robust public discourse."

To this end, the First Amendment has been repeatedly interpreted as centering on the role of public debate to democratic citizenship, with a special emphasis on robust deliberation, quality information, and, at times, listening. When, for example, *The New York Times* was sued by the Alabama governor in 1964, the Supreme Court ruled on behalf of the press by repeatedly mentioning the importance of public discussion: "Those who won our independence believed . . . that public discussion is a political duty, and that this should be a fundamental principle of the American government . . . Thus, we consider this case against the background of a profound national commitment to the principle that debate on public issues should be uninhibited, robust, and wide-open" (*New York Times Co. v. Sullivan*, 1964).

The Supreme Court has also repeatedly emphasized the press's role in providing the public with accurate and adequate information necessary for public deliberation. For example, in the aforementioned case, "the protection of the public requires not merely discussion, but information." In another case nearly ten years later, the court ruled that, "in the First Amendment, the Founding Fathers gave the free press the protection it must have to fulfill its essential role in our democracy. The press was to serve the governed, not the governors" (*New York Times Co. v. United States*, 1971).

Court decisions that interpret the First Amendment as affirming the constitutional right to listen are less commonly found but have been featured in a handful of rulings, one of which explicitly stated that "the freedom to speak and the freedom to hear are inseparable. They are two sides of the same coin" (*Kleindienst v. Mandel*, 1972).[2] These decisions echo the importance of listening as described by democratic theorist John Stuart Mill, who examined, among other things, the importance of the freedom to both speak and listen in the formation of public opinion. In his chapter "On Thought and Discussion," Mill (2001, p. 35) repeatedly emphasized the importance of listening in the art of government. For Mill, not only must the freedom to express opinions be treasured, but the freedom to hear others' opinions must constantly be guarded as well. Says Mill: "He who knows only his own side of the case, knows little of that."

One historically notable occasion featuring an assertion of the freedom to listen occurred in Boston in 1860, when a mob of wealthy White men charged into an abolitionist meeting featuring the question of "How shall slavery be abolished?" and violently broke up the meeting. Writing the following week in abolitionist William Lloyd Garrison's newspaper *The Liberator*, Frederick Douglass chastised the unruly mob for their violent censorship and stressed the importance of listening embedded in the right of free speech:

> There can be no right of speech where any man, however lifted up, or however humble, however young, or however old, is over awed by force and compelled to suppress his honest sentiments. Equally clear is the right to hear. To suppress free speech is a double wrong. It violates the rights of the hearer as well as those of the speaker.
> (Douglas, 1860)

Mediated Listening and the Fairness Doctrine

The introduction of new broadcast technologies in the early 20th century introduced, ironically, a new and complex set of challenges to the First Amendment. Unlike the printed press and public oratory, broadcasting was not only a highly technical and expensive enterprise, but perhaps more importantly, the broadcast spectrum was a limited resource that required rules and regulations for both allocation and use. In 1927, Congress passed the Radio Act, which determined that the newly commercialized radio airwaves were public resources, like air and water, that warranted regulation. As a result, broadcast stations were allocated specific frequencies through a process of government licensing. In part, this was an attempt to preserve the airwaves as a public rather than a privately owned utility. But it was also a recognition that, without such regulation, the radio spectrum was garbled and of "little use because of the cacophony of competing voices, none of which could be clearly and predictably heard" (*Red Lion Broadcasting Co., Inc. v. FCC*, 1969).

At the same time, Congress determined that since the air waves were public property, broadcasters must operate their stations "in the public interest, convenience, or necessity" (Radio Act, 1927). This declaration was largely interpreted as acknowledging the citizenry's need for both ample and high-quality information as well as for multiple and diverse opinions offered from a plurality of viewpoints. These propositions were later reflected in what came to be called the fairness doctrine, which required news and public affairs programming to not only air examination of matters of public interest to audiences but to do so from multiple (or at least two) competing perspectives.

In 1949, the Federal Communications Commission (or FCC, the governmental agency charged with regulating the broadcast system) held that "it is axiomatic that one of the most vital questions of mass communication in a democracy is the development of an informed public opinion through the public dissemination of news and ideas concerning the vital public issues of the day" (Federal Communications Commission, 1949). In several subsequent Supreme Court cases adjudicating this regulation, justices frequently underscored the importance of listening as a First Amendment consideration, repeatedly asserting that "it is the right of the viewing and listening public, and not the right of the broadcasters, which is paramount" (*Red Lion Broadcasting Co., Inc. v. FCC*, 1969).

Several arguments were proffered to justify this type of government regulation, which seemingly violated First Amendment prohibitions on government regulation of speech and the press – the foremost being scarcity, or the limitations of the radio spectrum itself, which restricted the number of stations that could exist. While public discussion was the overarching goal to be protected by the fairness doctrine, the fulcrum upon which it balanced was the issue of scarcity – the fact that very few could own or operate a broadcast station. In their adjudication of cases wherein fairness and the First Amendment seemed to conflict, the justices came to equate station ownership with point of view and, granting the paucity of available spots, required that these few licensed stations each present a plurality of opinions. As a result, fairness was quantified by a calculus that equated the limitation of broadcast stations with the limitation of possible points of view.

But with the advent and distribution of cable television in the late 1970s and early 1980s and the seemingly infinite capacity of the cable spectrum to accommodate a seemingly endless number of stations, the scarcity justification for the fairness doctrine began to erode. Finally, under President Ronald Reagan, the FCC eliminated the fairness doctrine in 1987. As a result, stations were then able to broadcast anything short of libel virtually unchecked, and the rise of Rush Limbaugh and hate radio began. That is, with the seeming increase in sheer quantity or number of stations, the FCC and justices reasoned that the public would have opportunities to hear a diversity of views as would be expected in any open "marketplace of ideas." What they did not consider, however, was that the broadcast spectrum was not the only scarce resource at play; that both the time and the attention of audiences were also limited and, hence, precious resources as well.

The rise of new technologies and the World Wide Web in the 1990s and beyond further expanded the virtual public square, which featured space for political deliberation. But soon, other questions arose, such as whether these forms of new media were to be understood as speech, press, or broadcast and whether any of it merited First Amendment protection. Currently, the FCC and the federal government have largely absented themselves from involvement in First Amendment questions regarding social media such as Facebook, Twitter, Instagram, Parler, and others. But the question remains of whether the profusion of conflicting and conspiracy-pedaling siloed stations, websites, and apps of today truly serve the public interest and offer opportunities for open and robust discussion.

Today, 30 years after the demise of the fairness doctrine, we can have some perspective on the suite of problems, compounded by new technologies, that have arisen in its absence. I see five central problems:

1. *The proliferation of broadcast stations, websites, and apps (such as Twitter and Instagram) has led away from, not toward, a greater diversity of views.* Competition has led to curated stations that cater to specific audiences – often by topic but frequently by point of view as well. Today, as in the past, every radio station, website, podcast, news organization is not simply curated for an audience; the mission of selling audiences to advertisers is nothing new. What is new is that audiences are now curated, with audiences becoming genres in themselves, each insulated and preserved separately from having to listen to anything other than to their already-existing, self-confirming views.
2. *While the scarcity of broadcast venues is no longer limited, human attention and time surely are limited.* Audiences do not generally engage with a plurality of stations or sites but rather tend to stick with familiar and self-confirming views. And as farmers well know, repeatedly broadcasting the same seeds creates a monoculture (too much of any one crop), which eventually leads to a profusion of failure, pests, and disease.
3. *The equation of quantity over quality has led to a dangerous insularity that simply equates more speech with better speech* – regardless of whether the speech is more of the same, reflects a diversity of views, or whether listeners can and will even hear this plurality of view and voice. This short-sighted equation has led to what many feel are disastrous decisions like *Citizens United* (2010), in which the Supreme Court equated money and speech (with complete indifference to listening). The result was that the speech of the monied interests simply drowned out other voices, making it impossible

for audiences to hear anything approximating a diversity of views. Moreover, if money is speech, then what is listening?

4. *The quality of information purveyed on broadcast stations and internet sites has vastly diminished, as has a lack of public accountability.* The resulting confluence of disinformation, misinformation, lies, and deception has rendered even the possibility of rigorous open debate untenable. As a result, this proliferation of untrustworthy material comes closer to what political theorist Bernard Crick (2002, p. 90) sees as characteristic of autocratic discourse: "Proclamations are typical of autocracies, newspapers of modern democracies. With no regular news, rumour and gossip become social institutions in autocracies." Crick (2002, p. 90) also adds that, "the populist mode of democracy is a politics of arousal more than of reason, but also a politics of diversion from serious concerns that need settling in either a liberal democratic or a civic republican manner."

5. *Polarization leads to demonization, which makes listening to one's opponents seem impossible to some, and downright immoral to others.* In today's lucrative age of "going viral," there is an ever-ready appetite for the sensational, the conspiratorial, and the hyperbolic, all of which are accompanied by a sense of righteous indignation. The result is the silencing of unwanted voices – not by exercising the freedom to not listen but by preventing others from listening. Whether in the form of banishing disliked journalists from the White House pressroom, posting viral ad hominem attacks on those with whom one disagrees, or, in the form of cancel or callout culture, ally theater, or deplatforming, the expressions of outrage are contagious, and the temptation to publicly shame and censor unwanted speech grows apace. There is thus not only a decreasing ability to listen to those whose ideas differ from one's own, but there are decreasing opportunities to listen to anything with which one disagrees. The freedom to listen is now threatened from both the right and the left, by both politicians and college students, and the sacrifice of listening on the altar of moral supremacy seems, at this moment in history, to be unrestrained.

Conclusion

Conceptualizing free speech and a free press solely from a speaking-centered perspective not only trivializes listening but also emphasizes the individual over the community. Free speech is considered important principally because it protects the personal freedom of the individual speaker, which is of course essential to liberty and democracy. The most serious problem occurs when the rights of the individual completely override the rights of the community and when genuine deliberation about the common good – the very essence of politics – is presumptively abandoned. We can see this dynamic at work in recent years when, in response to public health mask mandates, both individuals and governmental representatives refused to place community health above individual preferences. During such moments, the individual becomes sacrosanct, the plurality not so much.

So what does freedom of listening entail? Minimally, it would mean examining both the rights and responsibilities of freedom, and it would involve both public and private action. From a public perspective, democratic citizens need "access to reasonably accurate information" that can be trusted and relied upon (Crick, 2002, p. 98). As a recent *Saturday Night Live* skit parodically illustrated, a country that can depend on the reliability of sports scores surely ought to be able to depend on the reliability of election results, public health recommendations, census statistics, and myriad other forms of factual information upon which good governance depends.[3] Further, as the Supreme Court has repeatedly ruled, democratic citizens need opportunities for public debate and deliberation (i.e., the need to both speak *and listen*) that actually contain plurality and diversity. This might be accomplished by some kind of updated Fairness (or perhaps plurality?) Doctrine or some other legislative means that would promote and preserve a diversity of views on public media sites. Furthermore, a nationwide public civic education curriculum, with an emphasis on listening, would go a long way toward fostering dialogue and debate among citizens.

From an individual perspective, a commitment to freedom of listening requires both inner and outer awareness, an understanding of one's own limitations, and a recognition of the complexity of listening itself. *In other words, the time for listening education as an adjunct of citizenship is long overdue.* This does not mean tactical listening in order to win an argument but democratic listening that appreciates the plurality of perspectives needed in a robust democracy.

The freedom to listen therefore requires stamina and self-control. It entails a willingness to tolerate the disagreeable, the different, and the dangerous. Freedom of listening needs strength to sustain the blows of anger and resentment, of terrible ideas and misunderstandings, while remaining alert. It requires vigilance and courage, a willingness to respond, to question, and to debate (Lipari, 2014). Those who wish to exercise their freedom not to listen may, of course, do so. But the cost is high when we curtail the freedom of others. Refusing to accept *others as real persons* becomes toxic – to community, to justice, and to a lived and livable democracy.

In short, our laws are currently at war with our politics, and the manifestations are palpable – voter suppression, gerrymandering, disproportional land-based representation, Citizens United, revocation of the fairness doctrine, monopoly media ownership, infotainment, unconstrained propaganda and misinformation, unabated polarization, bitterly contested election results, the ability of unchecked autocrats to seize power, all of which is accompanied by an unwillingness to listen to those with whom we disagree. Some would argue that the United States has not witnessed such undermining of constitutional democracy since the eras of Secession and Reconstruction.

So what is wrong with our politics? I would amend Crick's (1992, p. 144) chilling caution, "Politics is not possible when most people do not want it," to include the phrase *or do not want to listen*. To listen is to actively participate in politics, to cooperate with diverse others simply because it is the right thing to do. In this historical moment, at a time of ceaseless violence and rising authoritarianism, speech-without-listening is not only wrong but dangerous. Without engaged deliberation, without real listening, our ability to discern the common good will invariably shrink our democratic potential. We cannot allow that to happen.

Notes

1. Many library advocates stress the importance of free public libraries to the genesis and sustenance of an informed citizenry. For example, the industrialist/philanthropist Andrew Carnegie, who built nearly 2,500 libraries, frequently referred to libraries as "the cradle of democracy." See Gregorian (2002, October 17).
2. See also *Lamont v. Postmaster General*, 381 U.S. 301 (1965), *Red Lion Broadcasting Co., Inc. v. FCC*, 395 U.S. 367 (1969), and *Thomas v. Collins*, 323 U.S. 516 (1945).
3. See *Saturday Night Live*, "Newsmax" [video]. YouTube. December 13, 2020. URL: www.youtube.com/watch?v=GP_K5czbny4

Bibliography

Citizens United v. Federal Election Commission. (2010). 558 U.S. 310.
Crick, B. (1992). *In defense of politics*. Chicago: University of Chicago Press.
Crick, B. (2002). *Democracy: A very short introduction*. New York: Oxford University Press.
Douglass, F. (1860, December 14). Frederick Douglass at music hall. *The Liberator, 30*, 50.
Federal Communications Commission. (1949). *In the matter of editorializing by broadcast licensees: Report of the commission*. No. 8516.
Gregorian, V. (2002, October 17). *Libraries as acts of civic renewal*. Speech to the Kansas City Club, Kansas City, Missouri.
Kleindienst v. Mandel. (1972). 408 U.S. 753.
Lamont v. Postmaster General. (1965). 381 U.S. 301.
Lipari, L. (2014). *Listening, thinking, being: Toward an ethics of attunement*. University Park, PA: The Pennsylvania State University Press.
Mill, J. S. (2001). *On liberty*. Electronic Resource. London: Electric Book Co.
New York Times Co. v. Sullivan. (1964). 376 U.S. 254, 270.

New York Times Co. v. United States. (1971). 403 U.S. 713.
Radio Act, Pub. L. (1927). No. 47 U.S.C. 4.
Red Lion Broadcasting Co., Inc. v. FCC. (1969). 395 U.S. 367.
Sandel, M. (2020). *The tyranny of merit: What's become of the common good?* New York: Farrar, Straus and Giroux.
Thomas v. Collins. (1945). 323 U.S. 516.

12 Hear the Presidency Differently

Vanessa Beasley

"I hate to say I told you so." It is a bad idea to start any essay like that, and it seems especially problematic in a chapter about how to fix politics within a diverse democracy. Still, I begin there to stake my ground before introducing my solution. I have argued previously that one of the most underappreciated functions of presidential rhetoric is its consistent promotion of traditional idioms of shared national identity among an increasingly diverse American people (Beasley, 2004). These idioms are so traditional as to be platitudinous, and yet I have maintained that they serve a valuable function: teaching generations of Americans a basic vocabulary for, and thus a way of understanding, who they are as well as who they might become as a united community.

When discussions of shared identity were suddenly gone, they were quickly missed. That is, when the bully pulpit stopped discussing such matters during Donald Trump's presidency, I could hear an eerie silence. It was not just that Trump's rhetoric violated norms, as it surely did (Siskind, 2020). To my ear, the issue was much more basic. The president wasn't constituting "the people" correctly. Actually, he was not constituting "the people" at all. From his inaugural address on – an example I will return to – there were always at least two Americas in Trump's rhetoric: his favored "us" positioned against a (sometimes literally) worthless "them."

To refer to a president's "us" and "them" is to evoke a conceptual view of rhetoric's constitutive function (Charland, 1987). In contrast to an instrumental view of public discourse, in which rhetoric is deployed to change public opinion, a constitutive view focuses on how public rhetoric creates or scaffolds identity formation, especially at the collective rather than the individual level. Any leader of a large group, including US presidents, necessarily engages in constitutive rhetoric, telling group members who they are. US presidents must pivot between an emphasis on various aspects of American national identity when they "go public," sometimes relying on regionalisms, for example (Beasley, 2001). Yet even then, presidents usually do not bifurcate "the people," at least not explicitly (Beasley, 2004).

Even if the concept of "two Americas" has been the way generations of scholars from Tocqueville (1996) onward have explained the persistence

DOI: 10.4324/9781003212515-16

of racial inequality in the United States, it has not been the way generations of presidents have invoked the nation's "imagined community" (Anderson, 1991). There has been a requirement instead for presidents to offer "civic ideologies, or myths of civic identity . . . [to] foster the requisite sense of peoplehood" (Smith, 1997, p. 6). This need is not new; it has been born of the citizenry's growing diversity, resulting from histories of enslavement, immigration, and disenfranchisement. Yet over time, as the *demos* has become more diverse, there has been a greater need for the steady rhetorical reaffirmation of *e pluribus unum* and, often, of a more perfect union (Obama, 2008).

My solution thus starts from the following framework: *To fix politics, we must change how we listen when presidents tell us who we are.* The "we" I refer to here is meant to be as inclusive as possible, not just partisans or citizens but anyone with a concern for who is included in the American polity and who is not. By the end of the Trump presidency, with its border walls, family separations, and executive orders for restricted narratives of US history, those implications seem clear enough.

Note, too, that "we" is the subject of the sentence in my solution. The audience has agency. I am not calling for presidents to change their rhetoric, even if I do have an informed sense of what would be better or worse for them to say. Instead, I am asking for citizens to think differently about what this discourse of "the people" means, how they process it, and how they might change their attunement to it. To that end, I will suggest three specific ways to listen to presidential rhetoric, discussed here in order of degree of difficulty: listen for what is different, listen to presidents as institutions instead of as individuals, and listen for something new.

Listening to What Is Different

To hear absences requires a deep familiarity with historical patterns; you cannot recognize what is missing without first knowing what was supposed to be there. Arguably, the most influential account of these patterns and their functions was written by Karlyn Kohrs Campbell and Kathleen Hall Jamieson (2008). They have argued that the presidency can be understood as something that comes into being via the rhetorical acts of the chief executives, including inaugural addresses, state of the unions, eulogies, vetoes, and farewell addresses. "As it now exists," they have written, "the presidency is an amalgam of roles and practices shaped by what presidents have done. At any given moment, an awareness of these roles and capacities shapes the practices of the incumbent" (Campbell & Jamieson, 2008, p. 2). What they would call "awareness" I would call listening not only to understand what has come before or what might be expected to follow but also for what these patterns might reveal about what is required to affirm unity within a diverse democracy. What do "we, the people" need presidential rhetoric to consistently *do* for us?

Some of the patterns in the literature suggest citizens expect presidential rhetoric to consistently be, well, more or less consistent (Hart, 1987; Hart et al., 2013). Likewise, some comparative studies of the presidency suggest that situational context can place highly differential constraints on individual officeholders and their rhetoric (Skowronek, 2020). There is also evidence that the mass media constrain political communication in fairly predictable ways, even if the force and scope of these constraints can change as new media enter the picture (Jamieson, 1988; Bennett, 2016).

These constraints and the similarities they engender are arguably most obvious when presidential speech becomes the centerpiece in the nation's rituals of governance. Consider the inaugural address. Among the four functions Campbell and Jamieson identify for this address is the restoration of feelings of unity, which is especially important after contentious elections. The speech "unifies the audience by reconstituting its members as 'the people,' who can witness and ratify the ceremony" (Campbell & Jamieson, 2008, p. 31).

Donald Trump's inaugural address needed to hit this mark. Given his political inexperience as well as his loss of the popular vote, the speech provided his first opportunity to show, on national television, that he understood the role of the president and how he could play the part. Many of his sentences sounded conventional, especially when he began: "We, the citizens of America, are now joined in a great national effort to rebuild our country and to restore its promise for all of our people. Together, we will determine the course of America and the world for years to come" (Trump, 2017). His speech contained multiple references to unity, including "[w]hen America is united, America is totally unstoppable," and "[a] new national pride will stir our souls, lift our sights, and heal our divisions" (Trump, 2017). It also had an explicit scriptural allusion, another common feature in inaugural addresses, taken from Psalms 133: "how good and pleasant it is when God's people live together in unity" (Trump, 2017). Apart from the informality of the phrase "totally unstoppable," much of this discourse fit the expected pattern.

Yet Trump's use of collective pronouns in other parts of the speech foreshadowed the possibility that his presidency would be atypical. Sometimes his "we" and "our" appeared to refer less to a united body of diverse Americans than to a particular subset of same, thereby producing a rhetoric reaffirming the nation's divisions and suspicions. "America will start winning again, winning like never before. We will bring back our jobs. We will bring back our borders. We will bring back our wealth. And we will bring back our dreams" (Trump, 2017). Note the direct objects in each case here. Whose jobs, whose borders, whose wealth, and whose dreams are to be "brought back" and from whom or where?

Likewise, a few lines later, Trump's use of "we" seemed to refer more clearly to himself and his administration: "We will get our people off welfare and back to work – rebuilding our country with American hands and American labor. We will follow two simple rules: Buy American and hire American" (Trump, 2017). Trump's reference to "our people" could have signaled unity among *all* US citizens; the repetition of the word "American" could signify as much. Yet it is also possible that his words underscored divisions *within* the country too. On the presidential campaign trail, Trump had often associated his "America first" slogan with a previous time in US history – the late 1900s and early 2000s – evoking what Jennifer Mercieca (2020) has called an "uncritical American exceptionalism steeped in nostalgia" (p. 66). It wasn't just America that was different at that time; it was that Americans were as well, with a very small and homogenous group of people holding most of the nation's economic and political power.

These examples from Trump's inaugural address show why even minor breaks from previous rhetorical patterns are worthy of attention. Other presidents have certainly hinted at nostalgia or, to state it less subtly, the "good old days" of racism and sexism in their public discourse, but it has not been typical to hear these same notes in an inaugural address during the late 20th and early 21st centuries as voters have become more diverse (Beasley, 2004). It might be that Trump had simply not yet learned how to sound like a president or that his staff had not yet determined why such rhetorical refrains were important. As months and then years went by in the Trump administration, his willingness to break rhetorical norms suggested otherwise. Just as Campbell and Jamieson's model (2008) would have predicted, Trump's words increasingly created a different kind of presidency and, as a consequence, a different kind of nation.

Listen to the President Institutionally

Like Trump, I have used personal pronouns often here. However, the next aspect of my solution requires eschewing the personal and thinking in more institutional terms. As discussed earlier, one way to think institutionally is to make comparisons across presidential administrations and to look for patterns and disruptions. But that is not enough. Citizens also must learn to listen to presidents *institutionally*, which is much more difficult in a radically pluralistic nation.

When listening is offered as a political solution in an era of polarization, the fix is often framed as a call for individual action or at least purposeful self-determination. We hear calls for civility, emotional regulation, and/or other habits of mind that would improve understanding among colleagues and kindreds. Think about advice commonly given on college campuses or at awkward Thanksgiving dinners, for example. Even when national attention is focused explicitly on institutionalized processes for partisan politics, such as campaigns and elections, we are often reminded that both the losing party and the winners should listen to what "the people" are saying – via their votes and their voices – and learn from those who have political beliefs and feelings different from our own (Hart, 2020).

Yet such counsel can sound quite different coming from your aunt or your professor than from your president. Drawing upon an extreme example to make the point, consider what different people heard when listening to Trump's response to the violent aftermath of the Unite the Right rally led by White supremacists in Charlottesville, Virginia, in August 2017. After suggesting that "counterprotestors" also should be condemned for violence ("What about the alt-left that came charging at, as you say, the alt-right? Do they have any semblance of guilt?"), the president said, as if to invite an exercise in perspective taking, "You also had some very fine people on both sides" (Trump, 2017, August 15).

It was unusual, to say the least, to hear a modern president state so plainly in televised remarks that there was something worth listening to from Nazi-quoting individuals. Again, while there have been prior presidents whose bigotry and/or sympathy for similar organizations was well known, the ubiquitous cameras of the mass media and then social media, along with the changing demographics of the electorate, have resulted in more recent chief executives using coded language to express racist-sounding sentiments (Haney Lopez, 2014). Throughout Trump's presidency, it became quite normal to hear him say all manner of things that were highly unconventional for a president. His repeated violation of discursive norms created the irresistible temptation to focus on him as an individual, someone who, by choice or compulsion, simply could not be contained. Increasingly, the nation began listening to Trump as an idiosyncratic individual who just happened to be the president of the United States.

As Hart (2020) has written, "Trump's platform was Trump," and this intense self-focus in his rhetoric contributed to a kind of "double listening" among his supporters, allowing them to discount problematic words they heard Trump saying and then concluding that he was not, in fact, a problem (p. 183). For example, if Trump said something sexist and/or misogynistic, his supporters might respond that he could not actually mean such things because of his status as a husband or as a father of daughters. In these contexts, listening to Trump as an individual turned a familial version of acceptance into a form of sense making. Put differently, listening to him as a person meant forgiving him as a president.

Second, listening to Trump as an individual is part of a larger trend Dana Nelson (2008) has called presidentialism, the glorification of individual presidents in ways that undermine citizens' senses of their own agency in a democracy. Nelson's fear is that when the president is viewed as something of a superhero, it becomes far too tempting for citizens to assume that he/she will solve all of the nation's problems. The rise of the mass media has contributed to this framing in steadily more comprehensive ways, according to her analysis. Hart's (1994) indictment of the impact of television's highly personalized coverage of electoral politics would also support this view, as would Lance Bennett's (2016) discussion of the frames most commonly used by the corporate news media when covering presidents.

Listening to a president as an institutional actor, in contrast, means forgoing the other ways we have been taught to listen to a "prime-time presidency" and paying less attention to the drama or the personalities in office at a given time (Parry-Giles & Parry-Giles, 2006). Instead of forgiving or anointing the presidential *person*, that is, we must decide to what the *office* of the presidency should be held responsible. I have argued that one of these responsibilities is defining American national identity in ways that show both fidelity to and respect for the diversity of the population, as well as the aspirational need to become more inclusive, a goal that has proved difficult to achieve, especially during the presidency of Donald John Trump.

Conclusion

The US presidency is a product of its own practices. The history of those practices, including rhetoric, can loom large in times of polarization, when a pull toward nostalgia is countered by discussions of the nation's founders (many of whom were slaveholders) and who, then, should not be regarded as the nation's bedrock or its North Star. By way of concluding this essay, I offer a third suggestion for a type of listening that is significantly more challenging than those already advanced: learning how to do something we don't know how to do but that must nonetheless be done.

Franklin Roosevelt called the presidency a place of moral leadership. The definition of moral leadership changed during Donald Trump's presidency against a backdrop of demands to dismantle systemic racism and other forms of structural inequality. In US institutions outside of politics, leaders seeking to claim the moral high ground normally admit to both what their institutions have gotten wrong in the past as well as how they will improve it. Some of these pledges involve acknowledging past practices, some involve making promises of different decisions moving forward, and some suggest letting new voices participate in decisions of consequence.

When compared to other institutions, US politics has been slower to make such admissions or changes. It is true, of course, that more women and people of color have been elected to office in the past decade. Yet the research I have cited here, including my own, suggests that some of the barriers those leaders face when assuming office are decidedly rhetorical. At all levels of governance, the need to promote unity is important; in the absence of a unifying rhetoric, xenophobia will take its place no matter who the leader is. However, in the realm of presidential rhetoric, the traditional ways of promoting shared national identity have been enacted and performed exclusively by White men. Citizens might want a president who consistently "sounds presidential," but, historically speaking, sounding presidential has often meant ignoring gendered and racial biases built into the office's performances.

For this reason, I doubt that all of our problems can be solved by listening exclusively to the past. History can teach us what is worth preserving, but it can also teach us what must now be forsaken if we want to build something new and better. To do that, we need to listen to new sources and new voices, even if that means reckoning with the limitations of our own knowledge, with our learned prejudices, and with how we, too, must become better attuned to the cultural nuances of one of the largest and most diverse nations in the history of the world.

Bibliography

Anderson, B. R. (1991). *Imagined communities: Reflections on the origins and spread of nationalism.* London: Verso.

Beasley, V. B. (2001). Making diversity safe for democracy: American pluralism and the presidential local address. *Quarterly Journal of Speech, 87*(1), 25–40.

Beasley, V. B. (2004). *You, the people: American national identity in presidential rhetoric, 1885–2000.* College Station: Texas A&M University Press.

Bennett, W. L. (2016). *News: The politics of illusion* (10th ed.). Chicago: University of Chicago Press.

Campbell, K. K., & Jamieson, K. H. (2008). *Presidents creating the presidency: Deeds done in words.* Chicago: University of Chicago Press.

Charland, M. (1987). Constitutive rhetoric: The case of the Peuple Quebecois. *Quarterly Journal of Speech, 73*(2), 133–150.

Haney Lopez, I. (2014). *Dog whistle politics: How coded racial appeals have reinvented racism and wrecked the middle class.* New York: Oxford University Press.

Hart, R. P. (1987). *The sound of leadership: Presidential communication in the modern age.* Chicago: University of Chicago Press.

Hart, R. P. (1994). *Seducing America: How television charms the modern voter.* New York: Oxford University Press.

Hart, R. P. (2020). *Trump and us: What he says and why people listen.* New York: Cambridge University Press.

Hart, R. P., Childers, J. P., & Lind, C. J. (2013). *Political tone: How leaders talk and why.* Chicago: University of Chicago Press.

Jamieson, K. H. (1988). *Eloquence in an electronic age: The transformation of political speechmaking.* New York: Oxford University Press.

Mercieca, J. (2020). *Demagogue for president: The rhetorical genius of Donald Trump.* College Station: Texas A&M University Press.

Nelson, D. D. (2008). *Bad for democracy: How the presidency undermines the power of the people.* Minneapolis: University of Minnesota Press.

Obama, B. H. (2008, March 18). *A more perfect union.* Philadelphia, PA. www.npr.org/templates/story/story.php?storyId=88478467

Parry-Giles, T., & Parry-Giles, S. J. (2006). *The prime-time presidency: The West Wing and U.S. nationalism.* Champaign: University of Illinois Press.

Siskind, A. (2020, October 16). This is not normal: A guide to what the next president will have to unwind. *The Washington Post.*
Skowronek, S. (2020). *Presidential leadership in political time: Reprise and reappraisal.* Lawrence: University Press of Kansas.
Smith, R. M. (1997). *Civic ideals: Conflicting visions of citizenship in U.S. history.* New Haven: Yale University Press.
Tocqueville, A. D. (1996). *Democracy in America* (J. P. Meyer & M. Lerner, Eds.). New York: Harper and Row.
Trump, D. J. (2017, January 20). *Inaugural address.* Washington, DC. www.whitehouse.gov/briefings-statements/the-inaugural-address/
Trump, D. J. (2017, August 15). *Remarks by president Trump on infrastructure.* www.whitehouse.gov/briefings-statements/remarks-president-trump-infrastructure/

13 Fix the "Cancel Culture" Mentality

Shawn J. Parry-Giles

In the fall of 2019, former President Barack Obama entered the culture wars. He did so by taking on "woke" culture and the belief that change happens by being "as judgmental as possible about other people." President Obama's words were cheered by unlikely opponents and jeered by supporters. Conservatives like Ann Colter of Fox News responded on Twitter, "Good for Obama," and another *Fox & Friends* guest called Obama, "the voice of reason" (Rueb & Taylor, 2019). Yet others like M. Arceneaux (2019) pushed back in *The Independent*, asserting, "I respect you immensely, Barack Obama, but I don't need lessons about 'being woke' and 'cancel culture.'" Arceneaux committed everyone to "call out wrong when spotted," refusing to "cower to the powerful and their righteousness."

Expressions of cancel culture are pervasive across social media. The practice is typically premised on the idea of canceling an individual, particularly a powerful person, who has expressed "offensive . . . ideas" that undermine "progressive" ideals and practices. Often attributed to the Left, the aim is to produce a public backlash to ideas that offend, hoping to cut short a career or undermine cultural cachet through boycotts and employer actions (Romano, 2019). Shane Gillis provides just one case in point. Because of offensive remarks made about LGBTQ+ people, women, and Americans of Chinese dissent, Gillis lost his spot on *Saturday Night Live* before any episodes featuring him could be aired (Vera, 2019). In capturing the debate over cancel culture, *Vox* writer Aja Romano (2019) asks, "Is cancel culture a mob mentality, or a long overdue war of speaking truth to power?"

Although associated with the Left, cancel culture cuts across the political spectrum. The Right and particularly Donald Trump have targeted it as a way to demean progressives during the 2020 election, shifting Trump's ire away from political correctness as candidate and president ("political correctness is just absolutely killing us as a country") (Cillizza, 2018) and toward antiracism initiatives in the 2020 campaign ("false belief that America is an irredeemably racist and sexist country") (Trump, Executive Order, 2020). Standing before Mount Rushmore on

July 4, 2020, Trump equated cancel culture with "totalitarianism" that demanded a strong leader to protect the nation's children and the country's liberty from "radical assault." Demeaning cancel culture while contributing to it represents a partisan strategy to muffle anyone on the Left who tries to cancel anyone on the Right. It also represents a defensive strategy to block a progressive resurgence – a common practice of conservatives throughout the nation's history (Robin, 2018, p. 20).

In this heightened period of cancel culture, we tend too often to silence those who champion principles different from our own. Deliberation and compromise, as instruments of democracy, become the casualties of devout principles and resolute identities. Such political divides precipitate the shouting across our airwaves, social media, and town halls, all of which requires an antidote for our ailing *civis*. In part, I make the case here for a greater elasticity of principles and identities that seek out commonalities and that privilege the diversity of discordant voices needed to achieve *rhetorical harmony*. Yet for deliberative commitments to flourish, we also have to fix the root causes of cancel culture – the inequities that gaslight the so-called culture of demagoguery and that thrive on an "us vs. them" mentality (Roberts-Miller, 2017, p. 36).

The Roots of Cancel Culture

Instances of cancel culture are broad and deep. Historically, those in power have worked to drive out the opposition from the nation's founding onward. The Federalists tried to cancel Republicans, slavery defenders tried to cancel abolitionists, presidents tried to cancel woman suffragists, and Joseph McCarthy tried to cancel anyone challenging anticommunist sentiments. In the contemporary moment, the empowered and the oppressed try their best to cancel the opposition (e.g., protesters shouting down speakers, Zoom bombings disrupting diversity and inclusion trainings).

Cancel-culture attacks can thus target those in positions of power and those critiquing it. Such canceling often condemns racist, sexist, and homophobic words and deeds but can also reinforce bigotry or misogyny in the process. Hillary Clinton has long served as a political target for conservatives but also for leftists who admonished her for reinforcing policies that propped up Wall Street over Main Street, undermined the poor (welfare reform of 1996), or disproportionately imprisoned Black and Brown people (Crime Bill of 1994) (Geier, 2016). Whenever Hillary Clinton spoke after her 2016 loss, she faced a chorus of requests from the Right and the Left to cancel her and thus deny her right to speak ("Go home. Close the door. Shut your mouth. Be quiet") (Schwartz, 2019). Even today, T-shirts continue to sport the phrase "Shut Up Hillary," Twitter brandishes hashtags such as "#GoAwayHillary," and press headlines like, "Why Won't Hillary Clinton Just Go Away?" still abound (Garber, 2020). Like other female presidential candidates, Clinton is often treated as an interloper who doesn't belong in politics (e.g., "#DropOut[Elizabeth] Warren") and whose talk irritates voters (Parry-Giles, 2014, p. 21). In the aftermath of her second failed presidential candidacy, Clinton defied her critics by writing books, starting a podcast, entering Twitter debates, going on talk shows, stumping for candidates, and starting a political action committee. Cancel culture often fails to silence people, but it still sends warning messages to female candidates and other public figures that you, too, will be mistreated if you dare to step into the presidential contests or if your principles contradict the principles of certain outspoken others (Garber, 2020).

Those committed to rooting out discrimination have also challenged cancel-culture practices. Author Meghan Daum challenges cancel culture ("social media mob") by calling out misogynists *and* feminists in the context of the Trump presidency. Daum expressed concern for the misogynist treatment of Christine Blasey Ford by Republican senators in the Supreme Court nomination hearings for Brett Kavanaugh. Yet Daum is also troubled by feminists who conflate violence against women with all forms of misogyny – equating rape with "lesser forms of male creepiness (groping, leering)." Daum, in particular, has grown impatient with "the smug vibe of many young activists" who cancel others (Brooks, 2019).

Others who have participated in cancel culture come to question their complicity in canceling others. Black feminist activist, Loretta Ross (2019), regrets the way she "called out" White feminists in the 1970s for not recognizing the oppressions that feminists of color faced. In trying to raise awareness of such oppressions, Ross came to see the act of calling out others as counterproductive because White women rarely "understood what it meant to be *White* women in the system of White supremacy." Ross eventually called on accusers and the accused to "work together to ascertain harm and achieve justice without seeing anyone as disposable people."

Political Cure Number One – Practicing Democratic Deliberation

Ross envisions a workable corrective in which we replace the popularity of cancel culture with a culture of deliberation. Democratic deliberation is said to be predicated on "reaching reasoned decisions among free and equal" peoples (Bohman, 1997, p. 321). One way to do so is by recognizing the plasticity of our own principles and identities and to look for areas of common ground among those with whom we disagree. Too often, we buy into a zero-sum game that divides us into winners and losers – if African Americans advance economically, White Americans lose economic stability; if LGBTQ+ Americans gain marriage rights, marriage for hetero-Americans is somehow desecrated; if women gain a stronghold in the workplace, men lose professional prestige (Bouie, 2019). We are left with a rubble of rage and resentment toward others blamed for our own grievances (Robinson, 2020). For deliberation to thrive, we must adopt instead a "public-goods" mentality that envisions a rising tide lifting all boats. To do so, we must explore commonalities and reduce anxieties tied to cultural change and group difference.

We must also make the case more convincingly that social-justice victories promote the public good versus social inequalities. The global status of women is a case in point. Global scholars argue that nations thrive when women's economic equity is prioritized and that nations struggle when women's economic rights are impeded. Addressing the 25th anniversary of the U.S. World Conference for Women in Beijing, Valerie Hudson (2020) elaborates two truisms from 25 years ago that remain in play today: "The fate of nations is tied to the status of women" and "What you do to your women, you do to your nation." The mission ultimately is for women to control their own reproductivity and productivity. When both women and men thrive, the nation as a whole prospers. The aim is to find the common ground (e.g., the well-being of all) needed to transcend identity (gender) division and overcome women's oppression collectively.

The classical concept of *harmony* provides an elixir for the harms associated with the inequities inspiring cancel culture. Historically, harmony interested not only musicians seeking a concordance of sounds but also students of rhetoric. As Aviva Rothman (2017) explains, harmony relied on bringing together different entities that made the "discordant" "consonant," thereby "reconciling . . . opposites." Rhetorical scholars have drawn on such classical conceptions of harmony, championing its ability to reconcile divergent epistemologies and styles into a "unified diversity" (pp. 10, 90, 178). Rather than canceling others, drowning out ideas, or holding others down, democratic deliberation aims to take seriously a diversity of ideas by harmonizing the colophony of voices in support of the common good. And rather than expecting consensus or the elimination of differences, the mission instead is to celebrate a diversity of identities and principles while also looking for slivers of common ground to sustain interpersonal engagement.

Political Cure Number Two – Advancing Political Equities

Democratic deliberation, as already established, presumes a free and equal people. Substituting deliberative ideals with acts of cancel culture alone will prove ineffectual unless we confront the structural conditions that fuel a culture of anger and demagoguery. Cancel culture, from this perspective, is symptomatic of larger cultural ills. An important intervention necessitates a structural realignment and a search for greater equity across differences. In recent years, the need for greater recognition of oppressions suffered across identity groups (Beauvais, 2018, p. 145) has taken on greater urgency after the deaths of so many Black and Brown people at the hands of police (e.g., Breonna Taylor and George Floyd).

Many view the current struggles for equity as a linear march across time toward progress. Yet, in practice, we have commonly seen spikes of progressive uplift (the 15th Amendment, the Civil Rights Act of 1964), followed by spikes of a reactionary backlash that deepens social injustice (Jim Crow, Nixon's Southern strategy). Such inequities were baked into our founding documents (U.S. Constitution, Naturalization Act of 1790), inequities that continue to rival efforts for progressive political realignment (e.g., erosion of the 1965 Voting Rights Act).

More recently, we have seen heightened expressions of cancel culture in the aftermath of an Obama administration that symbolized racial uplift and a Trump presidency that symbolized racial backlash. As the first woman candidate of Black American and South East Asian heritage pursued the 2020 vice presidency (Senator Kamala Harris – D-CA), we learn of a plot to kidnap the governor of Michigan – Gretchen Whitmer (D) – because of her response to the COVID-19 crisis (e.g., "stay-at-home orders"). Chants of "Lock her up" wafted across Michigan, reminiscent of Donald Trump's refrains about Hillary Clinton from his 2016 rallies (Bogel-Burroughs & Peters, 2020). In 2020, pro-Trump voters similarly chanted "lock her up" whenever the president associated refugees with Representative Ilhan Omar (D-MN), the first Somali-American woman in Congress. As women (Black, Brown, and White) gain a stronghold in American politics, we see a frightening backlash in which calls for silencing (canceling) have taken a very violent (kidnapping, murdering) and carceral (jailing) turn because of the angst over women's advancement. Such cultural whiplash – progress + backlash – reflects the push and pull of achieving these allegedly self-evident truths.

These kinds of backlash are most visible in one of the country's revered political practices – voting. Voting oppression, political gerrymandering, election interferences, and troll farms all point to the ways in which our democratic system is in crisis. When filling out the Census surveys every ten years and commemorating the anniversaries of the 15th Amendment, the 19th Amendment, the Voting Rights Act of 1965, and the 26th Amendment, we need to reenergize our efforts to achieve the core principles of democracy – the fulfillment of equality ("equal protection of the laws") and the guarantee of the vote. When becoming disenfranchised in the US, voters' options for redress are limited, resulting in a great deal of shouting, since indecorous speech can reliably be heard over the megaphones of the powerful.

While voting restrictions have plagued the country since its founding, the US Supreme Court decision of *Shelby County vs. Holder* (2013) has hardened such restrictions. In a tight ruling, the majority of the justices (5–4 decision) ruled in *Shelby County* that section 4 of the Voting Rights Act of 1965 was unconstitutional because past rulings had declared that "constitutional equality of the States is essential to the harmonious operation of the scheme upon which the Republic was organized." In reconciling state and federal powers, *Shelby County* challenged the "preclearance" clause of the Voting Rights Act and, in turn, awarded states greater authority in determining voting rights. The 2018 report of the US Commission on Civil Rights catalogs the consequences of *Shelby County*, identifying those state restrictions the federal government would have blocked under the Voting Rights Act. These restrictions include instituting stricter voter-ID policies, purging voter rolls, reducing the number of voting precincts and ballot drop-offs, and increasing requirements for proof of citizenship. The commission concluded that stricter voter ID laws often impact Black and Brown communities most appreciably.

For true deliberation culture to thrive, clear steps must be taken. We must reduce barriers to voting, increase Census representation among communities of color, recodify the Voting Rights Act to eliminate state-based restrictions, halt foreign interferences in US elections, and privilege the popular vote over superdelegates and the Electoral College. Following the recommendations of the U.S. Commission on Civil Rights (2018), the US Congress needs to "restore and/or expand protections against voting discrimination," and the Department of Justice should likewise "reinvigorate its efforts to protect voting rights." Congressional deliberation and action are integral to ensuring justice and breaking down these structures that scaffold the inequities that inflame cancel culture.

Conclusion

We need not look far for exemplars to guide us. In 2020, we mourned the loss of two role models who never stopped fighting on behalf of equality for all – John Lewis and Ruth Bader Ginsburg. Both broke barriers and were true believers in the social justice principles guiding their lives and careers. Both worked across identity groups in pursuing greater equity, lived out a commitment to coalition politics, and sought out commonalities over differences. Lewis spent a career supporting voting rights for people of color and for LBGTQ+ rights with the Equality Act before Congress. He showed us the importance of forgiveness and reconciliation, even showing mercy for those who harmed him (Dionne, 2020). And Ginsberg expanded women's rights by expanding men's rights in her landmark Supreme Court case *Weinberger v. Wiesenfeld* (1975). She, too, fought tirelessly for LBGTQ+ rights from the bench (Carmon, 2015). And both put into practice their commitment to work across different identities and principles without erasing anyone's self-worth. Ginsburg's commitment to expanding the tent of engagement is shown in her famous quotation: "Fight for the things that you care about, but do it in a way that will lead others to join you" (Vagianos, 2015).

Ginsburg showed us how one could disagree vehemently with one's biggest opponent (in her case, fellow Supreme Court Justice Antonin Scalia) without losing an ability to engage that person personally and professionally. Upon Ginsburg's death, Eugene Scalia (2020), Antonin's son, made clear that in spite of their combative relationship as justices, "not for a moment did one think the other should be condemned or ostracized." The younger Scalia argued that the relationship between his father and Ginsburg epitomized the importance of "how to welcome debate and differences" even while standing firm in one's own beliefs, especially when the national good was at stake.

Talking to others we disagree with does not mean that we must turn our backs on our political principles. It does mean that we must take the time to understand how others' principles differ from our own. Judith Butler offers poignant advice in this regard, advising that "we live in time; we err, sometimes seriously; and if we are lucky, we change precisely because of interactions that let us see things differently" (Ferber, 2020). In other words, we complicate our meaning making through conversations across difference. Along these same lines, Rabbi A. Suskin (2016) inspires us to practice "kindness in disagreement," giving us the opportunity to grow personally, politically, and intellectually.

Pursuing unified diversity also does not mean that all speech is equally worthy, especially, as Michael Roth (2020) notes, when it includes "hateful violence." And here is a real danger: When we abandon deliberative ideals, violence will take advantage of the silence and fill the void. Without talking to one another across our differences, we will surely be left with a splintered electorate, one in which people impugn one another's motives in an attempt to erase those with whom they disagree. More optimistically, says James Herrick (2013), public rhetoric of the right sort can blend the principles of harmony with the practices of deliberation to make social violence a distant memory.

Bibliography

Arceneaux, M. (2019, October 30). I respect you immensely, Barack Obama, but I don't need lessons about "being woke" and "cancel culture". *The Independent*. www.independent.co.uk/voices/obama-woke-meaning-michelle-cancel-culture-foundation-chicago-a9178436.html

Beauvais, E. (2018). Deliberation and equality. In A. Bächtiger, J. S. Dryzek, J. Mansbridge, & M. E. Warren (Eds.), *The Oxford handbook of deliberative democracy* (pp. 144–155). Oxford: Oxford University Press.

Bogel-Burroughs, N., & Peters, J. W. (2020, April 20). "You have to disobey": Protesters gather to defy stay-at-home orders. *The New York Times*. www.nytimes.com/2020/04/16/us/coronavirus-rules-protests.html?action=click&module=RelatedLinks&pgtype=Article

Bohman, J. (1997). Deliberative democracy and effective social freedom: Capabilities, resources, and opportunities. In J. Bohman & W. Rehg (Eds.), *Deliberative democracy: Essays on reason and politics* (pp. 321–348). Cambridge, MA: MIT Press.

Bouie, J. (2019, August 14). America holds onto an undemocratic assumption from its founding: That some people deserve more power than others. *The New York Times*. www.nytimes.com/interactive/2019/08/14/magazine/republicans-racism-african-americans.html

Brooks, R. (2019, October 24). Meghan Daum's merciless take on modern feminism, woke-ness and cancel culture. *The Washington Post*. www.washingtonpost.com/entertainment/books/meghan-daums-merciless-take-on-modern-feminism-woke-ness-and-cancel-culture/2019/10/24/77f47d40-efaf-11e9-8693-f487e46784aa_story.html

Carmon, I. (2015, April 27). How Ruth Bader Ginsburg helped pave the way for marriage equality. *MSNBC*. www.msnbc.com/msnbc/how-ruth-bader-ginsburg-helped-pave-the-way-marriage-equality-msna583326

Cillizza, C. (2018, October 30). The dangerous consequences of Trump's all-out assault on political correctness. *CNN*. www.cnn.com/2018/10/30/politics/donald-trump-hate-speech-anti-semitism-steve-king-kevin-mccarthy/index.html

Dionne, E. J., Jr. (2020, July 19). A tribute to John Lewis: In his own words. *The Washington Post*. www.washingtonpost.com/opinions/2020/07/19/tribute-john-lewis-his-own-words/

Ferber, A. (2020, September 22). Judith Butler on culture wars, JK Rowling and living in "anti-intellectual times". *New Statesman*. www.newstatesman.com/international/2020/09/judith-butler-culture-wars-jk-rowling-and-living-anti-intellectual-times

Garber, M. (2020, March 12). How Hillary Clinton became a postmodern menace. *The Atlantic*. www.theatlantic.com/culture/archive/2020/03/why-hillary-clinton-wont-just-go-away/607852/

Geier, K. (2016). Hillary Clinton, economic populist? Are you fucking kidding me? In L. Featherstone (Ed.), *False choices: The faux feminism of Hillary Rodham Clinton* (pp. 29–45). London: Verso.

Herrick, J. A. (2013). *The history and theory of rhetoric: An introduction*. Abingdon, UK: Routledge.

Hudson, V. M. (2020, March 6). What you do to your women, you do to your nation. *The New York Times*. www.nytimes.com/2020/03/06/opinion/global-womens-rights.html

Parry-Giles, S. J. (2014). *Hillary Clinton in the news: Gender and authenticity in American politics*. Champaign, IL: University of Illinois Press.

Roberts-Miller, P. (2017). *Demagoguery and democracy*. New York: The Experiment.

Robin, C. (2018). *The reactionary mind: Conservatism from Edmund Burke to Donald Trump*. Oxford: Oxford University Press.

Robinson, M. (2020, October 9). Don't give up on America. *The New York Times*. www.nytimes.com/2020/10/09/opinion/sunday/america-patriotism.html

Romano, A. (2019, December 30). Why we can't stop fighting about cancel culture. *Vox*. www.vox.com/culture/2019/12/30/20879720/what-is-cancel-culture-explained-history-debate

Roth, M. S. (2020, September 19). Colleges, conservatives, and kakistocracy. *The New York Times*. www.nytimes.com/2020/09/19/opinion/campus-free-speech.html

Rothman, A. (2017). *The pursuit of harmony: Kepler on cosmos, confession, and community*. Chicago: University of Chicago Press.

Ross, L. (2019, August 17). I'm a Black feminist: I think call-out culture is toxic. *The New York Times*. www.nytimes.com/2019/08/17/opinion/sunday/cancel-culture-call-out.html

Rueb, E. S., & Taylor, D. B. (2019, October 31). Obama on call-out culture: That's not activism. *The New York Times*. www.nytimes.com/2019/10/31/us/politics/obama-woke-cancel-culture.html

Scalia, E. (2020, September 19). What can we learn from Ginsburg's friendship with my father, Antonin Scalia. *The Washington Post*. www.washingtonpost.com/opinions/eugene-scalia-rbg-friendship-oped/2020/09/19/35f7580c-faaa-11ea-a275-1a2c2d36e1f1_story.html

Schwartz, I. (2019, November 12). Former Clinton advisor Doug Schoen to Hillary Clinton: "Go home, shut your mouth". *Real Clear Politics*. www.realclearpolitics.com/video/2019/11/12/former_clinton_advisor_doug_schoen_to_hillary_clinton_go_home_shut_your_mouth.html

Shelby County v. Holder, 570 U.S. 529. (2013). https://supreme.justia.com/cases/federal/us/570/529

Suskin, A. (2016, June 2). My havruta and I disagree on everything: And that's a good thing. *My Jewish Learning*. www.myjewishlearning.com/rabbis-without-borders/maybe-we-should-give-up-on-tolerance/

Trump, D. J. (2020, July 4). *Remarks by president Trump at South Dakota's 2020 Mount Rushmore's fireworks celebration*. Keystone, South Dakota. Whitehouse.gov. www.whitehouse.gov/briefings-statements/remarks-president-trump-south-dakotas-2020-mount-rushmore-fireworks-celebration-keystone-south-dakota/

Trump, D. J. (2020, September 22). Executive order on combating race and sex stereotyping. *Donald J. Trump Presidential Administration*. www.whitehouse.gov/presidential-actions/executive-order-combating-race-sex-stereotyping/

United States Commission on Civil Rights. (2018). *An assessment of minority voting rights access in the United States: 2018 statutory enforcement report*. U.S. Commission on Civil Rights. www.usccr.gov/pubs/2018/Minority_Voting_Access_2018.pdf

Vagianos, A. (2015, June 2). Ruth Bader Ginsburg tells young women: "Fight for the things you care about". *Huffington Post*. www.radcliffe.harvard.edu/news/in-news/ruth-bader-ginsburg-tells-young-women-fight-things-you-care-about

Vera, A. (2019, December 9). Here are just some of the people who were canceled or threatened with cancellation in 2019. *CNN*. www.cnn.com/2019/12/08/us/2019-canceled-stories-trnd/index.html

Weinberger v. Wiesenfeld, 420 U.S. 636. (1975). https://supreme.justia.com/cases/federal/us/420/636/

14 Cultivate Empathy for Outgroups

Nicholas A. Valentino

On January 6, 2021, a violent mob attacked the US Capitol during what would normally have been a routine ceremony recognizing the results of the presidential election of November 3, 2020. The furious group of Trump supporters toppled barricades, fought with police, broke windows, and occupied the building where the nation's laws are made. Some were armed, some carried Confederate flags or wore clothing with White nationalist symbols, and some stalked the halls, searching for specific lawmakers responsible for, in their words, "stealing the election." One protestor was shot and killed, a D.C. Capitol police officer died after being viciously beaten, and at least three others died of medical emergencies. At least 56 police officers were injured (Feuer, 2021, January 7). Scenes of the chaos were broadcast around the world, and many foreign leaders sent expressions of concern, alarmed by America's inability to peacefully transfer power after a free and fair election.

This tragic and shameful blow to America's reputation as a stable democracy is but part of a larger trend, a tributary linked to the broad river that drives politics here and around the world, a waterway often featuring racial and ethnic inequality, conflict, and injustice. Over the past few decades, racial conflict has become more salient, extreme, and consequential, both in the United States and around the world. Populist leaders increasingly deploy anti-immigrant policies and harsh racial rhetoric, unjustifiable in terms of economic benefits or national security, to mobilize supporters and undermine democratic norms and institutions. Police and criminal justice organizations shed too much blood, especially in minority communities (Knox et al., 2020), without sufficient cause or consequence. Criminal justice institutions ensnare too many (especially young) non-White men and too often strip them of their citizenship rights even after their debt to society has been paid (Lerman & Weaver, 2014). All too often, we erect physical and economic barriers to wall ourselves off from the rest of the world, as if that would make us safer, when in fact isolation drags down the nation's economy.

While all of this is surely happening, there are more positive signs as well. It is easy to miss how many citizens actively resist unfair, unjust, or unwise

DOI: 10.4324/9781003212515-18

policies that inflame group conflicts, even when they and their families might benefit by "going along" with the rampant prejudice. Evidence for this claim abounds: There is a great deal of variation in support for policies that redistribute benefits from some groups to other groups – affirmative action, social welfare redistribution, voter protection laws, support for immigration, and fair criminal justice policies – that cannot be explained by ingroup interests alone.

A great scholarly investment over the last quarter of a century helps us understand one side of this puzzle: Why do some people support policies that punish other groups, even when they derive no personal gain for doing so? Dimensions such as symbolic racism (Sears, 1988), authoritarianism (Feldman, 2003), social dominance orientation (Sidanius & Pratto, 2001) and group identity (Jardina, 2019) have been shown to drive citizens to behave in ways akin to cutting off their noses to spite their faces. The symbolic attachment to some groups and dislike of others often overrides narrow self-interest in public opinion formation. These forces surely help us understand why people sometimes refuse to help others.

But what explains some individuals' willingness to reach out to those who are different than themselves, even when they have much to lose? For example, why do African Americans oppose anti-immigrant policies (Brader et al., 2009; Sirin et al., 2016b, 2017), even when they are more likely than other groups to suffer job competition and wage suppression as a result of working-class immigrants surging into their communities? Why do they oppose the racial profiling of Muslims by airport security officials or Donald Trump's ban on visitors from predominantly Muslim countries even when they perceive themselves to be at a higher risk from terrorism than do other ethnic groups?

Is it simply group interest? Do all helpers come from groups that are suffering? No, there is a great deal of variation in *outgroup caring* among all persons across the socioeconomic spectrum. Among Whites, are the "helpers" simply those who do not hold negative racial stereotypes or who are low in authoritarian personality traits? Racism and authoritarianism matter, of course, but they are not the whole story. The absence of hostile racial stereotypes, a lack of authoritarian personality, or only weak identification with a dominant group does not guarantee that a person will reach out to others in need. Some individuals from all parties, religions, ethnic and racial groups, and genders *do* recognize the suffering of strangers and *do* support policies designed to reduce that suffering. These individuals are high in a rather rare but politically potent dimension called outgroup empathy.

Outgroup Empathy

The backlash to punitive policies directed at minorities, the tendency to welcome immigrants and protect refugees fleeing violence from other countries, to resist inequality and unfairness even when it might benefit our closest kin, and even, we would guess, to accept a free and fair election that one loses are all linked to outgroup empathy. In a forthcoming book entitled *Seeing Us in Them: Social Divisions and the Politics of Group Empathy*, Cigdem Sirin, Jose Villalobos, and I propose group empathy theory to help understand the roots of a broad domain of social conflicts and policy trends in our time.

So what is *outgroup empathy*? Empathy is often a slippery concept, defined in different ways by different writers and researchers. Some think empathy is purely affective or synonymous with sympathy: feeling bad for those who are less fortunate than ourselves. Others think it is a cold ability: to simply see the world through another's eyes. We think that both definitions are too simplistic. Our definition of outgroup empathy, building on a large number of previous studies in psychology, suggests that it is a long-term trait, probably learned early in life and consisting of both cognitive and motivational dimensions. It includes the ability to take the perspective of someone from another group but also the motivation to care about that individual once one begins to walk in their shoes. Our definition comes closest to that of Batson and Coke (1981), but unlike them, ours focuses on outgroups, not members of one's close family and friends.

How is outgroup empathy measured? We build on Davis's (1983) self-reported measurement of both perspective taking and empathic concern in the Interpersonal Reactivity Index (IRI). Perspective taking is tapped by noting how people react to statements like, "I try to look at everybody's side of a disagreement before I make a decision." Empathic concern is measured with statements like, "I often have tender, concerned feelings for people who are less fortunate than me." We modified several of Davis's items to focus not on individuals but on members of racial or ethnic outgroups. Our final Group Empathy Index (GEI) contains just four questions, short enough to be included in large national surveys (and indeed, it has been included on a wave of the British Election Study in 2018 and the American National Election Study in 2020). Two questions are *perspective-taking items*, including, "How often would you say you try to better understand people of other racial or ethnic groups by imagining how things look from their perspective?" and "Before criticizing somebody from another racial or ethnic group, how often do you try to imagine how you would feel if you were in their place?" The other two are *empathic concern items*, including, "How often would you say that you have tender, concerned feelings for people from another racial or ethnic group who are less fortunate than you?" and "When you see someone being taken advantage of due to their race or ethnicity, how often do you feel protective toward them?" Responses to these four simple questions form a highly reliable scale and are summed to create the GEI.

This resource, outgroup empathy, might be easy to mistake as another name for constructs like symbolic racism, social dominance, ingroup identity, authoritarianism, partisanship, and ideology, all of which are important for understanding our current moment. But empathy for those from different backgrounds, traditions, religious beliefs, and worldviews is unique and rather rare. While our scale's items do not mention specific groups, they do ask people how often they are transported into other people's lives and experiences. We find that some people do this more often and some less. And those differences, above and beyond all the usual suspects mentioned, are politically important.

While there is not enough space in this chapter to show the reader the proof, I am confident in our findings about outgroup empathy and invite consideration of the studies outlined in our book (Sirin et al., 2021). We find that outgroup empathy predicts support for a wide variety of policies across a range of domains beyond the explicitly racial to broader solutions for social welfare redistribution, immigration, and rights for women and LGBTQ individuals. It predicts opposition to Brexit in the United Kingdom above and beyond ideology, partisanship, and authoritarianism, as well as a host of sociodemographic factors like education, income, religion, and age. In short, outgroup empathy is real, and it has consequences.

The "Naivete" of Outgroup Empathy

We highly value skepticism in the social sciences, and so we tip our cap now to the skeptical reader who thinks, "Outgroup empathy sounds like a naïve and risky worldview, since anyone who spends their time thinking about the welfare of others is bound to be taken advantage of." In fact, political leaders often seem to encourage just such selfish thinking, scoffing at those who would sacrifice for others, especially those who hail from faraway lands, different ethnic backgrounds, and distinct cultural traditions. In some people's eyes, the credo of the day is this: "We must take care of ourselves first and foremost, restricting our generosity to 'real Americans.'"

All of that seems sensible, but there are also good reasons to call into question such a narrow worldview. Those who can take the perspective of others living in a diverse community, after all, are uniquely positioned to capitalize on economic opportunities and to solve the mounting problems they collectively face. Those who work well with others from distinct backgrounds are more likely to succeed in a global economy full of opportunities springing from collaboration, reciprocity, and compromise. They require partners able to listen, understand, learn, and build things together. In other words, it is not at all obvious that focusing inward rather than outward, never mind subjugating others for profit or security, will produce benefits even in the short term, not to mention the longer run.

Outgroup Empathy and Democratic Norms

Most of our work focuses on the role that outgroup empathy plays in support of policies directly impacting minority groups: immigration restrictions, foreign aid, support for affirmative action and social welfare redistribution, Black Lives Matter protests, LGBTQ rights, and so on. But we also suspect that outgroup empathy might have a lot to do with more abstract but foundational political beliefs, values, and norms as well.

Take, for example, the persistent and baseless claim that Donald Trump would have won the 2020 presidential election if not for massive and widespread electoral fraud. Dozens and dozens of lawsuits claiming election fraud, filed by GOP operatives around the country, were summarily rejected by courts at every level. Election officials from both parties in every state reviewed election procedures and certified results, repeatedly insisting that 2020 saw one of the most secure elections ever held. Yet millions of Americans still tell pollsters they believe the presidency was "stolen" by a cabal of "Deep State" actors, a conspiracy theory promoted by the president and those allied with him, sentiments amply broadcast over Twitter and right-wing media outlets. These beliefs were common among those who participated in the insurrection of January 6, 2021, which shook the historic American tradition of electoral losers humbly accepting the will of the people and then peacefully transferring power to the winner.

But how might group empathy be involved in this case? It is no coincidence, we think, that one of the pieces of "evidence" most often cited by those who believed in the conspiracy was that they did not personally know anyone who voted for Joe Biden (Bump, 2020, December 7). In fact, both sides of the aisle seemed to struggle with taking their opponent's perspective in the wake of the 2020 election. Thanksgiving dinners throughout the nation were thrown into a tumult as a result.

Outgroup Empathy and the COVID-19 Pandemic

There has been plenty of talk recently about the politicization of election procedures and the response to COVID-19. We would say, unfortunately, that the more basic effort has been to politicize, stigmatize, and dismiss the value of empathy for outgroups. The notion that helping outgroups is a sign of political weakness and that cruelty can be justified in the service of short-term political victory is a common thread in these debates. Wearing a mask to protect strangers is similar to accepting people from another political party as legitimate Americans. Both propositions require taking the perspective of distant others plus the motivation to care about what those folks are going through.

In a nationally representative survey taken in the spring of 2020, my student Francy Luna Diaz and I found a strong correlation between the

GEI and concern about COVID-19, above and beyond partisanship, ideology, and other factors. We think that it is no coincidence that concern about the pandemic, even the recognition of its very existence, is profoundly correlated with the ability to place oneself in the shoes of strangers who are suffering. We now know that racial disparities in human suffering as a result of the COVID-19 pandemic are vast. Our collective inability to appreciate the suffering taking place in hospitals around the country is staggering. The core of the problem, in other words, is that *outgroup empathy itself* is becoming politicized, stacking one tragedy on the back of another.

How to Cultivate Outgroup Empathy?

Psychologists have long argued that individual-level empathy is a naturally occurring human trait and that, therefore, it need not be actively cultivated. But it is also true that empathy is vitally important because, as social animals, we depend so much upon one another for our very survival. Empathy is a mechanism for strengthening the social bonds of the tribe so that its members will come together when attacked from without. That is why it is so important to remember that we are talking about a very different, rare, and complex phenomenon when discussing group empathy. How can we cultivate caring for others outside our family when doing so might put our own loved ones at greater risk?

According to leaders like Dr. Martin Luther King and John Lewis, nurturing the Beloved Community requires a society-wide commitment to justice, egalitarianism, and love among all members of the human family. Such abstract values are surely hard to disagree with, but how to achieve them? Most civil rights leaders believe that the first step toward reaching those goals is eliminating hunger, poverty, disease, and homelessness. Arguments in favor of equal political representation, social justice, and the elimination of economic inequality often start with addressing these basic needs. It is vital to debate which policies can actually accomplish this first step without undermining liberty and the reward for individual human initiative and achievement. To my way of thinking, the evidence plainly demonstrates how extreme poverty and injustice must be reduced before we can reasonably discuss the correct balance between the size of government and the benefits of individual hard work.

But beyond the evidently controversial call for a more equitable distribution of political rights and societal resources, what could individuals and their families do to increase outgroup empathy? Today, for example, our country's traditional divisions are growing as we become increasingly isolated as a result of the pandemic. We are isolated not just from our friends and loved ones but also from the world at large. Scholars have long suspected that physical contact, especially that which includes real conversation, collaboration, and cooperation, can strengthen trust and respect for those hailing from different cultural backgrounds, religious traditions, races, and ethnicities (Allport, 1954). But it is not enough simply to *exist* near other groups of people precisely because the very act of *seeing* people who are different from ourselves can be threatening to many (Enos, 2017). Accordingly, some set of positive conditions must be present for intergroup contact to trigger empathy, including equal status between groups and perceived common interests or goals (Pettigrew & Tropp, 2006).

More positively, the simple sharing of cultural traditions can help reveal our common humanity. One way to do so is by traveling broadly for the purpose of learning about other people and places. As Mark Twain (1835–1910) wrote in his memoir *The Innocents Abroad, Roughing It*: "Travel is fatal to prejudice, bigotry, and narrow-mindedness, and many of our people need it sorely on these accounts. Broad, wholesome, charitable views of men and things cannot be acquired by vegetating in one little corner of the earth all one's lifetime." Such travel, of course, is a luxury that many cannot afford, but we suspect that travel might be beneficial at any scale and on nearly any budget. As trite as it might sound, we must get out and see the world and talk to the people who live there. Most who have done so readily admit that the world itself seems to change as a result. And with the World Wide Web now at our fingertips, we can take virtual trips as well.

Less costly than physical travel is building something locally with those who are different from us. Working toward a shared goal exposes us to the skills, traditions, and perspectives of other groups. The benefits of group diversity for problem-solving are beginning to receive scholarly attention (Page, 2007). Performing community service, especially in an educational setting in which different groups are learning with and from one another, has been shown to carry significant benefits, as Mo and Conn (2018) have demonstrated when investigating participants in the Teach for America program. We find in our book that even brief service-learning courses in diverse communities might have a positive effect along these lines, although much more research needs to be done.

As mentioned before, COVID-19 made all these activities elusive, even impossible, for many Americans. To keep themselves and their communities safe, people had to forego the very activities that build empathy for those struggling the most. As soon as it is safe, then, we must begin to build things together again, across and not just within lines of difference. Government could actually help promote such activities, as it did when rebuilding after the Great Depression, and as other countries have done after wars ravaged their cities. Working alongside one another, creating value not just in our own communities but in the communities of others, is surely a realistic solution for all of us, at least in some way, at least for some period of time.

Conclusion

Once order was restored after the insurrection of January 6, 2021, several senators and more than 130 GOP House members resumed their effort to overturn the election by rejecting the Electoral College votes from states won by President-Elect Joe Biden and Vice-President Elect Kamala Harris. When opposing this effort, US Senator Ben Sasse, a Republican from Nebraska, rose to recognize the outcome of the presidential election. The speech was one of several that struck a common theme, recognizing the importance of community and neighborliness (KMTV Staff, 2021, January 6).

> Colleagues, today has been ugly. When I came to the floor this morning, I planned to talk about the lesson of 1801 because I'm kind of a history nerd, and I wanted to celebrate the glories of the peaceful transition of power across our nation's history. It feels a little naive now to talk about ways that American civics might be something that could unite us in bringing us back together . . . . You can't do big things together as Americans if you think other Americans are the enemy . . . . There are some who want to burn it all down. We met some of them today. But they aren't going to win. Don't let them be your prophets. Instead, organize, persuade, but most importantly, love your neighbor.

Loving thy neighbor is mandated in all holy texts. Unfortunately, group empathy theory shows us that neighborliness alone is insufficient. Empathy for those *close and dear* is important, but it is a much more difficult thing to build empathy across lines of difference in a pluralistic society.

In our book, we find that individual empathy enhances care and protection for the ingroup – our families, loved ones, and neighbors – but does little to promote intergroup equality and social justice. In the United States, individual empathy is unrelated to opposition to punitive immigration policies and only weakly related to rallying to defend the rights of other groups. In Britain, for example, empathy for close intimates, family, and friends does little to boost support for equal opportunities for ethnic minorities, members of the LGBTQ community, Muslims, or women. It is unrelated to support for social welfare policy and opposition to Brexit. Empathy for outgroups, on the other hand, strongly boosts policy support for all these groups, and it does so among White and non-White Britons alike.

Caring for those who are protesting racial injustice in their own neighborhood or attempting to decrease inequality and suffering far away cannot be achieved with simple exhortations to neighborliness. Interpersonal empathy does not facilitate and might even obscure our view of the injustices just over the horizon. Hopefully, more people will soon realize exactly how close and how interdependent our different neighborhoods really are. That notion was central to Martin Luther King, Jr.'s last Christmas sermon, given in 1967, when he explained, "If we are to have peace on earth, our loyalties must become ecumenical rather than sectional. Our loyalties must transcend our race, our tribe, our class, and our nation; and this means we must develop a world perspective." The evidence we have gathered in our studies bears out Dr. King's philosophy fully: We must work together to find the *us* in *them*.

Bibliography

Allport, G. W. (1954). *The nature of prejudice*. Cambridge, MA: Perseus Books.

Batson, C. D., & Coke, J. S. (1981). Empathy: A source of altruistic motivation for helping. In J. P. Rushton & R. M. Sorrentino (Eds.), *Altruism and helping behavior* (pp. 167–187). Hillsdale, NJ: Lawrence Erlbaum.

Brader, T., Valentino, N., & Jardina, A. (2009, September 3–6). *Immigration opinion in a time of economic crisis: Material interests versus group attitudes*. Presented at the American Political Science Association Meetings held in Toronto, Canada.

Bump, P. (2020, December 7). One possible reason Trump's false fraud claims took root: Many of his supporters may not know Biden voters. *Washington Post*. www.washingtonpost.com/politics/2020/12/07/one-possible-reason-trumps-false-fraud-claims-took-root-many-his-supporters-may-not-know-biden-voters/

Davis, M. H. (1983). Measuring individual differences in empathy: Evidence for a multidimensional approach. *Journal of Personality and Social Psychology*, 44(1), 113–126.

Enos, R. D. (2017). *The space between us: Social geography and politics*. New York: Cambridge University Press.

Feldman, S. (2003). Enforcing social conformity: A theory of authoritarianism. *Political Psychology*, 24(1), 41–74.

Feuer, A. (2021, January 7). Assaulting officers, illegal guns and unlawful entry: Violent protesters face federal charges. *New York Times*. www.nytimes.com/live/2021/01/07/us/capitol-building-trump/at-least-56-police-officers-were-hurt-during-the-chaos-at-the-capitol-the-dc-police-chief-says

Jardina, A. (2019). *White identity politics*. New York. Cambridge University Press.

KMTV Staff. (2021, January 6). Sen. Sasse delivers speech on Senate floor following DC chaos. *KMTV2-News Now*. www.3newsnow.com/news/political/sen-sasse-delivers-speech-on-senate-floor-following-dc-chaos

Knox, D., Lowe, W., & Mummolo, J. (2020). Administrative records mask racially biased policing. *American Political Science Review*, 114(3), 619–637.

Lerman, A. E., & Weaver, V. M. (2014). *Arresting citizenship: The democratic consequences of American crime control*. Chicago, IL: The University of Chicago Press.

Mo, C. H., & Conn, K. M. (2018). When do the advantaged see the disadvantages of others? A quasi-experimental study of national service. *American Political Science Review*, 112(4), 721–741.

Page, S. E. (2007). *The difference: How the power of diversity creates better groups, firms, schools, and societies*. Princeton, NJ: Princeton University Press.

Pettigrew, T. F., & Tropp, L. R. (2006). A meta analytic test of intergroup contact theory. *Journal of Personality and Social Psychology*, 90(5), 751–783.

Sears, D. O. (1988). Symbolic racism. In P. A. Katz & D. A. Taylor (Eds.), *Eliminating racism: Profiles in controversy* (pp. 53–84). New York: Plenum Press.

Sidanius, J., & Pratto, F. (2001). *Social dominance: An intergroup theory of social hierarchy and oppression*. New York: Cambridge University Press.

Sirin, C. V., Valentino, N. A., & Villalobos, J. D. (2016a). Empathic responses to non-verbal racial/ethnic cues: A national experiment on immigration policy attitudes. *American Behavioral Scientist, 60*(14), 1676–1697.

Sirin, C. V., Valentino, N. A., & Villalobos, J. D. (2016b). Group empathy theory: The effect of group empathy on US intergroup attitudes and behavior in the context of immigration threats. *Journal of Politics, 73*(3), 893–908.

Sirin, C. V., Valentino, N. A., & Villalobos, J. D. (2017). The social causes and political consequences of group empathy. *Political Psychology, 38*(3), 427–448.

Sirin, C. V., Valentino, N. A., & Villalobos, J. D. (2021). *Seeing us in them: Social divisions and the politics of group empathy*. Cambridge: Cambridge University Press.

Twain, M. (1835–1910/1984). *The innocents abroad: Roughing it*. New York: Library of America: Distributed to the trade in the U.S. and Canada by the Viking Press.

Part 4
Confront the Establishment

15 Counter a Reactive Media System

Dhavan Shah, Yini Zhang, Jon Pevehouse, and Sebastián Valenzuela

Americans currently live in two very different worlds, two halves of one country divided by media and politics. And while it might be appealing to think of these two halves as equally responsible for the gulf separating the political left from the political right, that has become an increasingly untenable position. Our media and politics are now defined by asymmetry, with the Left operating by one set of rules and the Right playing by another. On the left, political elites and journalistic outlets spend their time *reporting* the facts underlying news events and responding to public expressions of concern by their partisans. On the Right, media are not as responsive to discourse by their own partisans but spend more time *reacting* to moderate and liberal perspectives, reactions often uncoupled from the facts surrounding current events. Conservatives are motivated more by "liberal tears" than by informed action – belief trumped by incredulity.

How might we respond to a right-wing media ecosystem increasingly detached from the facts underlying events and that spends most of its time reacting to discourses from the political center and left? In this chapter, we argue that norms of reporting and modes of social media engagement must adapt to a changing media ecology made up of partisan voices that are asymmetric in their intensity, factuality, and responsiveness to one another. Instead of having the political left respond to this dynamic by mirroring the rhetoric of the right, we suggest a commitment by fact-checking organizations, news outlets, platforms, academics, and foundations to a new era of *frame-checking* to counter the efforts made by actors on the political right not only to mislead but also to distract and disorient.

Coupled with fact-checking, concerted efforts directed at frame-checking will shed light on how media outlets and political elites on the Right ignore events of relevance, highlight other topics, or counteract mainstream coverage to promote alternate accounts and spurious interpretations, to stoke moral outrage, and to stimulate opposition strategies among conservatives. Parallel efforts should be directed at the media outlets and political elites on the Left to confirm that these asymmetries merit a formal and organized response. Continuing to operate

DOI: 10.4324/9781003212515-20

"as usual" within a fractured media system will undermine democracy. Change is needed, and it is needed now.

A Fractured Media System

The contemporary media system in the US is characterized by both deep interconnectedness and stark polarization, with news and social media tightly bound together yet also deeply divided on a partisan basis. Some have claimed that the media system in the US is a blend of old and new media bound together in a web of linking and sharing (Chadwick, 2017). These media players have a variety of motivations, competing for audience attention while also being dependent on one another for generating interest in current events (Klinger & Svensson, 2015; Webster, 2014). Partisan cleavages also separate news audiences from social media audiences, with the political right and political left having different goals in this regard (Faris et al., 2017; Yarchi et al., 2020). Given these cleavages, deciding on how the events of the day should be discussed becomes a perplexing matter indeed.

Although traditional news formerly sets the agenda for public discussion of current events, communication flows have become less predictable in a shifting ecology featuring citizens' expressive powers (Shah et al., 2017). The factors driving communication flows across news and social media have been analyzed previously by using theories of agenda setting (e.g., Guo & McCombs, 2016), cascading frame activation (e.g., Entman, 2003), and networked discursive power (Jungherr et al., 2019).

Research has demonstrated "a complex and dynamic interaction" between news and social media (Neuman et al., 2014, p. 193; Valenzuela et al., 2017). According to many observers, the latter is gaining traction in determining how news attention is being shaped and reinforced (Wells et al., 2020). Added to this confusion are differences in the composition, structure, and norms of conservative media compared to center-left and liberal media (e.g., Benkler et al., 2018; Freelon et al., 2020). In our past research, for example, we have tracked communication flows related to mass shootings discussed widely on Twitter between 2012 and 2014 and shared across the political spectrum (Zhang et al., 2019; Pelled et al., forthcoming). We also studied similar communication flows related to #MeToo movement events in 2017 and 2018 (Suk et al., 2021; Ghosh et al., 2020). In both cases, we compared the specific facts surrounding those events (the input) with how the media system reacted to them (the output) and how they did so over time. We often found that the facts themselves did not always predict the resulting discussions in mainstream and social media. Instead, *preexisting preferences* within the different media best explained what audiences saw and heard about the events being covered.

In separate sets of analyses, we modeled news attention across conservative, moderate, and progressive outlets and Twitter discourses on the Right and Left in relation to the characteristics of mass shooting and #MeToo events. After accounting for the different facts and characteristics of these events, we tested the relationships between news attention and Twitter discourses concerning gun policy and women's rights (Zhang et al., 2021; Shah et al., 2021). Results show that the Left, in terms of both news coverage and social media discourse, is more responsive to the facts driving news events (e.g., the number of victims, the number of children killed, accusations against GOP politicians, and #MeToo announcements) than was the Right. In contrast, the Right spent its time reacting to reports by the political left and center, reframing its own content to counteract what the Left was saying. This reactive give-and-take clearly undermines any sense of a deliberative public sphere (Dahlberg, 2007). We need to understand the factors contributing to this corrosive dynamic and replace it with something better.

Hybridity and the Attention Economy

Multiple factors have displaced the late-20th-century media system (which operated under a different set of norms and logics), resulting in the hybridized and fragmented 21st-century version propelled by those on the political right. The rise of cable news outlets with clear political slants (e.g., FOX News, MSNBC), increasingly partisan online news outlets and aggregators (e.g., Breitbart, HuffPost), and social media platforms with ideological underpinnings (e.g., Parler, Instagram) now compete in media ecosystems previously dominated by print and broadcast media, legacy operations that abided by established journalistic norms of fairness, truthfulness, and completeness (Blumler & Kavanagh, 1999; Chadwick, 2017). The result has been increased exposure to political extremism, especially that of right-wing populists, who have collectively weaponized digital media to counteract what the mainstream media is saying in its coverage (Costello et al., 2016; Krämer, 2017).

With so much channel multiplicity and information overload, capturing audience interest has become increasingly challenging (Webster, 2014), thereby raising the stakes for interconnections between older media and newer media to drive traffic (Chadwick, 2017). One obvious result is that news outlets now actively court audience attention, using social media to distribute and amplify their content (Webster, 2014; Wu et al., 2020). Social media also now channel people's attention completely independent of the traditional news media (Tufekci, 2013). Widely followed elite actors (Harder et al., 2017), messages amplified through retweeting (Wells et al., 2016), discourses organized around hashtags (Freelon et al., 2018), and clickbait content (Munger, 2020) are especially powerful. Across all these venues, the Right and the Left operate differently, with the Right weaponizing the news in a constant battle against liberal and centrist perspectives. Two things result from these practices: (1) asymmetry – different news discussions fueled by different political purposes and (2) ideological rigidity – a concern for being politically consistent rather than for being politically informed. Both factors help explain what we see and hear each day in our medium of choice.

Asymmetry and Frame Diversion

Partisan media compete with legacy media to focus audience attention and, sometimes, to stoke outrage (Baum & Groeling, 2008). On social media, people interact with like-minded others, solidifying their existing policy positions and reinforcing their polarized sensibilities (Song & Boomgaarden, 2017; Yarchi et al., 2020). The result is that the political right is cloistered in a distinct subcluster, apart from – and yet responsive to – centrist and liberal outlets (Benkler et al., 2018). Conservative news sources, centered on Breitbart and Fox News, for example, are widely shared in right-wing networks on social media, while a much wider range of sources circulates in left-leaning networks (Faris et al., 2017). In short, media asymmetries between the Left and the Right could not be starker than they are today.

And the effects of these asymmetries are predictable. The right-wing media, for example, are more susceptible to disinformation operations (Hjorth & Adler-Nissen, 2019), and conservatives on Twitter are more likely to spread fake news (Bovet & Makse, 2019). Our research findings discussed earlier point to another effect – conservative outlets also regularly reframe news in response to fact-driven coverage from centrist and liberal outlets in an effort to counteract the reigning narratives. When doing so, conservatives not only share outright misinformation but also engage in *frame diversion* – the use of communication tools to distract and disorient rather than to select and inform. That is, conservative elites go well beyond conventional understandings of news framing (Entman, 1993, p. 52):

> To frame is to select some aspects of perceived reality and make them more salient in the communicating text, in such a way as to promote a particular problem definition, causal interpretation, moral evaluation and/or treatment recommendation for the item described. Frames, then, define problems.

We contend that the right-wing media ecosystem does not frame news in the conventional sense, since conservative coverage is often unconcerned with resolving specific policy issues. Instead, they seek to distort understanding, distract attention, foster outrage, and encourage opposition to solutions proposed by their political opponents without offering counter-proposals or making needed policy recommendations. The result of such a reactive gesture is frame diversion, a communication strategy adopted by the Right to distract, disorient, and halt substantive discussions and debates. In light of such moves, how can we possibly restore equanimity – or even mere sanity – in political communication writ large in the United States?

Conclusion

As mentioned, frame diversion is a reaction to center and left perspectives, a technique designed to garble their messages, mislead attentive audiences, and muddy the facts underlying the events of the day. To be effective, such efforts must go beyond the noble work of organizations like PolitiFact (www.politifact.com/), FactCheck.org (www.factcheck.org/), and Fact Checker (www.washingtonpost.com/news/fact-checker/), all of which hold public figures accountable for lies being told to the public (Graves, 2016). But we need considerably more if we are to undermine the toxic effects of frame diversion.

Heretofore, fact-checking had the power to demand political accountability from campaigns and politicians. The Trump era, however, has taught a generation of conservative operatives that deception through distraction can also be effective without outright lies having to be told. As a result, fact-checkers must now expand their mission to consider the journalistic malpractice caused by frame diversion, focusing more on what is *not* being said, on the issues being ignored, and on the distractions offered in their stead. It is also possible that a new set of organizations will need to engage in *frame-checking*, ensuring that both the Left and the Right are engaged in discussions and debates on the same substantive ground and that extraneous issues, issues particularly galvanizing to polarized voters, are called out for what they are – dangerous distortions of objective political realities.

It is also possible that frame-checking might not begin in the newsroom. Fact-checking, after all, evolved from independent bloggers who relied on their professional networks and who forged media partnerships over time, with strong connections into the academic and foundation worlds (Graves, 2016). Networks like these would need to be reactivated to track down the more insidious but also more nuanced effects of frame diversion. Those who distort frames, after all, always have interesting things to say; the problem is that what they are saying often has no connection to what is transpiring in the real world. What is needed are independent, nonpartisan watchdogs who are clever enough to observe and evaluate news outlets, news aggregators, and social media activists and to monitor the information flowing through their respective platforms, paying special attention to the proclamations being made and to the issues being obscured. Will the revelation of concerted efforts at frame diversion lead to changed views of those on the Right or a renunciation of such techniques? We are not naïve enough to believe that. But identifying the practice will help superintend political debates, exposing distraction and disinformation campaigns for what they are – a measure of political desperation.

If nothing is done, the conservative media ecosystem will grow apace, galvanized not by what is happening on the ground but by merely finding new examples for yesterday's claims. Think, for example, how many tales of outrage could be told about issues like gun policy and women's rights without ever mentioning, in the first case, police shootings, or in the second case, sexual aggression or job discrimination. Quite clearly, the fragmentation of our media system serves the goals of the political right more than those of the political left. That is especially true when ongoing events suddenly trigger preexisting left/right asymmetries as well as mainstream news/social media asymmetries, thereby producing a gaggle of reactive Tweets, narrow foci of attention, and a whirlwind of viral hashtags.

It is laudable that the political left travels the highways of news coverage rather than its byways, clinging to frame maintenance rather than to frame diversion. Given the Right's success, however, it can be tempting to follow their lead. Doing so would be something of a solution, but it would also add to the hyperpolarization of a hybridized media system already straining our democracy. Besides, choosing foolishness over wisdom is rarely a solution; we need to improve public discourse, not coarsen it further. And so the only real solutions are the oldest of them all – paying attention to what is really going on and not to what one might imagine, staying focused on issues and not being distracted by trivialities, and changing your mind when the facts demand it instead of retreating to a cramped world filled with prejudgments. Clearly, for all who care about democracy, there is much work to be done.

Bibliography

Baum, M. A., & Groeling, T. (2008). New media and the polarization of American political discourse. *Political Communication*, 25(4), 345–365.

Benkler, Y., Faris, R., & Roberts, H. (2018). *Network propaganda: Manipulation, disinformation, and radicalization in American politics*. Oxford: Oxford University Press.

Blumler, J. G., & Kavanagh, D. (1999). The third age of political communication: Influences and features. *Political Communication*, 16(3), 209–230.

Bovet, A., & Makse, H. A. (2019). Influence of fake news in Twitter during the 2016 US presidential election. *Nature Communications*, 10(1), 1–14.

Chadwick, A. (2017). *The hybrid media system: Politics and power*. Oxford: Oxford University Press.

Costello, M., Hawdon, J., Ratliff, T., & Grantham, T. (2016). Who views online extremism? Individual attributes leading to exposure. *Computers in Human Behavior*, 63, 311–320.

Dahlberg, L. (2007). The internet, deliberative democracy, and power: Radicalizing the public sphere. *International Journal of Media & Cultural Politics*, 3(1), 47–64.

Entman, R. M. (1993). Framing: Towards clarification of a fractured paradigm. *Journal of Communication*, 43, 51–59.

Entman, R. M. (2003). Cascading activation: Contesting the White House's frame after 9/11. *Political Communication*, 20(4), 415–432.

Faris, R., Roberts, H., Etling, B., Bourassa, N., Zuckerman, E., & Benkler, Y. (2017). Partisanship, propaganda, and disinformation: Online media and the 2016 US presidential election. *Berkman Klein Center Research Publication*, 6.

Freelon, D., Marwick, A., & Kreiss, D. (2020). False equivalencies: Online activism from left to right. *Science*, 369(6508), 1197–1201.

Freelon, D., McIlwain, C., & Clark, M. (2018). Quantifying the power and consequences of social media protest. *New Media & Society*, 20(3), 990–1011.

Ghosh, S., Su, M. H., Abhishek, A., Suk, J., Tong, C., Kamath, K., . . . & Shah, D. (2020). Covering# MeToo across the news spectrum: Political accusation and public events as drivers of press attention. *The International Journal of Press/Politics*. doi: 10.1177/1940161220968081

Graves, L. (2016). *Deciding what's true: The rise of political fact-checking in American journalism*. New York: Columbia University Press.

Guo, L., & McCombs, M. (Eds.). (2016). *The power of information networks: New directions for agenda setting*. New York: Routledge.

Harder, R. A., Sevenans, J., & Van Aelst, P. (2017). Intermedia agenda setting in the social media age: How traditional players dominate the news agenda in election times. *The International Journal of Press/Politics*, 22(3), 275–293.

Hjorth, F., & Adler-Nissen, R. (2019). Ideological asymmetry in the reach of pro-Russian digital disinformation to United States audiences. *Journal of Communication*, 69(2), 168–192.

Jungherr, A., Posegga, O., & An, J. (2019). Discursive power in contemporary media systems: A comparative framework. *The International Journal of Press/Politics*, 24(4), 404–425.

Klinger, U., & Svensson, J. (2015). The emergence of network media logic in political communication: A theoretical approach. *New Media & Society*, 17(8), 1241–1257.

Krämer, B. (2017). Populist online practices: The function of the Internet in right-wing populism. *Information, Communication & Society*, 20(9), 1293–1309.

Munger, K. (2020). All the news that's fit to click: The economics of clickbait media. *Political Communication*, 37(3), 376–397.

Neuman, R. W., Guggenheim, L., Mo Jang, S., & Bae, S. Y. (2014). The dynamics of public attention: Agenda-setting theory meets big data. *Journal of Communication*, 64(2), 193–214.

Pelled, A., Lukito, J., Foley, J., Sun, Z., Zhang, Y., Pevehouse, J., & Shah, D. (forthcoming). Death across the news spectrum: A time series analysis of partisan coverage following mass shootings in the U.S. *International Journal of Communication*.

Shah, D. V., McLeod, D. M., Rojas, H., Cho, J., Wagner, M. W., & Friedland, L. A. (2017). Revising the communication mediation model for a new political communication ecology. *Human Communication Research*, 43(4), 491–504.

Shah, D. V., Zhang, Y., Suk, J., Pevehouse, J., Correa, T., & Valenzuela, S. (2021). *The reactive right: Partisan news production in an era of social media*. Unpublished manuscript, Mass Communication Research Center, University of Wisconsin-Madison.

Song, H., & Boomgaarden, H. G. (2017). Dynamic spirals put to test: An agent-based model of reinforcing spirals between selective exposure, interpersonal networks, and attitude polarization. *Journal of Communication*, 67(2), 256–281.

Suk, J., Abhishek, A., Zhang, Y., Ahn, S. Y., Correa, T., Garlough, C., & Shah, D. V. (2021). #MeToo, networked acknowledgment, and connective action: How "empowerment through empathy" launched a social movement. *Social Science Computer Review*, 39(2), 276–294.

Tufekci, Z. (2013). "Not this one" social movements, the attention economy, and microcelebrity networked activism. *American Behavioral Scientist*, 57(7), 848–870.

Valenzuela, S., Puente, S., & Flores, P. M. (2017). Comparing disaster news on Twitter and television: An intermedia agenda setting perspective. *Journal of Broadcasting & Electronic Media*, 61(4), 615–637.

Webster, J. G. (2014). *The marketplace of attention: How audiences take shape in a digital age*. Cambridge: The MIT Press.

Wells, C., Shah, D. V., Lukito, J., Pelled, A., Pevehouse, J. C., & Yang, J. (2020). Trump, Twitter, and news media responsiveness: A media systems approach. *New Media & Society*, 22(4), 659–682.

Wells, C., Shah, D. V., Pevehouse, J. C., Yang, J., Pelled, A., Boehm, F., . . . & Schmidt, J. L. (2016). How Trump drove coverage to the nomination: Hybrid media campaigning. *Political Communication*, 33(4), 669–676.

Wu, A. X., Taneja, H., & Webster, J. G. (2020). Going with the flow: Nudging attention online. *New Media & Society*. doi: 10.1177/1461444820941183

Yarchi, M., Baden, C., & Kligler-Vilenchik, N. (2020). Political polarization on the digital sphere: A cross-platform, over-time analysis of interactional, positional, and affective polarization on social media. *Political Communication*. doi: 10.1080/10584609.2020.1785067

Zhang, Y., Shah, D. V., Foley, J., Abhishek, A., Lukito, J., Suk, J., . . . & Garlough, C. (2019). Whose lives matter? Mass shootings and social media discourses of sympathy and policy, 2012–2014. *Journal of Computer-Mediated Communication*, 24(4), 182–202.

Zhang, Y., Shah, D. V., Valenzuela, S., & Pevehouse, J. (2021). *Reactive asymmetry in a hybrid and polarized media system: Communication flows across partisan news and social media in the wake of mass shootings*. Manuscript submitted for Publication.

16 Create a Watchdog Branch of Government

J. H. Snider

A hundred years ago, Walter Lippmann argued that the news media, despite being "the bible of democracy" (2007, p. 28), were inadequate to meet the information needs of mass democracy. Since then, many thoughtful observers have concluded that the news media, especially investigative journalism, have the economic attributes of a public good, which causes the market to undersupply the democratically optimal amount of it (Baker, 2001; Chafee, 1947; Hamilton, 2016; McChesney & Nichols, 2011; Pickard, 2019).

In most people's eyes, the solution to gross market failure is some sort of governmental intervention. But an exception is made for news media. Just as it was assumed for thousands of years that it was impossible for humans to fly, it is now assumed, based on all known experience with government, that government has an inescapable and democracy-destroying conflict of interest in directly addressing this type of market failure.

In this chapter, I address this conflict-of-interest problem head-on by proposing the creation of a **Watchdog Journalism Branch** of government (hereafter, W.J.B.) independent of the legislative, executive, and judicial branches. To be sure, there have been numerous other public-policy proposals to reduce government officials' conflict-of-interest problems related to subsidizing aggressive, independent journalism. Numerous solutions have been proposed, including a profusion of nonprofits, special corporations, voucher programs, and other relatively content-neutral schemes – usually within existing constitutional frameworks (McChesney & Pickard, 2011; Murschetz, 2014; PEN America, 2019; Pickard et al., 2009; Waldman, 2020). Having spent decades studying such schemes, I believe that they have been unable to cleanse themselves of the conflict-of-interest stain. Thus, I propose a more radical solution, one that changes the DNA of government and its constitutional framework.

The problem of market failure in watchdog journalism is greatest for local media, defined as media covering America's 50 states and tens of thousands of local political jurisdictions, including towns, cities, and counties. There, we have witnessed a double market failure stemming from watchdog journalism's "public goods" nature but also its

DOI: 10.4324/9781003212515-21

monopolistic structure, with one-newspaper towns seemingly accepted as a law of nature (Abernathy, 2020; Hendrickson, 2019; Sullivan, 2020) even though such a system is anathema to both democratic pluralism and maximizing consumers' welfare (Noam, 2009).

But it is also true that national news, with its narrow focus on (profitable) presidential politics and its disregard of (unprofitable) coverage of congressional activities, the judicial system, and federal agencies, has also failed to meet the public's democratic information needs. A hundred years ago, Walter Lippmann studied that failure vis-à-vis national news coverage of World War I (Lippmann et al., 2007; Lippmann & Mertz, 1920). Lippmann's analysis reminds us that regardless of how much watchdog journalism might have recently declined from a presumed golden age, it has never really met the needs of citizens – and might be increasingly failing as an increasingly complex society places more demands on government.

Governments, of course, already include many so-called independent ("horizontal") overseers, including inspectors general, ombudsmen, and ethics offices (Keane, 2009; Schedler et al., 1999). What distinguishes my W.J.B. proposal from others is that my watchdogs would report to the people themselves and not to officials within the three governmental branches they are asked to monitor. Too, my watchdogs would have governmental monitoring as their sole function, not one of many competing duties.

Just as our increasingly complex and confusing governments have become unthinkable without some sort of horizontal accountability mechanism, one day, that same consensus might exist concerning a journalism-based branch dedicated to holding accountable the actors and actions of people at the very highest levels of government. Or so I hope, and so I shall propose.

Design Overview

My Watchdog Journalism Branch of government proposal is built upon the following general guidelines. The W.J.B. should be:

- Embedded in a constitution (or charter) guaranteeing it branch-level independence.
- Financially independent from the three existing branches of government.
- Funded solely by government, with no opportunity for nongovernment revenue sources to cause conflicts of interests or introduce unacceptable biases.
- Fostering First Amendment values of pluralism rather than today's model of government-sanctioned news media monopoly at the local (e.g., town) level of government.

- Vigorously competitive internally, including at least three different member "seats," thereby providing not only diverse viewpoints but also comparative performance information.
- Supportive of minority voices by using ranked-choice voting in multimember districts when members are being selected.
- Composed of members evaluated in a competitive setting by "watchdog juries" able to meaningfully share their evaluations with the general public.
- Subject to criticism by private media having both full US-style First Amendment rights with respect to such criticism and no direct competition by the W.J.B. for their nongovernment sources of revenue.
- Limited in scope to providing accountability information about government – as assessed by the aforementioned watchdog juries.
- Composed of members with special rights to certain types of governmental information in the covered political jurisdiction and with criminal penalties for officials who violate those rights.
- Subject to reporting deadlines that facilitate comparative citizen evaluation of news media and that discourage plagiarism and related free-riding problems endemic to today's watchdog journalism.

When imagining an implementation scheme for the W.J.B., I do so with the full recognition that no one-size-fits-all scheme for democratic institutions could be sufficient. That is, the design of a democratic government appropriate for a Vermont town covering fewer than 10,000 people must be different from one for the US government covering more than 300 million people. Similarly, watchdog schemes based on 18th-century technology should be different from one based on 21st-century technology.

The fleshed-out model of the W.J.B. builds upon current technologies available in developed countries and assumes the government jurisdiction of a small US state or large US city. As jurisdictions scale down to smaller units, implementation details would necessarily change; for example, individual watchdogs might shift from large teams of journalists to single journalists (and even part-time journalists) while still preserving competition among the various watchdogs involved.

W.J.B. Funding

My proposal, including a watchdog jury system, would be automatically funded by a fixed percentage of the relevant government jurisdiction's operating budget, as specified in the jurisdiction's constitution (known as a charter at the local level of government). No funding of the W.J.B. would derive from an outside funding source, including advertisers, subscribers, nonprofit donors, or customers from other lines of business, any one of which would create conflicts of interest while needlessly competing with private media. Finally, the suggested fixed percentage of the government operating budget would be 1 percent, an amount akin to the annual management percentage fee on assets that investors pay financial advisors. A Gallup poll found that Americans believe local government wastes 37 cents of every dollar spent and that state government wastes 42 cents (Riffkin, 2014). If the actual waste due to a lack of democratic accountability is even close to that – let alone all the other harms fostered by an unresponsive government – the 1 percent expense could result in a huge payback.

W.J.B. Seats

Three elected seats are envisioned, with each seat functioning as a separate and competing member of a single, multimember district. Larger jurisdictions could support more seats, but competition must be made possible for even the smallest jurisdictions.

At-large elections for the seats would be simultaneous rather than staggered, with their candidates being nominated (via a combination of citizen petitions and a Watchdog Jury; see what follows) and finally chosen (during a general election) via ranked-choice voting. This voting architecture would result in minority publics finding genuine representation. For example, in a three-member district, representatives would need, respectively, 50 percent +1, 33 percent +1, and 25 percent +1, to win a seat. Each seat would have the same term of office as the local legislature. But the election would not be held when governors and mayors are being chosen, thereby fostering greater watchdog independence.

W.J.B. Responsibilities

Each elected watchdog would have the following *minimum* reporting requirements:

- Report on all public meetings of major public bodies within 24 hours of a meeting's adjournment.
- Report on all campaign finance, lobbying, and other major periodic ethics improprieties within 72 hours of their being publicly disclosed.
- Submit an annual report on how well each of the three branches of government has fulfilled its democratic functions within 30 days of the end of the government's fiscal year. The report would include graded evaluations of how well each branch's accountability mechanisms have worked.
- Present an annual report to the citizens concerning its own operations in two formats: (1) a written report published online by a given deadline and (2) a report presented to a Watchdog Jury (see explanation that follows) within one month of the written report's submission.

- Publish all reports and corrections online, including a replica sent to an independent state archive with a validated time stamp and authoritative record of submission.
- Publish all reports in a machine-readable format with well-structured, standardized metadata allowing the reports to be automatically linked to referenced authors, legislation, rulemakings, public officials, government agencies, dates, budget items, ethics disclosures, and public meeting records.

W.J.B. Privileges

Elected watchdogs would have privileged access to government accountability-related information, including:

- Access to government employees in the covered political jurisdiction, including their contact information, the right to survey employees confidentially, and the ability to promote whistle-blower hotlines to all government employees.
- Access to citizens entering into governmental transactions, including those seeking permits, licenses, and other governmental privileges.
- With appropriate safeguards, contact information for governmental contractors and for participants in public proceedings (including those watching governmental proceedings remotely).
- Access to posttrial or postsettlement documents related to those directly involved in judicial proceedings, including jurors and private lawyers as well as government prosecutors and defenders.
- The right to attend all public meetings on the same terms as public officials, including the same seating rights and access to all meeting notices, agendas, and documents on the same terms as public body members; the right immediately after every vote of a public body to ask members – while the meeting is still in session – to explain for the public record (within 12 hours of their vote) why they voted as they did.
- For purposes of conducting deliberative polls, access to the judicial system's resources about potential jurors.
- Subpoena power, if two-thirds of the watchdogs in a given W.J.B. agree to a subpoena.
- The right to bring criminal charges against an official who violates any of these mandatory rights.

W.J.B. Jury

A Watchdog Jury is envisioned as a microcosm of the citizenry and would play a major role in holding watchdogs accountable to the public. A given Jury would be composed of a stratified, randomly selected group of at least two hundred citizens. Jurors, all of whom would be subjected to mandatory duty, would play a major role in nominating and ultimately electing watchdogs, as well as providing annual performance reviews during a given watchdog's term in office.

A three-judge panel, appointed like multijudge panels are currently appointed in disputed election cases, would administer the jury in charge of nominating watchdogs. Administration would include maintaining a public website with links to candidate web pages, public comments, and candidate debates.

W.J.B. Candidates

A watchdog candidate with either (a) a petition signed by at least 0.1 percent of the citizens voting in the last general election in the relevant political jurisdiction or (b) a nomination by the previous Nominating Watchdog Jury would become an eligible nominee for a Watchdog Jury. The names of eligible candidates, along with a statement of their qualifications, would be publicly posted on the Watchdog Jury's website at least one month before the Jury's first meeting to select nominees. In addition, a Watchdog Jury would meet to deliberate on at least two separate days before nominating a watchdog. Incumbent watchdogs would be automatically renominated but could also be asked to appear before the Nominating Jury to defend their records.

Using ranked-choice voting, the Watchdog Jury would select the nominees. It would ensure that the total number of nominees eligible for the general election would be twice the number of watchdog seats. That is, for three seats, for example, six nominees would be approved for the general election.

W.J.B. Elections

The general election campaign would include a second Watchdog Jury whose role would be to gather information and then provide information cues to voters. The selection and administration of the General Election Jury would resemble that of the Nominating Jury. At the end of the candidate debates and jury deliberations, the jury would cast a ranked-choice vote for candidates. The resulting selections would be printed adjacent to the candidates' names on ballots, just like party labels are currently printed alongside candidates' names for other elected offices. Citizens would vote for all candidates using ranked-choice voting.

W.J.B. Trustees

Each watchdog candidate would designate at least three trustees who would be responsible for designating a successor if the watchdog must leave office partway through a term of office. These designations would include a statement explaining each trustee's qualifications and be posted online at least one month before a General Election Watchdog Jury convened.

W.J.B. Immunity

Today, legislators are protected from being sued for all actions, including libel, in the sphere of legitimate legislative activity. Similarly, watchdog journalists would be protected from libel. On the other hand, like legislators, they would be treated as public figures, thus having negligible libel protection from criticism.

W.J.B. Reporting

Each elected watchdog would be required to publish an annual performance report on the Watchdog's Jury website by a specific deadline. The report would include a clear and verifiable statement of journalistic practices, links to a watchdog's publications, a budget for the current year and all previous years the Watchdog has been in office, and an affidavit from the State Archives that all watchdog documents have been submitted to it in compliance with the law. The presentations of the annual reports to the Watchdog Jury would be fashioned in debate format, permitting each watchdog to speak to the comparative merits of their performance. The jury would rank each watchdog's performance on a five-point scale and also hold a no-confidence vote. Private media would also presumably critique these presentations. A no-confidence super-majority vote would result in removal from office and a replacement chosen by the watchdog trustees.

W.J.B. Ethics

Watchdogs and their employees would be banned for at least four years after leaving office from running for, or in any way being hired by, a government office in their coverage area. Watchdogs would also be banned from accepting any revenue from advertisers, subscribers, and other sources that might cause ethical conflicts for privately funded watchdog media. In addition, watchdogs would be expected to be agents of the voters who elected them but not the voters who did not vote for them, even though they would be expected to want their support as well. Representing voters' interests would be considered a sign of fidelity and not bias. But hiding from voters any material information about conflicts of interest would be viewed as unethical.

W.J.B. Formatting

The scope of a watchdog's coverage would be limited to government accountability journalism. But there would be no restrictions on either the distribution or format of watchdog journalism, except that whatever information is provided must be available freely to all. Watchdogs would be allowed to utilize not only conventional news and opinion formats but also satire and comedy, as these latter formats for conveying government accountability information to the public are often the most effective.

W.J.B. Internal Competition

Today, when mainstream news media compete, they tend to differentiate themselves. For example, in New York City, one of the few competitive local newspaper markets remaining in the United States, the information niches vary along multiple dimensions. Based on socio-economic status and ideology, we have *The Wall Street Journal* (high socioeconomic, conservative), *The New York Times* (high socioeconomic, liberal), *New York Post* (low socioeconomic, conservative), and *New York Daily News* (low socioeconomic, liberal). But many other niches are also possible, and even these publications have sought to appeal to dramatically different interests from time to time.

Similarly, watchdogs would be expected to differentiate themselves. Two likely niches in the US would be based on liberal versus conservative ideologies, niches akin to what local US newspapers in the 19th century often occupied. But the watchdogs I propose would be considerably more independent. That is, 19th-century newspapers tended to be funded by political parties, by the candidates themselves, and even, at times, by the governments they covered. The diverse ideological brands of independently funded US think tanks might be a more apt model for the kind of watchdog branches envisioned here.

Conclusion

I believe that we need an entirely new paradigm for governmental oversight; hence the watchdog proposal sketched out here. The recent decline of local journalism has brought to the fore the need for the kind of "public goods" news coverage long recognized by media economists and other media specialists as central to a vibrant polity. Yet no practical way of achieving those ends has been introduced – until now.

The Watchdog Journalism Branch I propose would disrupt private-sector approaches but in a way that would spur it to desirable innovation and enable it to better pursue First Amendment values. Like other open government laws, the W.J.B. might well even strengthen the foundation on which private-sector journalism is currently built.

This chapter does not address the getting-from-here-to-there problem; that is, how can the W.J.B. be created given the seemingly overwhelming inertia of our current constitutional system? (This and other related questions are the subject of a book I am currently writing.) My hope is that my proposal will start a needed conversation, one that highlights the need for fresh media reform proposals and for keeping a watchful eye on those who make our laws and spend our money. Today's reporters often perform that function well, but journalism as a whole needs our help as never before, and it needs new ideas as well. My hope is that this chapter – and the kind of watchdog journalism it imagines – will serve that precise function.

Bibliography

Abernathy, P. M. (2020). News deserts and ghost newspapers: Will local news survive? *Center for Innovation and Sustainability in Local Media, School of Media and Journalism, University of North Carolina at Chapel Hill.* www.usnewsdeserts.com/wp-content/uploads/2020/06/2020_News_Deserts_and_Ghost_Newspapers.pdf

Baker, C. E. (2001). *Media, markets, and democracy.* Cambridge: Cambridge University Press. https://doi.org/10.1017/CBO9780511613227

Chafee, Z. (1947). *Government and mass communications.* Chicago: University of Chicago Press.

Downs, A. (1957). *An economic theory of democracy.* New York: Harper and Row.

Hamilton, J. T. (2016). *Democracy's detectives: The economics of investigative journalism.* Cambridge, MA: Harvard University Press.

Hendrickson, C. (2019). Local journalism in crisis: Why America must revive its local newsrooms. *The Brookings Institute.* www.brookings.edu/research/local-journalism-in-crisis-why-america-must-revive-its-local-newsrooms

Keane, J. (2009). *The life and death of democracy* (Illustrated ed.). New York: W. W. Norton & Company.

Lippmann, W., & Mertz, C. (1920). A test of the news. *A Supplement to the New Republic, 4.*

Lippmann, W., Wilentz, S., Blumenthal, S., & Steel, R. (2007). *Liberty and the news* (1st Princeton Pbk ed.). Princeton, NJ: Princeton University Press.

Manin, B. (2017). Political deliberation & the adversarial principle. *Daedalus, 146*(3), 39–50.

McChesney, R. W., & Nichols, J. (2011). *The death and life of American journalism: The media revolution that will begin the world again* (Illustrated ed.). New York: Nation Books.

McChesney, R. W., & Pickard, V. (Eds.). (2011). *Will the last reporter please turn out the lights: The collapse of journalism and what can be done to fix it.* New York: The New Press.

Murschetz, P. (Ed.). (2014). *State aid for newspapers: Theories, cases, actions.* New York: Springer.

Noam, E. M. (2009). *Media ownership and concentration in America.* Oxford: Oxford University Press.

PEN America. (2019). *Losing the news: The decimation of local journalism and the search for solutions,* 115.

Pickard, V. (2019). *Democracy without journalism? Confronting the misinformation society.* Oxford: Oxford University Press.

Pickard, V., Stearns, J., & Aaron, C. (2009). *Saving the news: Toward a national journalism strategy* (p. 50). New York: Free Press.

Riffkin, R. (2014). Americans say federal gov't wastes 51 cents on the Dollar. *Gallup*. https://news.gallup.com/poll/176102/americans-say-federal-gov-wastes-cents-dollar.aspx

Schedler, A., Diamond, L. J., & Plattner, M. F. (1999). *The self-restraining state: Power and accountability in new democracies*. Boulder, CO: Lynne Rienner Publishers.

Sullivan, M. (2020). *Ghosting the news: Local journalism and the crisis of American democracy*. New York: Columbia Global Reports.

Waldman, S. (2020). A replanting strategy: Saving local newspapers squeezed by hedge funds. *Center for Journalism & Liberty*. www.journalismliberty.org/publications/replanting-strategy-saving-local-newspapers-squeezed-by-hedge-fund

17 Modernize Health-Care Decision-Making

Amy Bunger

Political rhetoric in health care is still comprised of debates about privilege versus right, public versus private, profit versus nonprofit, yet other questions loom large. Is the right medical care going to places where it is needed, when it is needed, and is it producing the outcomes desired? A new language of health care is now weaving its way into the codification of reimbursement standards, accreditation expectations, scientific practices, grant awards, and above all, in the perspective of both provider and patient.

Prior to the COVID-19 pandemic, health care had fallen off the list of public topics receiving governmental or decision agenda attention, and there was little agreement on what constituted a problem for the local legislatures to solve. With Obamacare having been both heralded and vilified and with little majority political consensus about health issues, the banner to take up the cause of improving health care has been driven by other entities. With political elites being sharply divided and their associated networks remaining highly polarized, the administrative, regulatory, and accreditation entities within the medical sphere are now driving the effort to improve patients' individual health and to reposition health care in general. Debates are now focused on the kind of care needed and to whom it should be given. Providers are judged – and reimbursed – based on the quality of the care they provide, which is measured by patient outcome and patients' perceptions of satisfaction.

Seminal works such as *Crossing the Quality Chasm* (Institute of Medicine, 2001) and the *To Err Is Human* report (Institute of Medicine, 2000) have done a lot to refocus policy-level work, funding, and focus. These reports introduced the notion of *value* – what patient outcome was received at what cost? and *efficiency* – were the fewest tests used, and did the costs expended produce a timely outcome? Other standards have come into play as well: Were health-care services provided in a patient-centered way? Did people have equal access when they needed it? Did the care provided vary in quality because of personal characteristics like race, gender, or socioeconomic status (Agency for Healthcare Research and Quality)?

DOI: 10.4324/9781003212515-22

In this new world of medicine, there has also been an increasing shift in the concept of expertise. Gone are the days of a presumed, deferential relationship with one's physician. From the scientific point of view, expertise amasses to the highest level of precision, but in the context of how health-care providers do their work, several other factors come into play. Expertise is still prized but not at the expense of patient experience and communication. For example, substantial energy has gone into maximizing patient-centered care: Was the patient a partner in the solution? Was the patient willing or able to adhere to what the physician prescribed (number of shots or pills per day, the absence of nicotine or alcohol or red meat, exercising 30 minutes a day versus three times a week)? Were the physician's expectations realistic for the variables and barriers present in the patient's life? Did the patient have access to fresh produce, or did they live in a food desert? Did the patient have the transportation needed to get to the types of appointments required? How accessible were specialty services (infusion, dialysis, radiation and chemotherapy, physical therapy) by public transportation? Could the patient afford the provider's recommendation?

Patient experience is now heavily incentivized and is part of the hospital ranking system for reimbursement. Attention to customer service principles directly correlates to higher patient satisfaction scores, from which multiple benefits arise. First, patient satisfaction is tied to an institution's bottom-line reimbursement. Secondly, experience translates into loyalty measurements. Did a patient return to the same clinic? Did they recommend the facility to friends and family? In the age of social media, did they recommend the institution on various social media platforms or "neighborhood" chat boards?

The best clinical service, after all, can be negated by public perception and social media reviews. How hard was it to navigate the facility ("wayfinding")? Was there a range of food choices in the cafeteria? How hard was it to find a cup of coffee? How comfortable were the seats? How hard was it to navigate through the parking lot? These individual experiences make significant impressions, all of which relate to a medical facility's financial bottom line. Reimbursement for satisfaction measures can sometimes seem like a popularity contest or a media perception exercise. However, the tools, processes, and strategies followed by a high-reliability organization can likewise be leveraged for satisfaction measures. For example: "How can we limit standing in line for a cup of coffee to no longer than 5 minutes?" "Should directions be placed at each doorway?"

Communication between the patient and the provider is likewise measured and incentivized, another example of evidence-based measures being prioritized by regulatory and accrediting bodies, all of which makes medicine a *social and political matter*: Did the patient have the opportunity to ask questions? Did the physician treat them with courtesy and respect? Did the physician use language they could understand? Did the provider avoid the use of jargon and acronyms? What is important to recognize here is that the primacy of the patient (as opposed to the sheer expertise of the physician) is being recognized through mechanisms that are less centered in traditional understandings of authority and that rest more in transactional aspects of the administrative state.

Increasingly, medical expertise is not simply a matter of sheer invention but also a question of execution. Certainly, the variation in roll-out of the COVID-19 vaccine (invention) underscored the need for process and execution (vaccines in arms). Health care learned this lesson in the past two decades, as major scientific entities (like the Institute of Medicine) brought Toyota processes into the proverbial hospital parking garage. Manufacturing processes, that is, are repetitive and are expected to produce the same quality each and every time. When such processes are translated into other industries (like medicine), they are expected to produce greater reliability and to increase degrees of certainty as they have done, for example, in the airline and nuclear power industries. The language of this manufacturing mindset includes words like *predictable*, *standardize*, *generalizable*, etc.

This industry-based mentality has led to transformative outcomes in the field of medicine that were dramatized during the COVID-19 epidemic. For example, we have seen the creation of the "intensive-care checklist" made famous by Dr. Peter Pronovost (2006). The words and ideas in it are simple and painfully familiar ("wash your hands with soap," "wear a mask," "maintain social distance," etc.), but the complexity comes in the execution and in the need for such behaviors to be repeated reliably and consistently. As Atul Gawande (2007) stated in *The New Yorker*, Pronovost's "work has already saved more lives in the last decade than that of any laboratory scientist in the last decade." This moment has helped us see the range of roles in science, from invention to diagnostic accuracy to compassion and predictable execution. Medicine, that is, depends heavily on communication for its effectiveness.

Whom Do We Serve?

Part of the need to modernize our current health-care system has been painfully apparent in looking at the populations hardest hit during the COVID-19 crisis. Previously overlooked has been *who* is receiving the health care provided. It is not as simple as seeing things in black and white – brown also matters. Differing regulatory agencies and accrediting bodies speak differently when describing the problem, but all point in the same direction. Physicians' stated purposes and the very language used to describe those purposes are evolving from a focus on the "indigent safety net hospital" to actual physician training programs specializing in care of the underserved.

Embedded in accreditation standards and measured yearly in American Council on Graduate Medical Education, for example, is whether residents are "taught about health care disparities." This emphasis on population health is permeating the clinical milieu for a multitude of reasons. For some providers, it brings them back to the central purpose of medicine, away from coding and bureaucracy and toward actual care. The outcome of the work provided – patient health – predicts reimbursement, and so politics once again enters the health-care domain. Especially in a pandemic, we see clearly, and cruelly, how health-care deserts affect some segments of the population more than others, an outcome that is now galvanizing the attention of politicians serving minority communities and also the attention of all citizens concerned with living in a just, caring society.

Physicians as People

Media and social media have brought an issue to the political forefront that had been previously secreted away in the health-care community. Internally, health care and the corresponding accrediting bodies have been focused on ensuring that a pipeline of physician providers would be available where we need them and when we need them. This meant encouraging people to become physicians (which takes four years of undergraduate schooling, four years of medical school, and anywhere from three to ten years of residency and/or fellowship training), and to work throughout their careers as physicians. Today, however, the regulatory and political context in which physicians work has become onerous to many, compromising the desire to go into the medical profession – or the desire to stay in it, given the rate of physician burnout (West et al., 2016). Political pressures, that is, can often have unwanted side effects, even when well intended.

Because of various forms of political jockeying and policy proliferation, insufficient attention has been paid to how changes in health care are impacting physicians themselves, a component that had been previously taken for granted. This problem came into public consciousness with the story of New York City emergency medicine physician Lorna Breen, who died by suicide after treating coronavirus patients, even though the phenomenon of physician suicide was becoming well known inside the health-care community.

Now, however, because of the news media, we are getting a better look at the impact of physician burnout on providers. As a result, we must now consider how modern health care, and indeed the pandemic specifically, will change the course of physician-provider education. During training, for example, residents and fellows become excited when getting to do a procedure for the first time and well remember when they were certified to do it for themselves. One new attending physician once wrote to me about the paradigmatic shift in her thinking and of her gratitude when her progress note read "extubate" and "decannulate." As she said, "there is nothing more gratifying than taking tubes out as opposed to putting them in." Providers go into medicine to help people and to save lives. The inexplicable toll on them by the tidal wave loss of life during the COVID-19 pandemic proved to be more than some could bear, resulting in notable physician suicides seen during that period.

As a result, taking care of the caretaker has finally found its way into the health professions. Well-being inventories, computer apps, strategies, and tool kits have permeated the medical market in an attempt to stem or prevent burnout. Hospitals now have licensed teams who can help with critical-incident debriefing – from the first time a team experiences a suicide to the first time a unit has to care for one of their own or to the first time a physician realizes they made a mistake and unintentionally caused harm.

The story of the COVID-19 pandemic is truly the story of modern health care. Fortunately, the American medical system now has profound expertise in saving lives. It has also amassed amazing science to develop a panoply of vaccines. But none of these advances change the most poignant fact of all: In the end, what family members care about is who was with their loved one when they died. What were their last words? Did someone hold their hand or provide them comfort? In short, health care is no longer just about science, expertise, or execution. Especially in recent years, the "care" of health care has become a matter of renewed attention. As a result, the medical conversation is changing in the United States.

Conclusion

The COVID-19 pandemic has proven the public cost – in lives, resources, and dollars – of a strongly decentralized approach to health care. This decentralization harkens back to the language of rights, including states' rights, and autonomy. Increasingly, the medical community is no longer cut off from all of the political conversations being conducted in society at large. As a result, we now find a new language of quality improvement, effectiveness, and manufacturing entering the public conversation. We hear new demands for an increase in predictability of how supplies will be shipped, how vaccines (or flu shots) will be administered, and how treatment will be provided to those most in need of it. Equipment such as ventilators, clinical personnel, and protective personal equipment (PPE) have all needed to cross state lines to help the hospitals hardest hit, thereby affecting every citizen – and every politician – living in those states. Too often, unfortunately, work of this sort has been done in reactive fashion instead of in a planned, predictable way. But one thing is certain: The conversations of the medical community that had previously transpired in cloistered settings are now being brought out into the open.

The politics of medicine has now become palpable to all who read a newspaper or who watch cable news.

Changing medical routines will take investment in high-reliability processes, and that opens the door to politics as well. We now have effective high-reliability health-care systems throughout the country. These qualities have been incentivized by the regulatory and administrative agencies of government, showing once again that medicine is too important to be left on its own. COVID-19 exposed health-care delivery systems that were wholly unprepared for a health event of such magnitude. Fixing things will take dedicated, nonreactive planning to rebuild data-driven and evidence-based health-care delivery systems (Strazzabosco, 2020). Health care in the United States is no longer an island unto itself. It depends on science, primarily, but it also depends on a "manufacturing" mindset as well as the disciplines of psychology and sociology. And added to their mix is political communication itself, without which important things like health care simply cannot happen.

Bibliography

Agency for Healthcare Research and Quality. www.ahrq.gov/

Gawande, A. (2007, December). The checklist, if something so simple can transform intensive care, what else can it do? *The New Yorker*, 86.

Institute of Medicine: Committee on Quality of Health Care in America. (2000). In L. T. Kohn, J. M. Corrigan, & M. S. Donaldson (Eds.), *To err is human: Building a safer health care system*. Washington, DC, US: National Academies Press. PMID. 25077248.

Institute of Medicine: Committee on Quality of Health Care in America. (2001). *Crossing the quality chasm: A new health system for the 21st century*. Washington, DC: National Academies Press. PMID: 25057539.

Pronovost, P., Needham, D., Berenholtz, S., Sinopoli, D., Chu, H., Cosgrove, S., . . . & Goeschel, C. (2006, December). An intervention to decrease catheter-related bloodstream infections in the ICU. *New England Journal of Medicine*, 355(26), 2725–2732.

Strazzabosco, M. (2020, September). Value-based medicine, a compass to guide healthcare decisions in the COVID-19 aftermath. *Liver International*, 40(9), 2076–2078. doi: 10.1111/liv.14605. PMID: 32677111

West, C. P., Dyrbye, L. N., Erwin, P. J., & Shanafelt, T. D. (2016). Interventions to prevent and reduce physician burnout: A systematic review and meta-analysis. *Lancet*, 388(10057), 2272–2281.

18 Give Election Apps More Integrity

Jessica Baldwin-Philippi

Much of my scholarship has been dedicated to thinking about how political actors and institutions can use digital tools to help democracy flourish – to enable citizens not only to take civic action but to develop a more robust way of seeing their role in civil society. From assessing how political campaigns can use digital media to invite citizens to participate (Baldwin-Philippi, 2015) to investigating cities that have created games to encourage deliberation and build community connections (Gordon & Baldwin-Philippi, 2014) and to utilize apps that not only allow residents to report problems but also explore the civic actions of their neighbors and neighborhoods (O'Brien et al., 2016), my colleagues and I have highlighted channels for meaningful civic participation. Although this work has been productive, the intervening years have made it clear that in order to ensure robust citizenship, the design of social media platforms must first be recalibrated at a much more basic level: We must design such apps for democratic integrity before we can design them for civic flourishing.

The social media platforms the public uses on a daily basis serve basic functions of democracy: providing (or limiting) the information citizens have access to and enabling (or discouraging) productive speech. These practices – voicing political speech and information gathering – are important for everyday citizens as well as for institutional actors like elected officials and political campaigns. Until 2016, digital platforms' ability to encourage democratic participation were widely celebrated. While nuanced research pointed out how these democratic opportunities might be constrained by political campaigns and elected officials (Kreiss, 2012; Stromer-Galley, 2014), the dominant view was that the platforms themselves were to be sites of expanded political participation.

Much fanfare – by myself included – has been paid to how these platforms promote democratic practices, such as how Facebook's Voter Information and "I voted" tools allow users to learn about voting, publicize that they voted, and encourage those in their network to do so as well (Bond et al., 2012). Platforms like Google and Instagram have followed suit, redesigning how they present voting information and encouraging users to post about their voting experiences.

Successful though they may have been, these add-ons cannot make up for lapses in the more basic democratic functions. Only recently have academics begun to critique social media's role in democratic culture, and after 2016, the pendulum has swung in the opposite direction – wrestling with how social media can become a unique threat to democracy. Rather than framing social media platforms as either entirely a boon or a bust, we must consider what design interventions are needed to uphold the integrity of democratic practices and civic culture.

Following Donald Trump's win in the 2016 US presidential election, moral panics around particular digital tools – microtargeting, bots, deepfakes, and so on – and calls to ban them supplanted discussions of these broader principles. While these corrections benefit from having clear recommendations, efforts to prohibit particular tools or practices instead of focusing on broader principles of democratic integrity will fail to solve the larger problems involved as new tools and practices develop. In each of these cases, broader principles are at play. Democratic integrity means ensuring that information flows are not overrun by disinformation and requires that messages that circulate in social media platforms – whether paid or organic – are transparent about their creators and audiences. Ultimately, this not only amounts to a shift in how social media platforms currently work but also a shift in how we conceive of political participation. That is, some forms of political engagement can actually be antidemocratic. As a result, we cannot normatively assess participation in politics apart from the content of the messages or ideas involved. We must find ways to enhance the transparency of political speech and to limit the circulation and reach of antidemocratic speech as well.

Requiring Transparency in Political Messages

Following both the 2016 US election and the 2015 UK Brexit vote, digital platforms' ability to microtarget users, or send different advertisements to different groups of people based on increasingly specific identifying information (from voting records to demographic categories to perceived interests), became a dominant political anxiety. In the United States, most of the concerns about these practices assumed their effectiveness, believing that such practices necessarily meant that different people would receive different political information and therefore become open to manipulation. It was further assumed that such people might not encounter information they disagree with and hence would be less equipped to debate ideas or become informed about the range of relevant issues.

As a result of these concerns, calls to ban microtargeting in political contexts or to ban political ads entirely became popular among those concerned about the role of social media in democracy. Such blanket bans are easy for platforms to execute but ultimately fail to assure democratic integrity by leaving some candidates and organizations at a disadvantage and thereby reducing turnout. Alternatively, building transparency into this system of targeting is a better way to discourage antidemocratic content while also ensuring that information is not hidden from some groups.

In the lead-up to the 2020 election, Facebook banned all political ads from its platform and left this rule in effect for months following the election amid serious concerns that Donald Trump would amplify his claims of a rigged election and delegitimize Joe Biden's victory. Unfortunately, blanket bans like this do nothing to stop how organic content circulates, and they have other detrimental effects as well. For example, such actions leave more modest political actors – especially those in down-ballot races who cannot afford television ads – at a clear disadvantage, leaving them with one less channel for persuasion and mobilization and hampering their fundraising efforts in addition. Similarly, the widely proposed policy of banning microtargeting, whether by eliminating the use of certain variables like race, or banning political content from using microtargeting altogether, has consequences that can diminish political participation.

Research has shown that these normative concerns do not actually play out due to microtargeting. Most significantly, microtargeting is unlikely to explain why people are entrenched in their respective ideological stances. Studies repeatedly show that digital media do not increase our "filter bubbles" or affect our offline information-seeking and -avoidance behaviors (Dubois & Blank, 2018; Fletcher & Nielsen, 2017). Research also casts serious doubt on the effectiveness of microtargeted messages on changing or informing political beliefs or opinion formation (Endres & Panagopoulos, 2019; Hersh & Schaffner, 2013; Kalla & Broockman, 2018).

Normatively speaking, for every instance of targeting voters with messages designed to get them to stay home on Election Day, there are contrary attempts to mobilize them. Research into targeting for mobilizing indicates that, on net, political participation among those being targeted to vote has become more efficient thanks to data-driven targeting practices. Of course, a party or campaign does not encourage all votes equally. Those whose political leanings are more difficult to decipher are less likely to be targeted by either side during a campaign due to the risk of mobilizing someone who might support one's opponent. Somewhat perversely, improvements in targeting are what have expanded campaigns' outreach to less obviously partisan potential voters; abandoning that practice would reverse these trends, thereby producing no net difference.

In 2016, political groups that bought significant amounts of Facebook advertising concealed the political organizations of which they were a part and yet published some of the most egregious ads fomenting racism, xenophobia, and polarization (Kim et al., 2018). This case shows that the root of the problem does not necessarily lie in targeting but in a lack of transparency of both authorship and audience. Such transparency is needed whether messages are paid for or organically circulated. The state of information circulating in a public must be knowable and sharable across groups, and its authors must be held accountable. Efforts to ensure transparency of authorship, content, and audience have so far only applied to paid advertising content and are not regulated by any reputable outside organization. As a result, problems of transparency still abound.

In order to make authorship clear, platforms need to go beyond identifying users when they purchase advertising to ensuring that their identities are published and/or connected to the relevant sponsorship groups. Moreover, if a political consulting firm is buying an ad as part of its work for a particular candidate, this must be made clear to the platform and made searchable by interested users. While platforms have gone to considerable lengths to verify individual identities, issues remain with identifying which individuals are connected to which political groups and what their relationship is to the candidate involved. Platforms must also verify the accounts of political groups so that in cases in which groups break terms of service, the offending group cannot simply create another account and thereby circumvent the ban.

To make content and audiences transparent, more substantive and searchable databases of ads need to be made public. Taking a page from the FCC, which mandates that information about television and radio ads be made public, social media platforms should ensure the following information for any targeted content is made available. First, the *content of messages* must be made available. Second, the broad *targeting categories* used must be publicized – most notably geography, demographic categories, and if list-matching or lookalike audiences are used (as when a user uploads a list of particular email addresses it wants targeted or when a platform creates a broader audience based on that list). Third, the reach of any message and, if paid content, the *size of the ad buy* must be made public.

Perhaps even more importantly, these disclosures must be *regulated by a third party* like the FCC and not merely entrusted to self-governance by tech firms. Research I have conducted with colleagues indicated that political consultants on both sides of the aisle are supportive of such rules (Baldwin-Philippi et al., 2020) and even supportive of governmental regulation to ensure adherence by political consulting firms and platform companies alike. Although microtargeting abilities are currently limited to paid content, these rules about disclosure should apply to any targeted content moving forward.

Finally, transparency should not only mean that the collected information exists in public but that it is locatable, that the databases are searchable in such a way that the public can easily explore the range of content contained within them. While current ad databases are literally searchable, the way they return results makes it difficult to sift through the information because each variation of an ad (whether a single word change or a change in the background color of an ad) is displayed separately, requiring a user to scroll through dozens of minor variations before getting to a substantively different campaign message. Instead, results should be displayed to users so that the campaigns of different groups are displayed prominently, letting users drill down to the relevant differences within each campaign. Only substantive changes to words and images of the ads should be displayed to prevent too much information from becoming no information at all.

Redesigning Circulation to Get Better Information

While disinformation, conspiracy theories, and propaganda have long been part of the information environment, they have recently taken on a more substantive role and gained greater attention due to social media platforms' design choices about how to circulate and amplify content. Designing to reduce circulation of disinformation requires a four-pronged approach: (1) correct such content within the interface of the platform itself, (2) prohibit users from recirculating such content, (3) prohibit a platform's own algorithm from circulating such content, and (4) ensure that artificial tools (e.g., bots) are unable to circulate content widely and do not contribute to algorithmically promoted content. While the first and last approaches have been adopted in various ways by the major social media platforms, they have proven to be imperfect solutions thus far.

Although removing content and accounts from problematic platforms has proven to be effective, it also provides users who peddle such information with an opportunity to gain the attention of partisan news sources by claiming censorship (Lewis, 2018). Additionally, choices about which content or users to ban is both politically and pragmatically difficult for platforms to navigate. When censorship does occur, it happens on an ad hoc basis, and often only after news coverage of particularly egregious content has been aired. In explaining their reasons for a censorship decision, social media companies have traditionally leaned on democratic norms of freedom of speech, claiming that more speech will counter bad speech. But more speech is a poor substitute in an information environment in which the offensive speech is likely to get amplified. Algorithmic filtering, after all, means that not everyone gets the same soapbox whenever they choose.

Fact-checks – a particularly celebrated form of counterspeech that has been viewed as a solution when executed by either nonpartisan media outlets or platform companies themselves – have often been portrayed as the answer to disinformation. Without redesigning circulation protocols, however, such efforts will fall short. This is primarily because, as studies have shown, the circulation of the correction pales in comparison to the availability of the original disinformation (Bell, 2019; Margolin et al., 2018). Moreover, Alice Marwick's (2018) work has shown that sharing disinformation is less likely to occur because of a deeply held belief in the veracity of the original content displayed. Because of these ideological commitments and the associated sense of in-group belonging, fact-checks are unlikely to work. While platform-designed fact-checks are an important addition to the corrective landscape, designing to reduce the original circulation of offensive messages and accounts will ultimately be the most meaningful intervention in the current information environment.

Popularly discussed as limiting "reach not speech," the design interventions discussed here can take a variety of forms that limit users' ability to recirculate content that a digital platform deems unacceptable. They can also prohibit algorithmic surfacing of that content, which often occurs in users' feeds when others in their network have liked or otherwise interacted with that content previously.

Such strictures can take a number of forms, from outright prohibition of recirculation or other engagement (e.g., liking, replying to, etc.) of content to forcing people to read a warning label. Both Facebook and Twitter have begun to do the latter, using pop-up displays to highlight fact-checks or by acknowledging that the content is disputed, forcing users to click through the warning before they can engage. In late 2020, Twitter prohibited users from retweeting a message from President Trump (2020) claiming that he won the election. While these implemented policies are a start, more stringent design choices of prohibiting the recirculation of such messages as well as replies to them are needed. Moreover, banning a given topic from trending algorithms or from being recommended must also be part of this effort to reduce misinformation from being shared on the web.

Conclusion

At this point, the first step in designing apps for democratic integrity must be to stop the current harm from proliferating. These are big requests to make of tech companies; altering such design choices, after all, often goes against the platforms' self-interests. Redesigning circulation will almost inevitably decrease the flow of widely engaged content – whether that circulation is artificial or organic – content that platforms rely on to maintain attention.

Designing for transparency in a meaningful way will also take more resources than are currently deployed by companies like Facebook. These changes would require that social media companies see their roles differently, as influential providers of information with responsibilities to the public rather than as open clearinghouses where the best information is allowed to rise to the top and become widely circulated without stoppage. That said, with these platforms having long espoused exalted political ideals – free speech, public deliberation, and political participation – it is now time to hold them to account and to make them design their apps for democratic integrity.

Scholars have long praised those most active in politics, with citizenship levels commonly assessed by the sheer amount of political speech shared or by the number of political actions taken (e.g., how often someone attends a public meeting or writes to an elected official). The *substance* of their actions, however, has been less commonly assessed. Previously, I myself have argued that promoting social media channels for citizens to talk back to their leaders is an inherent good, without having given due consideration to how often these voices might become antidemocratic, dehumanizing, exclusionary, or a repository for disinformation. Moving forward, we must explore the intricacies of political participation, asking pragmatic questions about how to redesign platforms so that citizens are not led astray by the torrent of disinformation descending upon them daily.

Bibliography

Baldwin-Philippi, J. (2015). *Using technology, building democracy: Digital campaigning and the construction of citizenship*. Oxford: Oxford University Press.

Baldwin-Philippi, J., Bode, L., Kreiss, D., & Sheingate, A. (2020). Digital political ethics: Aligning principles with practice. *UNC Center for Information, Technology, and Public Life*. https://citapdigitalpolitics.com/?page_id=1911

Bell, E. (2019, Fall). The fact-check industry. *Columbia Journalism Review*. www.cjr.org/special_report/fact-check-industry-twitter.php/

Bond, R. M., Fariss, C. J., Jones, J. J., Kramer, A. D. I., Marlow, C., Settle, J. E., & Fowler, J. H. (2012). A 61-million-person experiment in social influence and political mobilization. *Nature*, 489(7415). https://doi.org/10.1038/nature11421

Dubois, E., & Blank, G. (2018). The echo chamber is overstated: The moderating effect of political interest and diverse media. *Information, Communication & Society*, 21(5), 729–745. https://doi.org/10.1080/1369118X.2018.1428656

Endres, K., & Panagopoulos, C. (2019). Cross-pressure and voting behavior: Evidence from randomized experiments. *The Journal of Politics*, 81(3), 1090–1095. https://doi.org/10.1086/703210

Fletcher, R., & Nielsen, R. K. (2017). Are news audiences increasingly fragmented? A cross-national comparative analysis of cross-platform news audience fragmentation and duplication. *Journal of Communication*. https://doi.org/10.1111/jcom.12315

Gordon, E., & Baldwin-Philippi, J. (2014). Playful civic learning: Enabling lateral trust and reflection in game-based public participation. *International Journal of Communication*, 8. https://ijoc.org/index.php/ijoc/article/view/2195

Hersh, E. D., & Schaffner, B. F. (2013). Targeted campaign appeals and the value of ambiguity. *The Journal of Politics*, 75(2), 520–534. JSTOR. https://doi.org/10.1017/s0022381613000182

Kalla, J. L., & Broockman, D. E. (2018). The minimal persuasive effects of campaign contact in general elections: Evidence from 49 field experiments. *American Political Science Review*, 112(1), 148–166. https://doi.org/10.1017/S0003055417000363

Kim, Y. M., Hsu, J., Neiman, D., Kou, C., Bankston, L., Kim, S. Y., . . . & Raskutti, G. (2018). The stealth media? Groups and targets behind divisive issue campaigns on Facebook. *Political Communication*, 0(0), 1–27. https://doi.org/10.1080/10584609.2018.1476425

Kreiss, D. (2012). *Taking our country back: The crafting of networked politics from Howard Dean to Barack Obama*. Oxford: Oxford University Press.

Lewis, B. (2018). Alternative influence: Broadcasting the reactionary right on YouTube. *Data & Society*. https://datasociety.net/wp-content/uploads/2018/09/DS_Alternative_Influence.pdf

Margolin, D. B., Hannak, A., & Weber, I. (2018). Political fact-checking on Twitter: When do corrections have an effect? *Political Communication*, 35(2), 196–219. https://doi.org/10.1080/10584609.2017.1334018

Marwick, A. E. (2018). Why do people share fake news? A sociotechnical model of media effects. *Georgetown Law Review*, 2, 474–511.

O'Brien, D. T., Offenhuber, D., Baldwin-Philippi, J., Gordon, E., & Sands, M. (2016). Uncharted territoriality in coproduction: The motivations for 311 reporting. *Journal of Public Administration Research and Theory*, Online first. https://doi.org/10.1093/jopart/muw046

Stromer-Galley, J. (2014). *Presidential campaigning in the internet age*. Oxford: Oxford University Press.

Trump, D. [realDonaldTrump]. (2020, December 12). *I won the election in a landslide, but remember, I only think in terms of legal votes, not all of the fake voters and fraud that miraculously floated in from everywhere! What a disgrace!* [tweet]. https://twitter.com/realDonaldTrump/status/1337745268591259648

19 Shake Up the FCC

Bartholomew H. Sparrow

Most of the profound problems of American journalism stem from the near triumph of neoliberalism. I write "near triumph" because there remain indicators of the government's vital role in ensuring that the media serve the public "interest, convenience, and necessity" (per the 1934 Communications Act). The US government has promoted the quantity and diversity of the news by subsidizing the mailing of newspapers and magazines since 1790 (Pickard, 2019, p. 158).[1] It has limited the concentration of local and national newspaper and broadcast-media ownership, and established – and funded – the Corporation for Public Broadcasting. It has set up an Emergency Alert System for television and radio broadcasters and mobile phones.[2] And it has rejected an array of media mergers: DirecTV (now AT&T) and Dish (Echostar) in 2002, AT&T and T-Mobile in 2011, and Sinclair Broadcast Group and Tribune Media in 2018.

"Neoliberalism," of course, refers to the widespread belief in market efficiency. Neoliberalism presumes that the quality and quantity of news can be addressed through the cumulative choices made by free and rational individuals. It also assumes that news supply will match consumer demand. Conversely, neoliberalism denies the desirability or efficiency of governmental action because of its monopoly power and potential for coercion. "The business of America is business," in Calvin Coolidge's inimitable words. For neoliberals, the news is just another kind of business and hence has no need of governmental meddling.

Still, governmental tinkering in the media business is inevitable – through passing new legislation, enforcing existing policies, rendering legal rulings, regulating or deregulating the media, or privatizing otherwise governmental functions. And all these things have happened. The controversial fairness doctrine, which mandated that broadcasters present both sides of a controversial public issue, was ended in 1987. The Telecommunication Act, which facilitated media concentration locally and nationally and implemented a "$70 billion" giveaway to media companies (Sunstein, 2018, p. 179), was passed in 1996. Net neutrality, which enabled Internet service providers, such as Comcast, Charter Communications (which owns Spectrum), and Verizon (which owns Yahoo),

DOI: 10.4324/9781003212515-24

to use their market power to block, slow, prioritize, or subsidize certain consumer choices over others, was terminated in 2017.[3]

Hence, it is important to understand how neoliberalism has impacted the news industry. In this chapter, I will focus on the central role played by the Federal Communications Commission (FCC) in creating the current media economy and then propose how the FCC might be reformed to better represent the public interest, consistent with its original mandate.

Media Amok

The dominance of neoliberalism in the American political economy has put the media under severe stress. To wit:

- GateHouse Media (with Gannett), Digital First Media (51 percent owned by Alden Global Capital), and other investment companies have purchased newspaper groups and eliminated staff, abandoned news bureaus, cut other costs, sold assets, and either closed newspapers or left them as "ghost papers" with minimal staff and scant news content (PEN America, 2019, p. 29). The United States has lost more than 1,800 local print outlets since 2004, including *The Tampa Tribune* and the *Rocky Mountain News*. More than 200 counties are now without a newspaper, and over half of the remaining US counties (1,528) have only a weekly newspaper.[4] "News deserts" dot the country (Abernathy, 2016; PEN America, 2019, pp. 24–25, 38–39).[5]
- As of 2019, US television media are dominated by only six companies: AT&T (which owns TimeWarner), Charter Communications, Comcast (which owns NBC Universal), Disney (which owns ABC), News-Corp (which owns Fox, *The Wall Street Journal*, and *New York Post*), and National Amusements (which owns ViacomCBS). In 1983, by comparison, 90 percent of the US media was controlled by 50 companies. Because the six companies own both the "pipes" and the content of the news, they have cartel power and are at once able to control the production and dissemination of the news (Pickard, 2019, pp. 114–115). In the lead-up to the 2003 Gulf War, for instance, the media widely promoted false information, Fox and CBS News most egregiously (Kull et al., 2019).[6] "If Comcast, News Corp., Viacom, Disney, CBS, and Time Warner collectively or informally decide a U.S.-backed invasion of Iran will help keep their corporate revenues growing," one media observer asks (Kroeger, 2018), "what independent news outlet or journalist is going to have the coverage and market share to challenge them?"
- The digital media have become highly concentrated both vertically and horizontally. Amazon, Apple, Facebook (with Instagram, WhatsApp), and Google (with YouTube) have been able to buy up hundreds of companies over the past 10 years and now have a combined

stock market valuation of more than $5 trillion as of 2020, or more than one-third of the value of the S&P 100. Because they are able to dictate how online content is accessed and prioritized and because they produce news themselves, they have immense influence on and material stakes in the news. The tech giants "exploit their gatekeeper power to dictate terms and extract concessions that no one would reasonably consent to in a competitive market," an investigative report by the House Committee on the Judiciary stated (*Investigation*, 2020, pp. 10–11). In the absence of viable alternatives, however, these demands and concessions are simply "the cost of doing business."

Yet timely and measured political information is not just another commodity, unlike cars, carpets, or clothing. The existence of accessible, accurate news is fundamental to the well-being of a democratic society; it allows individuals to understand their lives, know their community, become familiar with their state and nation, and understand the world at large. It keeps those in power accountable, whether politicians, government officials, military leaders, or business executives. And the lack of a robust, high-quality local/national news system leads to further political polarization and ever-louder echo chambers (Pickard, 2019, pp. 14–17; Sunstein, 2018, p. 25).

The news is a public good. A healthy print, television, and digital media is of crucial importance to all those who read a newspaper, watch television, use the Internet, or have a smartphone. Too, the news benefits the public at large. The news is analogous to grade schools, national parks, and academic research – things that might not pay for themselves but that nonetheless improve our lives. Children and their parents might not want to pay for a world history class, for example. Few philanthropists would reserve forests, protect canyons, or create wildlife sanctuaries. And important basic research would never be conducted were scientists left to fend for themselves (Pickard, 2019, pp. 63–66, 175). Once provided, however, these services and goods are available to all and therefore enrich American society.

Public Goods, Public Agency

The word "crisis" is often overused, but the unhappy condition of the US media is more than evident. Not only is the quality of journalism deteriorating worldwide, as the World Press Freedom Index scores reveal, but there is less journalistic freedom and greater media concentration in the United States than in other wealthy countries (Kroeger, 2018).

At the center of media policy is the Federal Communications Commission (PEN America, 2019; Pickard, 2019). Whereas elected officials are effectively beholden to the news media and hence reluctant to challenge them (Pickard, 2019, pp. 65, 160; Snyder, 2007), the FCC exists as an independent government agency to do precisely that, acting as a trustee for the American public, the ultimate owner of the airwaves (per the 1934 Communications Act). The FCC oversees US radio, television, wire, cable, and satellite communications and is responsible for protecting "broadcast localism," encouraging media competition, and promoting diversity in news sources (Michael K. Powell, quoted in PEN America, 2019, p. 60).

Despite the FCC's authority to oversee broadcast licenses and to approve or reject mergers (PEN America, 2019, p. 60), it has not acted as a vigilant watchdog in recent years (PEN America, 2019; Pickard, 2019, pp. 51–56). In 2017, for example, the FCC contravened its obligation to "foster localism" by eliminating restrictions on media concentration. These rules included the prevention of broadcasters from owning two TV stations and a radio station in the same market (the Radio/Television Cross-Ownership Rule), the prohibition of the joint ownership of a daily newspaper and a radio or TV broadcaster in the same market (the Newspaper/Broadcast Cross-Ownership Rule), and the requirement that broadcasters keep a local studio in the town they service (the Main Studio Rule). The FCC's new rules also removed the requirement that at least eight independently owned TV stations exist in a market before any broadcaster can own two TV stations (the "Rule of Eight"); the prohibition of an entity owning two of the top four stations in a market (the Top-Four Prohibition or "Rule of Four"); and, by permitting stations to count only half of their ownership of ultra-high frequency stations, the cap preventing any one broadcaster from reaching more than 39 percent of the United States (the "UHF Discount") (PEN America, 2019, pp. 60–61). Worse, as the World Press Freedom Index reveals, media concentration coincides with decreasing journalistic freedom (Kroeger, 2018).

Another problem is that the FCC has not held broadcast stations "accountable for their public interest obligations" (PEN America, 2019, p. 62). In the 1940s and 1970s, the FCC gave instructions to broadcast stations on how to meet local needs by featuring programming for children, providing educational and religious content, and promoting public affairs (e.g., agricultural news in farming communities) (PEN America, 2019, p. 63). Despite granting "over 100,000 license renewals" since 1934, however, the FCC has denied "only four" because "a station failed to meet the public interest requirement" (PEN America, 2019, p. 63; Brotman, 2017).

The FCC has also failed to promote ownership diversity, despite it being one of the "Commission's core missions and policy goals," according to former FCC Chairman Michael Powell (PEN America, 2019, p. 60). As of 2017, people of color own only 5.8 percent of commercial AM stations, according to the FCC, 2.3 percent of commercial FM stations, and 2.6 percent of television stations. These were almost all small broadcast stations, moreover, the total value of which came to only 1 percent of the industry's worth (FCC, 2017, p. 4; PEN America, 2019, p. 34).

Instead, the FCC has supported media concentration under the rationale of "market efficiency" (Figliola, 2019, pp. 4, 8–9). "While claiming boldly to be a forum where complaints about monopolistic practices would be received and vigorously pursued," per the House Judiciary Committee's Antitrust Reform Act of 1992, the FCC has "become a regulatory 'graveyard' for telecommunications competition policy" (Antitrust, 1992, p. 39; *Investigation*, 2020, p. 35). It failed to prevent the former regional Bell Companies from committing anticompetitive violations "eerily reminiscent" of Bell System abuses before its breakup in 1982 (*Investigation*, 2020, p. 35). Bell Atlantic bought NYNEX in 1996, for example, and since 2000, Bell Atlantic has been part of Verizon (formed in 2000 when Bell Atlantic merged with GTE); AT&T acquired Ameritech and Bell South in 2006; and Southwestern Bell, which became SBC Communication in 1995, acquired AT&T in 2005.

As of this writing, the FCC has failed to halt AT&T's abandonment of its DSL service beginning in October 2020, thereby allowing it to jettison the 3 percent to 6 percent of its customers who can only get the internet via DSL (Tagland, 2020). As of 2017, the FCC has made broadband internet service a top priority, outweighing "whatever harms this might do to public safety, or how it might impact access for rural and poor Americans" (Tagland, 2020). Today, at least 10 percent or as many as one-third of Americans do not have broadband, especially affecting rural residents and Tribal populations. Notwithstanding the FCC's declaration that "broadband access is critical to economic opportunity, job creation, education and civic engagement," it is unclear how rural Americans and the poor will fare (FCC, 2019; PEN America, 2019, p. 63).

Meanwhile, the digital divide has only worsened during the COVID-19 pandemic because so many Americans depend on home connectivity, even as their incomes decline and as many risk eviction or foreclosure of their homes (Tagland, 2020). According to media scholar Victor Pickard (2019, p. 54), the FCC has "internalized the logic of market libertarianism."[7]

Reforming the FCC

Reforming the FCC has two parts: reform of the agency and reform of its policies.

Bureaucratic Changes

Changes in the structure of the FCC leadership would dampen the ideological and partisan leanings of the agency, particularly following the election of a new president, and would lessen the influence of the corporate media.[8]

- *Return to seven commissioners, per the FCC's original 1934 mandate.*[9] (In 1983, the FCC was reduced to five members.) Select the new commissioners from public-interest groups and/or media employees' organizations. This reform would make the FCC more representative of the many stakeholders in US media policy by reducing the numbers of politicians and business affiliates on the commission and by adding the voices of consumers, journalists, and other employees. Examples of media-related public-interest organizations include Common Cause, the Institute for Local Self Reliance, National Digital Inclusion Alliance, and PEN America. Examples of journalist advocacy groups include the American Press Institute, Committee to Protect Journalists, Investigative Reporters and Editors, and Media Law Resources Center. Organizations that promote media employees' interests include the Communication Workers of America (which incorporates the NewsGuild), Tech Workers Coalition, UNITY: Journalists for Diversity, and the Writers Guild of America (East and West).
- *Increase the length of the commissioners' terms in office.* Because of the five-year terms, President Donald Trump was able to appoint or renew all of the FCC commissioners. Appointing them to seven-year terms would help to depoliticize and professionalize the FCC and approach how Congress has handled the appointments of other public officials who need to be insulated from outside influence (such as the FBI director's 10-year term and the Federal Reserve Board members' 14-year terms).
- With the media companies' own interests in media regulation (e.g., the disposition of the broadcast spectrum), the FCC must report on what the industry is doing so that such information is no longer publicized solely at the media's discretion (which, at present, gravely underreports news on the political economy of the media). So the FCC would issue public-service announcements about any major changes to its personnel, rule interpretations, and technological developments, for example, and the broadcast media would have to carry such announcements as a condition of their FCC licenses; the FCC could then also disseminate these public-service announcements via social media.

Policy Changes

The FCC's changes as a public agency need to be accompanied by policy reforms.

- *Increase the number of separate owners within media markets* (PEN America, 2019, pp. 61–62). Use the FCC's own directives, and, if necessary, antitrust laws, to break up the six large media companies and thereby promote local TV and radio ownership and more national news sources. As with Ma Bell, so too with Google and Facebook (Pickard, 2019, pp. 128–133; Vaidhyanathan, 2018, pp. 211–220). Encouragingly, on October 20, 2020, the Justice Department filed a civil antitrust lawsuit against Google in the D.C. District Court, and on December 9, 2020, the FTC sued Facebook for illegal monopolization.

- *Increase funding for local and regional news providers.* American public media funding as of 2014 ranked the lowest among 18 high-income democracies. Higher-ranking countries provided an average level of direct and indirect public funding for the news media almost 30 times more than the United States did (Nielsen et al., 2016; PEN America, 2019, pp. 67–68; Pickard, 2019, pp. 137–138, 151–154). This includes funding for public and nonprofit broadcasters, for small commercial companies that represent quieter "voices," and for other news sources (Matsa, 2018; PEN America, 2019, pp. 67–68; Pickard, 2019, pp. 169–172).
- *Improve broadband by returning to net neutrality* (and expanding it nationally). This would be consistent with the FCC's new ten-year, $1.6 billion program to address the digital divide (FCC, 2019, pp. 2, 4; PEN America, 2019, p. 63). Making broadband nationally available is especially important because the big media firms have been promulgating 5G service, even as it is not cost effective to extend 5G throughout much of the United States because of the high fixed costs of erecting local 5G communication towers.
- *Raise revenues by taxing online advertising revenue.* A mere 2 percent tax would, by one estimate, raise about $2 billion (Karr & Aaron, 2019; PEN America, 2019, p. 64). This would help fund the listed policies.

Conclusion

President Calvin Coolidge's proclamation that "the business of America is business" came in a speech he gave to the American Society of Newspaper Editors. In fact, the aphorism was a paraphrase of Coolidge's statement that "the chief business of the American people is business," in reference to the fact that Americans were "profoundly concerned with producing, buying, selling, investing and prospering in the world" (Coolidge, 1925; Terrell, 2019). The president welcomed the fact that the "great newspapers are great business enterprises," and he was sanguine that a prosperous press would not betray the American people. In particular, Coolidge trusted in the wall of separation between the newspapers' editorial shops and their business personnel. As long as the owners were "sincerely trying to serve the public interests," promoting "the general welfare," and using their papers "for the support of popular government," he was happy for them to earn sizeable profits (Coolidge, 1925). But the implication of

Coolidge's comment was that if publishers did not act in the public interest, then their businesses should be subjected to regulation – the bottom line be damned.

That was a different era. The United States today has one-tenth the number of newspapers – 1,279 in 2018 as opposed to 14,065 in 1925 (Dill, 1928) – 25 times the number of AM radio stations (15,451 stations in 2019 versus 571 radio stations then), and now, almost 1,800 TV stations. But the greatest difference between the two is the collapse of the wall of separation. Today, nearly all media personnel are employed in large for-profit businesses, dedicated to increasing advertising sales above all else, with the result that they promote more sensationalist, edgy news and less serious, in-depth reportage. This push for readers and viewers explains the billions of dollars in free media received by Donald Trump during the 2016 election. The Trump campaign "may not be good for America," CBS News's Leslie Moonves notoriously declared, "but it's damn good for CBS." "The money's rolling in," Moonves noted – thanks to Trump's celebrity and showmanship – "bring it on, Donald. Keep going" (Collins, 2016; Pickard, 2019, pp. 2–3). The public interest in how the candidates and issues of the 2016 election were being covered and how Facebook skewed its treatment of the candidates scarcely mattered (Sunstein, 2018; Vaidhyanathan, 2018). By Coolidge's measures, the news media was not acting in the public interest and was poorly serving the "general welfare."

In his classic *Capitalism and Freedom*, Milton Friedman (1962, p. 35) remarked that the FCC's "implicit censorship and violation of free speech" by means of "the control of radio and television" exemplified government activity that "cannot . . . validly be justified" on the basis of his free-market principles. But Friedman added an all-important caveat. In instances of "technical monopolies" having a single provider (such as telephone services), Friedman calls for governmental intervention to promote competition (Friedman, 1962, pp. 28, 34). And today, the technology, scale, and reach of the extremely large media and technology firms have effectively created an oligopolistic media that profits from Friedman's "technical monopoly." President Coolidge would have worried greatly about such developments; so, too, would even a free-enterpriser like the famed economist Milton Friedman. So should we all.

Notes

1. 1790 (11% of mailing costs in 2006, or less than $300 million, as opposed to 75% of postal costs in 1970, or about $2 billion [PEN America, 2019, p. 67; Cowan & Westphal, 2010).
2. The Emergency Alert System was previously called the Emergency Broadcast System (1963–1997) and, previously, existed as the Control of Electromagnetic Radiation (CONELRAD), which was established early in the Cold War

for the communication of civil defense information in the event of a nuclear attack (1951–1963).
3. Comcast, for example, for three years blocked placing the Bloomberg business channel adjacent to CNN, CNBC, MSNBC, or Fox, contrary to the conditions of the 2011 Comcast-NBC Universal (Kroeger, 2018).
4. Most of these papers had a circulation of less than 5,000.
5. The news deserts vary greatly in population, from areas with fewer than 1,000 residents to others with more than 1 million residents – all without community newspapers. Even some cities – including Detroit, Cleveland, and New Orleans – have no daily newspapers (except for online versions). *The Detroit News* and the *Detroit Free Press* do publish three print editions a week, however, including a joint Sunday newspaper (PEN America, 2019, pp. 38–39).
6. Although not one of the big six, the Sinclair Broadcast Group, which owns 294 television stations and reaches 40 percent of U.S. households, offers another example. Sinclair compelled its stations to carry conservative commentary, broadcast a series of exclusive interviews with President Trump, and, in 2004, spread the Swift Boat attacks against Democratic presidential candidate Senator John Kerry (PEN America, 2019, pp. 30–31; Pickard, 2019, p. 109).
7. Pickard was specifically referring to the FCC's 2011 report, which, despite its thorough and accurate analysis, severely pulled its punches with respect to recommending reform.
8. The politics of FCC appointees and media policy do not necessarily hinge on partisanship. President Obama appointed Ajit Pai, who President Trump instated as FCC chairman, and President Clinton signed the 1996 Telecommunications Act; both presidents furthered neoliberal policies.
9. The FCC's commissioners, including the chairperson, are appointed by the president (subject to Senate confirmation) to staggered five-year terms. They may be reappointed.

Bibliography

Abernathy, P. M. (2018). *The rise of a new media baron and the emerging threat of news deserts*. Center for Innovation & Sustainability in Local Media, UNC School of Media and Journalism. www.usnewsdeserts.com/wp-content/uploads/2016/09/07.UNC_RiseOfNewMediaBaron_SinglePage_01Sep2016-REDUCED.pdf

Antitrust Reform Act of 1992. H. Comm. on the Judiciary, H. Rep. No. 102–850.

Brotman, S. N. (2017, March 23). *Revisiting the broadcast public interest standard in communications law and regulation*. The Brookings Institution. www.brookings.edu/research/revisiting-the-broadcast-public-interest-standard-in-communications-law-andregulation/

Collins, E. (2016, February 29). Les Moonves: Trump's run is "damn good for CBS". *Politico*. www.politico.com/blogs/on-media/2016/02/les-moonves-trump-cbs-220001

Coolidge, C. (1925, January 17). *Address to the American society of newspaper editors*. www.presidency.ucsb.edu/documents/address-the-american-society-newspaper-editors-washington-dc

Cowan, G., & Westphal, D. (2010, January). *Public policy and funding the news*. University of Southern California Annenberg School for Communication and Journalism. niemanlab.org/pdfs/USC%20Report.pdf

Dill, W. A. (1928). *Growth of newspapers in the United States* (M.A. Thesis), Department of Journalism, University of Kansas, Lawrence, KS.

Federal Communications Commission. (2017). *Third report on ownership of commercial broadcast stations.* bit.ly/2OROcz4

Federal Communications Commission. (2019, July 11). *FCC fact sheet.* https://docs.fcc.gov/public/attachments/DOC-358432A1.pdf

Figliola, P. M. (2019). *The federal communications commission: Current structure and its role in the changing telecommunications landscape.* CRS Report RL32589. Washington, DC, Congressional Research Service. www.everycrsreport.com/files/20190418_RL32589_8ba17da6c717de4c60f12a03c2e79071ad5d2824.pdf

Friedman, M. (1962). *Capitalism and freedom.* Chicago: University of Chicago Press.

Investigation of Competition in Digital Markets. (2020). Majority staff report and recommendations, subcommittee on antitrust, commercial and administrative law of the committee on the judiciary, U.S. House of Representatives, Washington, DC.

Iyengar, S., Curran, J., Lund, A. B., Salovaara-Moring, I., Hahn, K. S., & Coen, S. (2010, August). Cross-national versus individual-level differences in political information: A media systems perspective. *Journal of Elections, Political Opinion and Parties, 20*(3). pcl.stanford.edu/research/2010/iyengar-cross-national.pdf

Karr, T., & Aaron, C. (2019, February). Beyond fixing Facebook. *Free Press,* 8. freepress.net/sites/default/files/2019-02/Beyond-Fixing-Facebook-Final.pdf

Kroeger, K. R. (2018, October 18). Press freedom is declining worldwide and media mergers are part of the problem. *Medium.* https://kentkroeger.medium.com/press-freedom-is-declining-worldwide-and-media-mergers-are-part-of-the-problem-ee2730e3bcea

Kull, S., Ramsay, C., & Lewis, E. (2019). Misperceptions, the media, and the Iraq war. *Political Science Quarterly, 41*(3), 221–234.

Matsa, K. E. (2018, June 8). Across Western Europe, public news media are widely used and trusted sources of news. *Pew Research Center.* pewrsr.ch/2URzmtM

Nielsen, R. K., Fletcher, R., Sehl, A., & Levy, D. (2016, November 11). Analysis of the relation between and impact of public service media and private media. *Reuters Institute for the Study of Journalism.* bit.ly/2ZQ1Es3

PEN America. (2019). *Losing the news: The decimation of local journalism and the search for solutions.* New York: PEN America.

Pew Research Center. (2019, June 12). *Mobile fact sheet.* www.pewresearch.org/internet/fact-sheet/mobile/

Pickard, V. (2019). *Democracy without journalism? Confronting the misinformation society.* New York: Oxford University Press.

Snyder, J. H. (2007). *America's $480 billion spectrum giveaway, how it happened, and how to prevent it from recurring: The art of spectrum lobbying.* Paper presented at the TPRC Conference, Washington, DC: New America Foundation. https://papers.ssrn.com/sol3/papers.cfm?abstract_id=2117560#

Sunstein, C. (2018). *#Republic: Divided democracy in the age of social media.* Princeton: Princeton University Press.

Tagland, K. (2020, October 16, Friday). AT&T, FCC abandon rural broadband customers. *Weekly Digest*. Evanston: Benton Institute for Broadband & Society. www.benton.org/blog/att-fcc-abandon-rural-broadband-customers

Terrell, E. (2019). When a quote is not (exactly) a quote: The business of America is business edition. *Inside Adams: Science and Technology & Business*. The Library of Congress Blogs. https://blogs.loc.gov/inside_adams/2019/01/when-a-quote-is-not-exactly-a-quote-the-business-of-america-is-business-edition/

Vaidhyanathan, S. (2018). *Anti-social media: How Facebook disconnects us and undermines democracy*. New York: Oxford University Press.

Part 5
Upgrade Political Campaigns

20 Study the Electorate Thoroughly

Daron R. Shaw

In the summer of 2006, a group of Republican consultants gathered at The Oasis restaurant overlooking Lake Travis. The picturesque Hill Country of Texas was a favorite of Dave Carney's, a New Hampshire-ite whose probing mind and blunt manner made him invaluable to Texas Governor Rick Perry. Carney was serving as Perry's campaign manager in the 2006 reelection campaign, a colorful race featuring four candidates.[1] Carney was aiming not only to win but to change the relationship among political data, political vendors, and political campaigns.

Earlier that year, Carney had read *Get Out the Vote*, a scholarly monograph written by political scientists Alan Gerber and Donald Green (2019). The book detailed the results of innovative field experiments in which campaign "treatments" were randomly assigned to different groups of voters, with their subsequent behavior compared to that of a control group. Gerber and Green offered a tantalizing set of findings: Paid phone calls had little effect on voters; direct mail had small effects; and in-person canvassing had substantial effects. Carney contacted the political scientists and made them an offer: Come to Texas and use the Perry campaign as an experimental site, thereby gathering data about a major statewide election.

Green was both surprised and intrigued by the offer. Prior to that time, the "Get Out the Vote" experiments had been conducted in nonpartisan elections in New Haven and other local settings. But Carney's offer came with limits. The campaign was not willing to randomize its television or radio outreach, but Carney would let the researchers publish their findings in academic outlets after the election. For ethical reasons, Gerber and Green could not be compensated for their work, and they would not be rendering strategic advice. Ultimately, a deal was struck: Two fine scholars got a chance to do important research, and Carney could assess what really works in a campaign, thereby having an empirical way of auditing his vendors.

Jim Gimpel, a professor at the University of Maryland, and I joined the research team to test the effects of phone calls, direct mail, and in-person canvassing. Our findings largely corroborated what Gerber and Green had found in earlier experiments – modest effects for everything but in-person canvassing. As Green described the results to the assembled group on that fated day in June, the consultants grew restless and then nitpicked the results. While this was going on, Carney had a self-satisfied look on his face – the consultants were found to be adding minimal value at maximal cost.

Research in Campaigns

Carney's commitment to testing campaign strategies in real life was (and remains) unusual. To be sure, data gathering had always been the hallmark of smart campaigns, with surveys being used in the 1960s and '70s and then focus groups in the 1980s and '90s. By the turn of the century, big data – in the form of voter files – and computer modeling were being used to target voters. Field and survey experiments were also added to the mix. In some ways, what was happening in politics resembled the "money ball" revolution in baseball – hard data were being used to determine what had been overlooked before. In baseball before the early 2000s, that is, certain skills were undervalued – getting on base via walks or hitting for power (even at the expense of striking out a lot). In politics, data analyses clearly showed that face-to-face communication with voters had been seriously undervalued.

Not everyone loves the "money ball" approach. Traditional consultants say they "just know" their approach works (because they get their candidates elected) and that, at root, politics is an art, not reducible to regression coefficients or difference-of-means tests. Other naysayers argue that serious, systematic research costs time, energy, and money. Today, for example, a probability sample can require upward of a thousand interviews, with a price tag in the $25,000 to $75,000 range. For field experiments, it takes inordinate time to identify the appropriate target population, segment the voter list, assign people to treatment and control groups, and then analyze the effects. Data analysis requires computer hardware (servers, systems, etc.) and software (statistical packages). Good research also requires intellectual firepower, and that, too, can be costly.

My argument here is that the cost of *not* doing this research is far greater. For one thing, such research is cost effective. Consider, for example, what campaigns costs. In 2020, the Trump and Biden campaigns spent $372.8 million and $350.4 million, respectively; the average US Senate campaign spent $1,001,434; $273,175 for a House race. And yet, according to Federal Election Commission figures, campaigns spend only 5.2 percent of their money on research versus 45 percent of their funds on broadcast and cable TV advertising.[2] In 2020, for example, the Trump campaign spent $67.7 million on TV ads in Florida alone. The Biden campaign spent $82.3 million.[3] In 2018, Republican Ted Cruz spent $4.1 million on TV ads defending his US Senate seat in Texas. His opponent, Democrat Beto O'Rourke, spent $5.3 million.[4] When pressed, campaign managers inevitably cut back on research to afford more advertising. This chapter explains why that is manifestly unwise.

What Should Campaigns Do?

Polling? Yes!

Let us say, for argument's sake, that you are running a campaign and believe in discovering what voters think. What should you do? My advice: Start with a survey research program. True, polls are hardly new, and since the advent of cell phones, people have become reluctant to respond to pollsters. With response rates being shockingly low these days, some are skeptical about the accuracy and reliability of surveys even though the right sort of probability sample can provide invaluable information about voters.[5] By taking the right precautions, however, campaign polls offer a positive return on investment if two key guidelines are followed:

- Be sure that the poll has a substantial cell phone component. Moreover, the cell phone lists that a survey research organization uses must be up to date and accurate.
- Avoid relying on nonprobability samples such as automated phone polls (so-called robo-calls), online polls, and social media polls. While they are popular and less expensive, not enough is known about the errors associated with such approaches, making them hard to rely on for key campaign decisions.

What does a good survey research program look like? Initially, a campaign should conduct a "benchmark" survey that gauges voters' attitudes about how things are going where they live, what they think of the candidates, which issues are most important, what their policy preferences might be, and how they will vote in the upcoming election. Polls drawing on a large number of interviews are especially helpful for understanding subgroups within the electorate. By focusing on key indicators like race/ethnicity, education, income, etc., a campaign can create microtargeted messages for use during the race. Also helpful are "brushfire" or "trial ballot" surveys run during the summer and fall of an election year, surveys that track the fundamental dynamics of the race, detecting any attitudinal changes among key voting groups.

During the last month of the campaign, daily "tracking" polls can capture the ups and downs of the race. Consisting of a few hundred interviews each day, tracking polls roll three to four days of interviewing into a single estimate. The next day, the most distant day of interviewing is dropped and replaced by the most recent day's, thereby exposing voters' mood swings or their reactions to the most recent ads or campaign event.

Big Data Is Not Just a Catchphrase

In addition to polls, a savvy campaign examines lists of registered voters to identify individual-level targets. Such lists were mandated by the Help America Vote Act (2002) and are curated and maintained by secretaries of state. Campaigns take these data lists and augment them with political information provided by political parties and outside groups. The lists can also be augmented with commercial data purchased from outside vendors.

Smart campaigns will also talk to voters. Paid phone calls designed to persuade voters can also render information about their preferences. Door-to-door contacting can be used similarly, as can digital outreach. The goal here is to continually refine a conceptual "model" for the campaign by adding individual-level data from a variety of sources. In some cases, data additions can be made via smartphones so that new information automatically updates voters' estimated priorities, preferences, and behaviors.

Qualitative Data Works, Too

Perhaps the most attractive aspect of survey data is that generalizable results can be gleaned from relatively small samples. But polls rarely allow a campaign to get deeper impressions from voters. Focus groups, on the other hand, provide considerable depth. Focus groups typically consist of 8 to 20 voters convened by the campaign to discuss the candidates and the issues of the day. The discussion is led by a carefully trained moderator who follows a script: *What do you like about the Democrat? What do you like about the Republican? What do you dislike? Would you want to have a beer with this candidate? What issues do you want them to discuss?*

Group members' responses are then analyzed by the campaign, with an eye to adjusting the candidate's positioning. A key element of focus groups is making participants feel comfortable expressing their opinions. It is especially important for them not to feel intimidated lest their valuable perspectives are lost. Most focus groups are conducted in person, but video (or "virtual") focus groups are not uncommon.

A famous example of the importance of focus groups occurred in April 1992 when Bill Clinton's presidential campaign was languishing in the polls behind President George H.W. Bush and independent challenger Ross Perot. Clinton had been bloodied by a series of unhelpful news stories, and his advisers needed to divine the key problem.[6] To do so, they convened a series of focus groups in battleground states (which they dubbed "the Manhattan Project") and came away stunned. It turned out that voters did not particularly care about stories of Arkansas real estate deals or Clinton's alleged infidelity. But they did have a strong (but wrong) impression that Clinton was a privileged White male who had used his connections to avoid the military draft and make a bunch of money, an impression that dissipated quickly when focus group participants were told about Clinton's humble origins in Hope, Arkansas. Clinton's advisers immediately shifted their messaging to emphasize Clinton's origin story, expertly captured by the short film *The Man From Hope*. A surge in the polls followed in June of 1992.

The main downsides of focus groups are that they are not necessarily representative of the overall electorate and can be expensive. Today, a single 12-person focus group, with in-person (behind the glass) viewing, a trained moderator, videotaping, a transcription, and a write-up can cost up to $12,000. Polls provide breadth and focus groups provide depth, but in politics, nothing is free.

Focus groups are not the only option for obtaining qualitative data. For example, since 2008, campaigns have been dabbling with "tele-townhalls." These events provide outreach and data-gathering opportunities with a given group of voters. After voters dial into an event, the candidate or a surrogate engages them via telephone, hoping to learn from them as well as connect them to the campaign. Attendees are often asked a small battery of questions upon entering and leaving the event so any newly formed impressions can be calibrated.

Social Media Is Not Just the New Kid on the Block

Increasingly, social media platforms have become a source of information about individual voters. Facebook and Google are well known for collecting data on their platforms to deliver content tailored to users' interests. Data of this sort is much less available for use in (commercial or political) advertising than it once was, but it can sometimes be used by campaigns to drive outreach.

Social media provide other benefits as well, establishing the kind of feedback loop Dave Carney was interested in during the 2006 gubernatorial race in Texas. Social media platforms, for example, provide metrics that tell a campaign what interests voters. Google searches, Facebook shares and likes, Twitter retweets, Instagram shares, and YouTube memes – all of these creatures tell us what voters are thinking and do so unobtrusively. Smart campaigns learn from such things.

What Do Campaigns Learn About Voters?

People's preferences vary considerably by place and across time, which is why research is critical to a smart campaign. Twenty years into the new millennium, however, a wide array of social scientific research demonstrates that certain voters' attitudes have become remarkably stable in certain ways. As a result, anyone running a political campaign (or anyone studying political communication) needs to understand these continuities.

Politics? Corruption and Incompetence!

Disaffection with political institutions has grown apace in recent years, and ratings of the U.S Congress are particularly abysmal. Feelings about the news media are even more negative. But such opinions are not altogether recent. One need only look to the plethora of well-worn quotes from Mark Twain or Will Rogers to see how poorly politicians have traditionally been regarded. But something new is going on as well.

Two biases are especially popular. The first is a belief that public officials are corrupt (Shaw et al., 2021), a second that they are incompetent to boot (Gibson & Shaw, 2019). Together, they suggest a broken political system in need of reform. Candidates who are able to tap into this set of beliefs attract a great deal of attention. Ross Perot did so in 1992 and 1996 by talking about the budget deficit, and John McCain did so in 2000 by discussing campaign finance reform and governmental corruption. In 2016 and 2020, Bernie Sanders joined the chorus by describing the wiles of special interest groups. These appeals are frequently labeled (and often dismissed) as "populist." Surprisingly, however, these "little guy versus big shots" narratives are popular with a good many Americans, not just those in the lower socioeconomic class.

Whither the Parties?

One also finds widespread disaffection with political parties these days. Since the 1980s, we have seen partisans' ratings of the "out-party" decline precipitously. In other words, Democrats have become much more unfavorable toward Republicans than they are attracted to their fellow Democrats. The same is true of Republicans. In the parlance of political science, this is known as "affective polarization" – people are more likely to be motivated by hatred of the other side than by their in-group enthusiasm. Surprisingly, *policy issues* are not the key variable here. While there is some disagreement on the matter (Abramowitz, 2011, 2018), there is compelling evidence that Republicans and Democrats are not all that far apart on many key issues and that the gulf separating partisans has not widened over time (Fiorina et al., 2010).

Like the parties, political leaders are also highly polarized these days, and that has happened for a number of reasons: more partisan primary campaigns, the rise of candidate-centered politics, and the elimination of competitive districts through gerrymandering. The upshot: voters must now choose between a very liberal Democrat and a very conservative Republican. In the absence of moderate candidates, partisan voting dominates, and swing voting has become less common (it has especially declined since the 1990s). Unfortunately, partisan candidates now find little reason to appeal to the middle-of-the-roader. Increasing enthusiasm and turnout among "the base" has become the sine qua non of contemporary politics.

But Swing Voting Is Not Dead

Casting a ballot for Party A's candidate in one election and then voting for Party B's in the next election is virtually nonexistent in the 2020s. Roughly 9 in 10 voters identify with (or lean toward) one of the major parties. It is also true that partisan defection rates in the 2020 presidential election were extraordinarily low – only 4 percent of Democrats voted for Donald Trump, and only 8 percent of Republicans voted for Joe Biden.[7]

Yet *Swingus Americanus* is not an extinct species. Table 20.1 shows what 2016 voters did in the previous (2012) presidential election. Thirteen percent of Donald Trump's voters backed Barack Obama in 2012, while 4 percent of Hillary Clinton's support came from voters who voted for Mitt Romney in 2012. Overall, roughly 8 percent could thus be classified as swing voters.[8] Given the overall turnout numbers from 2016, this would yield 10.9 million swing voters nationwide (8.4 million Obama 2012–Trump 2016, and 2.5 million Romney 2012–Clinton 2016), a sizeable number indeed.[9] And this does not even consider the 1 in 5 who voted in 2012 but either didn't vote in 2016 or who could not recall their 2012 vote choice. *Swingus Americanus* is endangered but still drawing breath.

The implications for campaigns are considerable. If there are voters who *could* side with candidates from either party, then a campaign ought to research how to get them to side with their candidate. Conversely, contemporary campaigns should not assume that mobilizing their own partisans is the only game in town.

Table 20.1 Swing Voting in Presidential Elections, 2012–2016

		2012 Vote			
		Obama	Romney	Other	Don't know/ No 2012 Vote*
2016 Vote	Clinton	77%	4%	1%	19%
	Trump	13%	66%	1%	20%
	Other	35%	29%	8%	29%

Notes: * "DK/REF/No 2012 vote" includes those who did not recall their 2012 vote, refused to answer about their 2012 vote, or said they did not vote in 2012. Rows may not add up to 100% due to rounding.

Source: American National Election Studies' 2016 Time Series Study.

Boredom With the Old Issue Wars

Finally, it seems increasingly evident that the issue debates that animated party politics in the United States since the 1960s have grown stale. The analogy often used in campaigns is that there are three broad issue clusters in America, which act as legs on a three-legged stool:

1. Social welfare issues, encompassing the scope of government, taxes and spending, and redistributive programs;
2. Social issues, encompassing values, religion, and diversity;
3. Foreign policy and defense issues, encompassing military spending, national security, and (more recently) terrorism.

These three clusters have defined party conflict for the better part of the last 50 years, with Republicans taking more conservative positions on spending, values, and defense, and Democrats taking more progressive positions on the same issues.

Yet defense issues have become largely amorphous, with the policy positions of Republicans and Democrats shifting based on the specific conflict being addressed or by which party controls the presidency. For their part, social issues have become synonymous with tolerance of non-traditional lifestyles. Issues such as school prayer, religious rights, and the role of the family have faded. In their stead, gay marriage and LGBTQ rights have become pivotal. Public opinion has moved decidedly in favor of tolerance, giving Democrats a decided edge on a dimension that formerly showed a greater diversity of opinion.

With two legs of the stool somewhat disabled, then, candidates of both parties tend to relitigate the efficacy of tax policy and social program spending. Many voters find these debates compelling. Many other voters – especially younger voters and groups not firmly ensconced in the existing party coalitions – are less enthralled. How these issue alignments will change in the future remains an intriguing issue indeed.

Conclusion

My argument in this chapter is that American political campaigns should invest considerable resources in getting to know the American voter. I suggest three specific investments:

> *Campaigns should invest in better measurement of qualitative opinion.* While there is a great deal of public and private information about the preferences of the American voter, we do not have a full understanding of *why* they hold the attitudes they do. Answering that question could help campaigns know what to say and how to say it.

Campaigns should measure individual-level change. It is one thing to predict the opinions of a broad-based electorate but quite another to know *who*, specifically, has changed their minds. The practical step here is to invest in panel studies in which individual voters' preferences are assessed and then remeasured throughout the campaign.

Campaigns should use information from microtargeting to inform their voter contact programs. Yes, this is already done in many political campaigns, but investing in more nuanced surveys and building more capacious statistical models is the surest pathway to more effective campaigning.

Steps like these can make political campaigns more efficient, but greater investment in the measurement of public opinion would also produce societal benefits. The 2016 and 2020 cycles, for example, showed how latent issues can reshape the dynamics of a campaign. The 2016 Trump campaign's focus on, first, immigration and, then, international trade proved critical to its success in the primaries and later on in the general election. As we look to the future, it is clear that issues like political and economic reform, cybersecurity and terrorism, and diversity and inclusiveness have not yet been effectively incorporated into the platforms of the existing two-party system. Accordingly, political entrepreneurs should invest time, energy, and money in learning what is driving these still-amorphous but very real issues. In short, knowing who the American people are and why they are that way is a worthy goal for political campaigns but, more importantly, a way of ensuring that the nation's leaders keep in touch with the people they govern, an outcome that would be good for all Americans.

Notes

1. Perry was running against Democrat Chris Bell and independents Carole Keaton-Strayhorn (former mayor of Austin) and Kinky Friedman (country-western singer and raconteur, whose motto was "Why the hell not?").
2. Breakdowns of 2020 FEC campaign expenditures data are provided by www.opensecrets.org/campaign-expenditures (last accessed Oct. 8, 2020).
3. Estimates are based on October 22, 2020, data from Advertising Analytics.
4. Breakdowns of 2020 FEC campaign expenditures data are provided by www.opensecrets.org/campaign-expenditures (last accessed Oct. 8, 2020).
5. See Pew Research Report on response rates.
6. Among other things, Clinton was accused of shady real estate dealings, dodging the draft in the 1960s, and having several extramarital affairs.
7. Estimates are from the 2020 Fox News Voter Analysis/AP VoteCast.
8. This estimate (1) takes the percentage of voters who defected from Obama to Trump and multiplies this by the total percent of Trump voters in 2016, (2) takes the percentage of voters who defected from Romney to Clinton and multiplies this by the total percentage of Clinton voters in 2016, and then (3) adds these together.

9. There are reasons to be skeptical of reported past vote. Overall, 58 percent of respondents to the 2016 ANES who said they voted in 2012 (including those who didn't vote in 2016) claimed to have voted for Obama, 7 points more than the 51 percent Obama actually won in 2012. Meanwhile, Romney only won 40 percent of the vote of those who said they cast a ballot in 2012, 7 points fewer than the 47 percent Romney really won in 2012. Although there might have been a sizable number of voters who cast ballots in 2012 but didn't vote in 2016 and vice versa, it would not be surprising if Obama's percentage were somewhat inflated and Romney's a bit diminished. This would be due to some of the complications associated with voter recall of past votes. If so, this would mean the 8.4 million Obama 2012–Trump 2016 figure is exaggerated, while the 2.5 million Romney 2012–Clinton 2016 figure is probably too small. Still, the weighted ANES data slightly undershot Trump's 46 percent of the popular vote and overshot Clinton's 48 percent, so that could mean the data aren't especially exaggerated.

Bibliography

Abramowitz, A. (2011). *The disappearing center: Engaged citizens, polarization, and American democracy*. New Haven, CT: Yale University Press.

Abramowitz, A. (2018). *The great alignment: Race, party transformation, and the rise of Donald Trump*. New Haven, CT: Yale University Press.

Federal Election Commission. (2020). *2020 FEC campaign expenditures data*. www.opensecrets.org/campaign-expenditures (accessed October 8, 2020).

Fiorina, M. P., Abrams, S. J., & Pope, J. C. (2010). *Culture war? The myth of a polarized America* (3rd ed.). New York, NY: Longman Press.

Gerber, A., & Green, D. (2019). *Get out the vote! How to increase voter turnout* (4th ed.). Washington, DC: Brookings Press.

Gibson, N. S., & Shaw, D. R. (2019). Politics as unusual? Exploring issues and the 2016 presidential vote. *Social Science Quarterly*, *100*(2), 447–465.

Shaw, D. R., Roberts, B., & Baek, M. (2021). *The appearance of corruption: Testing supreme court assumptions about campaign finance reform*. New York, NY: Oxford University Press.

21 Talk About Voters Thoughtfully

Sharon E. Jarvis

Elections are a hallmark of American democracy. They are the method by which we choose our representatives. They have long been a source of national pride. And yet they are susceptible to multiple threats.

Some foes are obvious. At the international level, United States intelligence agencies have confirmed foreign efforts to tamper with American elections. At the national level, the recipients of the popular vote in the 2000 and 2016 presidential contests failed to win the Electoral College vote. At the state level, gerrymandered districts, worries about potential illegal voting, and alarms about aging voting machines have received heightened media attention. And on the political level, President Donald J. Trump spoke repeatedly about "rigged" elections. These pressures are largely public and, unfortunately, now overly familiar to most voters.

Other adversaries are less apparent. Many Americans might not know that the US Constitution does not feature the affirmative right to vote, a right that appears in the foundational documents for democracies created after ours. Even though there are multiple subsequent amendments addressing discrimination in electoral processes, the founders struggled with the idea of expanding the franchise. Their ambivalence endures in powerful ways today. Consider, for example, how (1) political parties routinely insert barriers to turnout for citizens when it benefits the party's majority status, (2) presidential candidates have been critiquing voters' choices since the 1960s, (3) American schools gutted civics instruction in the 1970s such that students no longer receive lessons on democratic values or how to vote, and (4) news organizations have long struggled with how to cover voters in their reporting (Jarvis & Han, 2018; Keyssar, 2009). The lack of advocacy from these sources has now become normalized, a clear danger to the United States.

A third set of troublemakers might be guilty of blind-spots having emerged from the growth, sophistication, and interpretation of survey research tools. Prominent scholars have raised this concern in various ways over the years. V. O. Key (1966), for example, has worried that the picture of the voter emerging in "the new electoral studies," contributing to "political folklore" and "being spread to a larger public by reporters" was not pretty (p. 4). Survey research findings used by "public relations" consultants to advise candidates, he feared, were being interpreted and acted upon in ways that cast voters as "fools" who could be "managed by campaigns" (pp. 4–6). Key also saw such a mindset as problematic, for it could shape how people see their roles in the polity as well as influence how leaders and the government treat them.

Gerald Pomper (1968) was also apprehensive about the "pessimistic portrait of the voter" emanating from survey data (p. 69). Like Key, he was uneasy that scholarship had begun to "ridicule the electorate," potentially portending a research trajectory that could become a self-fulfilling prophecy. Failing to be mindful of how elections offer citizens opportunities to protect themselves, he cautioned, might lead to actions that could "minimize the power of ordinary citizens" by "restricting their roles in elections," for "if elections are not respected, they could become unworthy of respect" (pp. 14–15).

Larry Bartels (2001) further warned that the subjection of the electorate to "microscopic analysis" tends to make electoral study a "nonpolitical endeavor" (p. 59). In his mind, this development divorces survey data on real people from their place in the larger political situation (p. 59). For Bartels, an important challenge for political scholars is to pay more attention to the power and place of elections in a political system more broadly (pp. 60–61).

The Problem to Be Fixed

The problem this chapter addresses is how to communicate about threats to elections in ways that do not make them worse. As reviewed earlier, there are highly visible and highly subtle menaces to consider. In a democratic republic, these dangers must be addressed. But how?

The Solutions to Be Advanced

The following paragraphs review three lines of research conducted as part of the Electorally Speaking Project in the Annette Strauss Institute for Civic Life at the University of Texas at Austin.[1] All of this work is guided by communication-based assumptions: (1) citizens come to know their political lives through language; as a result, the attractiveness of the labels connected to electoral participation are consequential, (2) the public conversation is led, but not fully determined, by the language used by elites such as political leaders, the legacy media, and widely followed voices on social media, and (3) the meanings of political terms can shift from time to time, becoming broader or narrower or changing entirely – often as a result of the elite voices who use such words (Jarvis, 2005, p. 42). Thus, one goal of these studies is to attend to how the words of electoral participation are used and if such uses are helpful or harmful in democratic life.

A second goal has been to be mindful of context. Elite voices operate in systems with professional norms and demands. Additionally, as other chapters in this book address, American citizens are living in a contentious political climate housing partisanship and cultural division. To honor these realities, my colleagues and I listened to the voices of everyday Americans, employed real news articles and actual tweets in our experiments, and worked with journalists and editors to respect the newsroom pressures. We wanted our prescriptions to fit the needs and tone of the time. In the spirit of *Fixing American Politics*, then, the content that follows offers an overview of the motivations, design, findings, and implications of the research I have conducted.

Are Elections "Rigged?" – Limit the Noise

A first study addressed one of the obvious threats mentioned in the introduction: How did Americans respond to former President Trump's charges that elections were "rigged" (Park-Ozee & Jarvis, 2020)? This analysis was driven by how the meanings of words can shift based on how they are adorned (Jarvis, 2005), as well as how the president of the United States has the power to turn word meanings into arguments (Zarefsky, 2004). Here, we wondered if Trump's using the word "rigged" in connection with "election(s)" might have shaped how people regarded the latter label.

Methodologically, we used computational analysis to identify dominant themes in open-ended responses to the survey question: "When people say that elections are rigged, what do you think they mean?" Offering people opportunities to discuss elections in their own words can reveal subtleties in meaning that closed-ended studies would miss. Further, individuals may "react to cues" (Iyengar, 1996, p. 64) in closed-ended surveys that parrot what elected officials from their party have previously advocated. The question appeared in a population-based survey supported by the Democracy Fund, run by Survey Sampling Inc. (SSI), and was in the field October 11–15, 2018.

A topic modeling program identified four key themes in the responses. The most common theme related to the notion that electoral outcomes are "predetermined." Democrats (32.1%) and Republicans (33.8%) voiced this concern at equal rates. It struck us as meaningful that the most top-of-mind response to our prompt had little to do with election mechanics, foreign influence, partisan stances, or Trump's rhetoric. Instead, it had more to do with a perceived lack of agency and influence within the electorate.

These data suggest that the "rigging" argument mostly featured raw political power, at least as recently as 2018. It is notable that most Americans, when answering an open-ended prompt, did *not* put a specific elite face on the term "rigged." Even though pundits worried that prior survey data showed that Trump's charges of rigging were having an effect, our data show that by 2018, they had yet to become a top-of mind concern nor had they chipped away at the meanings of the term "election" in ways that Trump had perhaps desired.

A communication model offers food for thought when interpreting these data and considering what to do when a politician advances baseless claims about elections being "rigged." The concept of rhetorical sensitivity addresses when and how to send messages (Hart & Burks, 1972). Rhetorically sensitive people are mindful of when to speak and what to say – distinguishing between all information and information that should be shared. Our data show that after three years of Trump questioning the integrity of elections, the concern that elections were "rigged" was not immediately salient for the people in our study. In this instance, news or social media attention to his charges would only recirculate baseless charges. A far better approach, based on the Hart and Burks model, is to limit the noise.

Are Dangers Insurmountable? – Balance Threats and Solutions

Another project, also supported by the Democracy Fund, was guided by a fundamental question: How might we talk about the threats to elections in ways that would still make people want to participate in them? To answer this question, we assembled an interdisciplinary team of researchers, including a former reporter and editor, and conducted two experiments.

The first focused on print news coverage and was inspired by research on solutions journalism (Albertson et al., 2019). Work in that arena holds that the press has an ethical duty to focus on more than just bad news, for when audiences only see negative aspects of a topic, they might tune out everything smacking of politics (McIntyre & Gyldensted, 2017). Accordingly, it is important to report on problems as well as efforts to address them.

To test if audiences reacted differently to reporting that only featured threats – versus coverage that addressed threats and efforts to safeguard elections – we conducted an online experiment of 1,787 adults in October 2018. Experimental stimuli were created by editing real articles that had appeared in *The New York Times, The Washington Post*, and *USA Today*. The topics of the articles included cybersecurity, voter purges, and aging voting machines. Participants were randomly assigned to one of two conditions: (1) traditional reporting (threat condition) articles only addressing threats to elections, and (2) solutions journalism (threat + solution condition) articles covering threats and efforts to address such threats.

Results show that solutions content in stories about threats to elections increased enthusiasm and optimism while decreasing anxiety, sadness, anger, and disgust. These findings provide insights for journalists wanting to cover threats to American elections in a manner that does not negatively impact readers. These results also advance a "best practice" for elections administrators and political advocates when asked to speak about threats to elections with the press: craft messages, and quotable soundbites, that explain both threats to elections and what organizations *and* individuals are doing to address them.

The second experiment addressed tweets and was driven by work on boomerang effects (Haenschen et al., 2019). Scholarship in that area addresses how many well-intentioned messages may lead to unintended results (Cialdini et al., 2006). To test if tweets addressing voter suppression might have accidental effects, we conducted an online experiment of 1,447 adults in October 2018. Survey respondents were shown screenshots of 25 real tweets that had been posted between October 3 and 22, 2018, by nonprofit organizations, elected officials, and other Twitter users with substantial followings. All of the tweets received at least 1,000 retweets, suggesting that the messages had substantial reach among Twitter users. Participants in our study were randomly assigned to one of three conditions: (1) threat condition: tweets mentioned potential voter suppression, (2) threat and solution condition: tweets mentioned potential voter suppression and actions people can take, such as requesting a provisional ballot or providing a hotline number, and (3) control condition: tweets that made no mention of elections.

In comparing the threat condition to the control condition, tweets highlighting voter suppression (and not offering solutions) depressed trust in elections. That is, tweets written to increase awareness of voter suppression without offering individual-level solutions people could use to protect their vote decreased trust in the election. We do not believe that tweets about voter suppression were sent with the intent to dampen trust in elections – they were likely sent in an effort to inform the public of potential problems and to garner media attention on the issue. Tweets that emphasized the problem and lacked a solution, however, backfired by decreasing trust in elections. These findings lead us to encourage Twitter users to make the public aware of future problems at the polls to include individual-level solutions in messages about voter suppression.

Do Voters Count? – Emphasize Their Agency

A third undertaking took a longitudinal and multimethod approach to the language of electoral participation (Jarvis & Han, 2018). It began with an analysis of how 36,400 instances of the words *vote(s)*, *voter(s)*, and *voting* were portrayed in six major newspapers spanning the 18 presidential campaigns between 1948 and 2016. It also included an experiment and focus groups testing how people respond to various portrayals of politics, as well as interviews with more than 50 reporters to learn more about why journalists write the stories they do.

A key finding from the content analysis addressed how words about voting have been used over time. Between 1948 and 1968, the term "votes" appeared 6 times more often in headlines and articles than the word "voters." That subtle word choice might seem unimportant, but the term "votes" signaled the very essence of campaigns – how people could affect electoral outcomes and hence the central role they had in election narratives. When the term "votes" was prevalent, as in news stories between 1948 and 1968, readers were subtly being urged to *participate*, reminded of their opportunity to influence the political system, and told how they could use the franchise to protect themselves and their interests. In other words, news stories suggested that people decide – and benefit from – elections. The difference between the words "votes" and "voters" may seem trivial. But in campaign reporting, *these two words may send entirely different messages about who decides what*. After 1972, the term "voters" was used more prominently in the news, largely to discuss individuals who were measured, predicted, and *acted upon* by pollsters and strategists. Suddenly, voters were no longer in the driver's seat.

Another takeaway from the experiments also highlights the importance of emphasizing voter agency. We conducted an online experiment with Polimetrix (now YouGov) in 2008. One group of respondents read a generic story about the 2008 primaries. A second group read that story, but this time, it also included a paragraph portraying voters as active participants by describing how "votes" were being solicited and how "voters" were being urged to act. A third group read a story that portrayed voters more as spectators subsumed under public opinion polls, including the very types of interpretations that troubled Key and Pomper.

People who read the "active participants" story, including both Democrats and Republicans, were more likely to express a desire to vote and less likely to express frustration with the press, compared to those who read the "spectators" story.

Steven Pinker (2015) has noted that when a person becomes an expert on something, it becomes easy to fall prey to a "curse of knowledge" – forgetting what it was like to not know something and, consequently, to omit such important background when communicating with others. The reliance on polling data in political science, as well as in the news, has led to a situation in which voters are often treated as mere pawns of survey data, strategists, and pundits – thereby undermining their role in the story of elections in the United States. When voters are given a more robust role to play in discussions of politics, on the other hand, democracy becomes the beneficiary.

Conclusion

Elections are central to American democracy, so it is important for people to know about the potential threats surrounding them. But how should we *talk* about such matters? Our research documents ways to discuss such concerns without making things worse. Our data offer the following prescriptions:

- President Trump's charges that elections were being "rigged," at least as recently as 2018, did not take hold as he had hoped. Such baseless charges should not be repeated, lest they eventually influence how individuals regard electoral integrity.
- Journalists should know that coverage focusing exclusively on the threats to elections has negative effects on the public, whereas reporting that features both threats and efforts to defend elections leads to less negative effects.
- Election administrators and advocates should be mindful that, when speaking to the press, quotable soundbites on election problems can decrease trust, whereas soundbites that feature problems *and* solutions can inform readers without having negative consequences.
- Social media users, such as those on Twitter, should not exclusively address threats to casting a ballot. They should also provide steps that people can take to protect their votes, including confirming registration, requesting a provisional ballot when denied the opportunity to vote, and reminding people what types of information to take to the polls.
- All advocates are encouraged to spell out the power and potential of voters rather than to treat citizens as pawns of surveys and strategists. Equipping people with agency and giving them a role to play in the campaign narrative has multiple benefits, the most important of which is to make voters the principal figures in the story of American democracy.

In sum, then, how we talk about voting matters. How we talk about voters matters as well. In a cynical world, it is easy to say that voting doesn't matter and that voters are unimportant. It is also your God-given right to talk that way. So will you?

Note

1. See https://moody.utexas.edu/centers/strauss/electorally-speaking-project.

Bibliography

Albertson, B., Haenshen, K., Jennings, J., Cutbirth, J., & Jarvis, S. (2019, January). *First do no harm: How reporters can cover threats to American elections without negatively impacting voters*. Paper presented to the Southern Political Science Association, Austin, TX.

Bartels, L. (2001). An agenda for voting research. In E. Katz & Y. Warshel (Eds.), *Election studies: What's their use?* (pp. 59–81). Boulder, CO: Westview.

Cialdini, R. B., Demaine, L. J., Sagarin, B. J., Barrett, D. W., Rhoads, K., & Winter, P. L. (2006). Managing social norms for persuasive impact. *Social Influence*, *1*(1), 3–15.

Haenschen, K., Albertson, B., & Jarvis, S. (2019, January). *Inviting a backlash: Testing the effect of boomerang messages on efficacy, interest, and trust*. Paper presented to the Southern Political Science Association, Austin, TX.

Hart, R. P., & Burks, D. M. (1972). Rhetorical sensitivity and social interaction. *Speech Monographs, 39*, 75–91.

Iyengar, S. (1996). Framing responsibility for political issues. *ANNALS of the American Academy of Political and Social Science, 546*(1), 59–70.

Jarvis, S. E. (2005). *The talk of the party: Political labels, symbolic capital, & American life*. Lanham, MD: Rowman & Littlefield.

Jarvis, S. E., & Han, S. (2018). *Votes that count and voters who don't: How journalists sideline electoral participation (without even realizing it)*. State College, PA: Penn State Press.

Key, V. O. (1966). *The responsible electorate*. Cambridge, MA: Harvard University Press.

Keyssar, A. (2009). *The right to vote: The contested history of democracy in the United States* (Revised ed.). New York: Basic Books.

McIntyre, K., & Gyldensted, C. (2017). Constructive journalism: Applying positive psychology techniques to news production. *The Journal of Media Innovation, 4*(2), 20–34.

Park-Ozee, D., & Jarvis, S. E. (2020). What does "rigged" mean? Partisan and shared perceptions of threats to elections. *American Behavioral Scientist*. doi: 10.1177/0002764220979777

Pinker, S. (2015). *The sense of style: The thinking person's guide to writing in the 21st century*. New York: Penguin Books.

Pomper, G. (1968). *Elections in America*. New Brunswick, NJ: Rutgers University Press.

Zarefsky, D. (2004). Presidential rhetoric and the power of definition. *Presidential Studies Quarterly, 34*(3), 607–619.

22 Vote When Voting Really Counts

John C. Tedesco

Nearly 160 million eligible voters participated in the 2020 US presidential election. Data from the U.S. Election Project at the University of Florida estimates that voter turnout represented about 66.7 percent of the voting-eligible population, which is the highest turnout rate for a US presidential election in more than a century (McDonald, n.d.). Whether motivated by the coronavirus public health pandemic, by the Black Lives Matter movement and social protests about racial injustice, by a polarizing president impeached by the House of Representatives, or by the affordances brought about by voting changes that turned Election Day into an election season in many states, more voters participated in the US presidential election than ever before.

Due to the coronavirus public health pandemic and the risk it posed to poll workers and voters, many states adjusted voting procedures in an effort to foster a safe election. Several states expanded early-voting opportunities, while other states allowed same-day voter registration, removed requirements for in-person absentee ballot requests, eliminated requirements for voters to demonstrate voting-related hardships, or extended the number of days after Election Day for acceptance of postmarked mail-in ballots. Republicans, generally not in favor of the voting extensions or procedural changes, alleged that some of the changes made to voting measures invited voter fraud. Democrats, buoyed by examples of fair elections in states like Washington that have for years distributed vote-by-mail ballots to all registered voters without significant fraud, argued that Republicans were focused on suppressing votes, particularly from racial and ethnic minorities. President Donald Trump and other Republicans, despite losing more than 80 lawsuits contesting vote counting, election procedural changes, or the vote certification process, asserted that Trump won the election and alleged that Democratic challenger and former Vice President Joe Biden and his cohorts "stole" the election.

While important, these are not the sorts of voting problems addressed in this chapter. Instead, I discuss a problem closer to home: Too many American voters do not vote when their vote counts the most – during local elections. Naturally, voting matters at all levels of government, although it stands to reason why conservative voters in New York or California remain unconvinced about the importance of their vote, since those states have not supported Republican presidential candidates since Ronald Reagan in 1984 and George H. W. Bush in 1988, respectively. It is also understandable why liberal voters in Oklahoma or Wyoming are dismayed, since neither Wyoming nor Oklahoma has voted for a Democrat in a presidential election since supporting President Lyndon Johnson in 1964.

But even in these partisan strongholds, turnout matters in down-ballot races. After all, New York had a Republican governor as recently as 2006 and California as recently as 2011, while Wyoming and Oklahoma each had Democrat governors from 2003 to 2011. When presidential election outcomes in a state appear predictable or when polls show seemingly insurmountable gaps between candidates (as we see in these examples), it stands to reason why some voters become discouraged. While many citizens consider voting a civic duty, others weigh the costs and benefits of voting (Downs, 1957), coolly calculating whether their vote will make a mathematical difference (Riker & Ordeshook, 1968).

Voting is the ultimate display of civic engagement in a democracy regardless of a citizen's voting calculus. Political pundits, journalists, and scholars for decades have expressed concern for the health of the US democracy, since voting rates among the adult population lag behind those of other democratic nations in the Organisation for Economic Cooperation and Development (OECD). A Pew Research Center comparison of voting rates among adult populations of OECD nations shows that the United States ranks 26th out of the 32 nations for which data were available (DeSilver, 2018). Some of these concerns are assuaged when we consider that the US rate is actually the highest among OECD nations that do not impose compulsory voting. Further concern about the state of our democracy is alleviated when the voting-eligible rates are assessed during the past 50 years, which show no significant decline since the 1972 presidential election (McDonald & Popkin, 2001). Essentially, 50 percent to 60 percent of eligible voters participate in our quadrennial presidential elections.

On the other hand, the rate for midterm or off-year elections generally hovers around 40 percent. Midterm elections include the biennial elections for US House of Representatives and about a third of US Senate elections. Gubernatorial elections are held during a midterm election in many states and, in a rarity, during off-year elections in Virginia and New Jersey. While the lower voting rates for midterm elections are worrisome, research on municipal elections is the most distressing of all. Turnout across 57 city elections showed an average 34 percent turnout rate (Wood, 2002), while voting across 38 mayoral elections saw only 27 percent of the local population showing up to vote (Caren, 2007). To make matters worse, turnout averages declined from about 25 percent in

1999 to 21 percent in 2011 across 340 mayoral elections in the 144 largest US cities (Holbrook & Weinschenk, 2014). Dallas, one of the nation's 10 largest cities, is widely referenced when poor turnout examples are discussed because of the paltry 5 percent turnout rate found in that city's 1999 mayoral election. All of this is quite ironic, because a citizen's vote makes much less difference in a presidential election than it does in local or municipal races. When voters vote locally, their votes contain enormous power.

At the presidential campaign level, a campaign can last as long as two years and cost candidates and parties upward of $1 billion. Presidential campaigns garner a large amount of media attention, and candidates use sophisticated techniques and message strategies to target voters, and as a result, citizens have a hard time avoiding campaign communication. In contrast, local elections, which may include races for school board candidates, judges, state legislators, sheriffs, or mayors, garner little attention from the media even though local elected officials directly impact citizens' daily lives. School board members, for example, allocate school funding, influence programming and planning for students and teachers, and set policies regarding student behavior in areas like bullying and dress codes.

As witnessed during the COVID-19 public health pandemic in 2020, mayors are also important. They can impact businesses and consumers via mandates about wearing face masks, through restrictions on openings and closures, or by setting service capacity limits for stores, restaurants, and gyms. Additionally, local judges can deliver strict or lenient sentences, and the county treasurer can affect local taxation rates. Despite this influence, turnout rates at the local level remain depressingly low. Why do citizens fail to vote when their votes count so much?

Researchers acknowledge that local election turnout rates are problematic, but "few studies have even begun to suggest ways in which the problem might be alleviated" (Hajnal & Lewis, 2003, p. 646). One explanation for low turnout is the simplest – citizens are perfectly satisfied with their local officials. Studies on community satisfaction (Parker et al., 2018, May 22) typically find that most Americans are fairly pleased with how their communities are governed. Low turnout at the local level, then, might be good news indeed, with residents feeling little need to shake things up.

Before celebrating, however, we must note that structural considerations also play a role, with election cycles affecting those who want to participate but who cannot. In many communities, for example, elections for school board members, county clerks, sheriffs, comptrollers, judges, state legislators, and mayors do not coincide with quadrennial or biennial elections (which typically occur on Election Day in November). As a result, even the most engaged citizen might become burdened by the calendar, with local elections in May, primary elections for state or federal offices in June, general elections in November, and special elections in January. Too, it is often the case that local campaigns will be visited by little media attention, thereby depriving citizens of information about the candidates and the issues. During such times, *voters themselves* (or their neighborhood groups) must do all the work needed to locate, analyze, and process the needed data. Information costs, that is, can be costly indeed.

Additionally, in many municipalities, mayoral elections have been replaced by council manager or city manager styles of leadership. In these models, in which promotions instead of elections determine leadership, the importance of elections is diminished further as is the likelihood of voter participation below the mayoral level. The result: Low turnout suggests that the "voice of the people in municipal elections is likely to be severely distorted" (Hajnal & Lewis, 2003, p. 646). When fewer citizens vote, organized special interests take over, potentially affecting the texture of local politics quite dramatically.

While the structural barriers to voting can be significant, the Knight Foundation (2015) asserts that the biggest obstacles to local voting are information based. A survey of millennials, for example, showed that insufficient information about candidates, lack of knowledge about community issues, and insufficient news coverage had the greatest impact on their likely involvement. The Knight Foundation's findings are especially important when they are coupled with the fact that local newspapers have struggled mightily during the last 15 years. Data from PEW reveals that newspapers have been hit hard by loss of ad revenue and decreased circulation and have lost about half of their employees since 2008 (Grieco, 2020). A comprehensive report on the newspaper industry reveals that more than 2,000 newspapers have folded, leaving hundreds of counties in the United States without a credible source of information on important community issues (Abernathy, 2020).

Loss of local political news coverage means that citizens at all levels are less likely to vote (Hayes & Lawless, 2015). In fact, these scholars assert that the "media environment has an important, independent effect on citizen engagement," meaning that when local political coverage declines, knowledge and participation go with it (Hayes & Lawless, 2015, p. 455). These data are especially important when we realize that as much as 98 percent of local political news comes to consumers from their local newspapers (Hindman, 2011).

Given the importance of local voting but also the barriers with which it must contend, how can the problem be solved? Here, I focus specifically on civics education, hyperlocal news, nonprofit news, and structural changes to voting laws.

Civics Education

A Brookings Institution Policy 2020 report called for increased civics education in 21st-century schools. Citing declining civic engagement and low levels of public trust in government as especially troubling, along with political scandals and polarizing news reports, Brookings called for incorporating social values into the school civics curriculum. Incorporating recommendations from CivXNow, a bipartisan coalition of researchers and academic institutions, Brookings urged increasing civic knowledge and skills, civic values and dispositions, and civics behaviors (Winthrop, 2020). These three pillars highlight governmental processes and constitutional rights, civil discourse and free speech, increased interaction among people with differing viewpoints, and building a greater sense of civic agency and voting efficacy. They also urge schools to model civic values through experiential pedagogy or service-learning projects in local communities, places where students would be able to observe democratic processes directly. Civics education at the community sphere, where issues are typically not as complex as they are at the federal level, enables young people "to develop the dispositions needed to actively engage in civic life and maintain the norms by which Americans debate and decide their differences" (Winthrop, 2020, p. 4).

Hyperlocal News

Hyperlocal news is generated by "geographically-based, community-oriented, original-news-reporting organizations indigenous to the web and intended to fill perceived gaps in coverage of an issue or region and to promote civic engagement" (Metzgar et al., 2011). Following the collapse of many local newspapers, AOL launched its Patch service aimed at filling the news void for cities and towns. Presently, the news template used by Patch serves more than 1,200 hyperlocal websites. After some challenging years getting a following and because of layoffs of their own, Patch now reaches upward of 20 million citizens and employs more than 100 full-time journalists. Many independent hyperlocal news sites now compete with Patch. Hyperlocal online news sites exist in a range of formats but typically generate a mix of original community news, blogs, and user-generated content aimed at fostering interaction between community members.

Content for hyperlocal sites typically is populated with news from volunteer or "citizen" journalists or through partnerships with journalism schools, but some larger or more successful hyperlocal sites have raised resources to hire reporting and editorial staff. In a comprehensive report of more than 40 such hyperlocal community news startups, research acknowledges that these sites have "filled gaps in news coverage, informed voters and increased voter turnout, spun into new projects, trained citizens to be journalists, mentored other news startups, produced award winning faculty research, upended journalism school curricula – and garnered begrudging respect from local officials" (Schaffer, 2010, p. 3). Although hyperlocal news sites rarely replace local news, they can supply information that would have been otherwise unavailable. Most hyperlocal news sites are sustained through a mix of revenue streams, including paid memberships, advertising, grants, sponsorships, and crowd-funded stories. Some of the most successful hyperlocal news sites, like *Voice of San Diego* and *The Austin Bulldog*, are nonprofit organizations. In many cases, voluntary content providers cover town council meetings, municipal courts, police and fire departments, traffic, and community improvements, along with local arts, entertainment, and sporting events. Although not an equivalent to legacy newspapers, hyperlocal news sites can fill the information gap in communities where newspapers have folded.

Nonprofit News

The Institute for Nonprofit News (INN) currently has about 250 member news outlets in a nonpartisan, public service model. According to the values of the INN, "nonpartisan newsrooms have a unique role in journalism because they are created as public trusts, with a mission to serve communities' information needs and benefit the public rather than generate private wealth. They seek to convey the truth, build community ties, inspire and inform people so they can make decisions in their own lives and in civic life" (INN, n.d., para 5). Since nonprofit news organizations are generally free from influence by corporate interests and funders, special interests, or government, they foster public trust. Additionally, community foundations can play an important role in creating funding partnerships for local journalism and news as well. Since community foundations aim to enrich the lives of members of the community in which they operate, partnerships to support journalism help ensure that local news has investigative journalists who (1) can hold elected officials accountable by ensuring that someone is present at meetings of town council, planning commissions, and zoning boards or who (2) can ask questions of police, fire, or public-works officials in person-to-person interviews, getting them on record and thereby providing important information for the local electorate. Soliciting financial help from private foundations, which often prioritize social justice, the arts, community health, or economic development, can be a challenge for news organizations. However, projects like New Voices from the Knight Foundation and the Institute for Nonprofit News provide recommendations, insight, and social support for communities while also meeting citizens' information needs.

Structural Change

Structural changes for increasing local voting can appear to benefit one political party more than another, which might explain why several states currently purge voters from their registration rolls during periods of non-voting. An alternative approach is to offer portable registration, letting voters remain on voting rolls when they move and automatically transferring their registration to their new residence. After all, the public health pandemic of 2020 taught Americans that multiple pathways are needed to make voting more accessible. Voting by mail, advance in-person voting, and eliminating evidence of hardship requirements for absentee ballots – all of these strategies can remove barriers to voting even while proving that they are safe and fair ways of ensuring robust turnout at the local level.

Conclusion

Two things seem clear: Democracy is enriched when voters have access to trusted sources of information and when obstacles to their electoral participation are minimized. That is no less true at the local level. The changes recommended here – renewed civics education, hyperlocal news, nonprofit news, and structural changes to voting access – can help ensure that democracy continues to be overseen by its most trustworthy protectors – those who live next door to us.

Bibliography

Abernathy, P. M. (2020). *News deserts and ghost newspapers: Will local news survive?* Center for Innovation and Sustainability in Local Media. Chapel Hill, NC: University of North Carolina Press. www.usnewsdeserts.com/wp-content/uploads/2020/06/2020_News_Deserts_and_Ghost_Newspapers.pdf

Caren, N. (2007). Big city, Big turnout? Electoral participation in American cities. *Journal of Urban Affairs, 1,* 31–46.

DeSilver, D. (2018, May 21). U.S. trails most developed countries in voter turnout. *Pew Research Center.* www.pewresearch.org/fact-tank/2018/05/21/u-s-voter-turnout-trails-most-developed-countries/ (accessed August 16, 2020).

Downs, A. (1957). *An economic theory of democracy.* New York: Harper & Row.

Grieco, E. (2020, April 28). Ten charts about America's newsroom. *Pew Research Center.* www.pewresearch.org/fact-tank/2020/04/28/10-charts-about-americas-newsrooms/

Hajnal, Z., & Lewis, P. G. (2003). Municipal institutions and voter turnout in local elections. *Urban Affairs Review, 38*(5), 645–668.

Hayes, D., & Lawless, J. L. (2015). As local news goes, so goes citizen engagement: Media, knowledge, and participation in US House elections. *Journal of Politics, 77*(2), 447–462.

Hindman, M. (2011). *Less of the same: The lack of local news on the Internet.* Washington, DC: Federal Communications Commission. https://docs.fcc.gov/public/attachments/DOC-307476A1.pdf

Holbrook, T. M., & Weinschenk, A. C. (2014). Campaigns, mobilization, and turnout in mayoral elections. *Political Research Quarterly, 67*(1), 42–55.

Institute for Nonprofit News. (n.d.). *Institute for nonprofit news* [About INN: Mission]. https://inn.org/about/

Knight Foundation. (2015). *Why millennials don't vote for mayor.* https://knightfoundation.org/reports/why-millennials-dont-vote-mayor/

McDonald, M. P. (n.d.). *National general election VEP turnout rates, 1789-present.* United States Election Project. http://electproject.org/national-1789-present

McDonald, M. P., & Popkin, S. L. (2001). The myth of the vanishing voter. *The American Political Science Review, 95*(4), 963–974.

Metzgar, E., Kurpius, D. D., & Rowley, K. M. (2011). Defining hyperlocal media: Proposing a framework for discussion. *New Media & Society, 13*(5), 772–787.

Oliver, J. E., & Ha, S. E. (2007). Vote choice in suburban elections. *American Political Science Review, 101*(3), 393–408.

Parker, K., Horowitz, J. M., Brown, A. Fry, R., Cohn, D., & Igielnik, R. (2018, May 22). Americans' satisfaction with an attachment to their communities. *Pew Research Center, Social & Demographic Trends.* https://pewsocialtrends.org/2018/05/22/americans-satisfaction-with-and-attachment-to-their-communities

Riker, W., & Ordeshook, P. (1968). A theory of the calculus of voting. *American Political Science Review, 62*(1), 25–42.

Schaffer, J. (2010). New voices: What works: Lessons from funding five years of community news startups. *J-Lab.* www.j-lab.org/wp-content/pdfs/new-voices-report.pdf

Winthrop, R. (2020). The need for civic education in 21st-century schools. *The Brookings Institution Policy 2020.* www.brookings.edu/policy2020/bigideas/the-need-for-civic-education-in-21st-century-schools/

Wood, C. (2002). Voter turnout in city elections. *Urban Affairs Review, 38,* 209–231.

23 Make Ads Safe for Democracy

Glenn W. Richardson Jr.

Political advertising lies at the vortex of several noxious currents that have riven American democracy: polarized division, pervasive disinformation, frightening levels of data-mongering, and searing inequality. Efforts to fix such things run aground almost instantly in the face of constitutional impediments or simple lethargy on everyone's parts. So if we cannot make political advertising safe for democracy, perhaps we can make democracy safe for political advertising. This essay explores ways of offsetting political advertising's worst qualities – ads untethered to fact or reality, the incessant monitoring of voters' innermost selves, and real-time attempts to divide them against their neighbors. Ads like these are converting economic power into political power, reinforcing profound inequities that already threaten to weaken democratic legitimacy. Something must be done.

By 2020, certain problems with political advertising were widely recognized and had generated responses from giant tech platforms, news organizations, and fact-checkers, as well as legislators at the state and federal levels. At the same time, the nature of campaign communication was metastasizing through the body politic in ever-more-novel ways. Once, political advertising could be defined as paid communication in a handful of media formats: TV, radio, print, public signage. Today, campaign communication presents across a multitude of platforms, including social·media, content streaming, direct-to-phone texts, and even in the virtual space of video games. And when the coin of the digital realm is attention based and not necessarily monetary, defining political advertising in terms of purchase seems inadequate, if not archaic and ineffective. So where to begin our political triage? What are the most worrisome threats to democracy? Let us consider each in turn.

Disinformation

The 2016 presidential campaign heightened awareness of the spread of misinformation. In 2016, Russian operatives bought ads and used fake accounts to generate misinformation, relying on bots and unwitting users to spread it. But by 2020, Russia turned to the American people themselves to do their work, in part because tech platforms (and the security community) had by that time become more adept at disabling foreign accounts. Although federal law now bans foreign election interference, it does not supervise what sort of information Facebookers share with their friends or what naïve Americans choose to retweet.

Disinformation may pose the most vexing threat to democracy because it is so difficult to prevent. The Constitution protects free speech, and according to the Supreme Court, this includes false political speech. (False commercial speech does not enjoy this protection.) We are compelled, then, as Justice Oliver Wendell Holmes Jr. once noted, to seek salvation from disinformation via the marketplace of ideas. Yet the idea market may be subject to some of the same failures plaguing markets generally – underinvestment in infrastructure, education, and basic research and development. These market failures may be even more problematic as campaign communication continues to shift to for-profit platforms.

Surveillance Campaigning

Democracy's information wars have taken a turn toward the personal, both in the data collected about citizens and in the messages aimed at them. Advertisers now possess powerful tools for behavioral modification. Advertising companies like Google and Facebook know where we are, with whom we interact, what we're thinking about, and what keeps us up at night. Extreme microtargeting can undermine democratic accountability, serving to manufacture the consent of the governed. Further consequences of the commodification of personal data are somewhat less evident. If nothing else, our political parties have become surveillance machines that, after the election, can blend into the State itself. Data, coupled with AI-driven algorithms, have, for example, already driven voter-suppression efforts. Those tactics (such as the 2016 effort to tamp down Black turnout) emphasized political or cultural arguments, but it may not be far-fetched to imagine more personal data being utilized as well, including health, court, and financial records.

Polarized Division

Division, too, is inherent in democracy. Despite the national motto (*E pluribus unum*, "from many, one"), sharp political arguments have defined the nation since the founding. Indeed, in the case of the Civil War, those arguments turned deadly and existential. Thus, one must not discount the possibility of grave damage being done via our divisive politics. Some scholars even suggest that *ideological polarization* – sharp differences people harbor on policy issues – has remained fairly constant over time while *affective polarization* (personal disdain for people on the other side) has grown exponentially. While the evidence is inconclusive as to social media's role in all of this, algorithms driven by engagement patterns and intense passion are reasonable suspects. When done at scale, these emotional effects can become pronounced. By 2018, Facebook claimed to have recalibrated its News Feed and reduced clickbait in an effort to diffuse polarization, but the 2020 presidential campaign surely proved that much more work needed to be done.[1]

Division, of course, is the very purpose of elections – deciding which side of the argument should govern us. Negative ads, as unpleasant as they may be, are integral to democratic discourse. Negative information is easier to recall, more capable of altering existing impressions, and (sadly) carries more credibility than positive information. That candidates and parties have chosen to frame their attacks in stark – often apocalyptic – terms, woven within the audiovisual fabric of popular culture, makes these appeals all the more powerful. With the cardinal principle of First Amendment jurisprudence being content neutrality, even vicious attacks cannot be banned and, as a result, are likely here to stay.

In short, campaign communication, both that driven by paid political advertising and its more organic cousins, is flooding the information space as never before with divisive misinformation, oppositional attacks, and partisan rancor, thereby undermining both comity and an informed citizenry. This has been true throughout American history. As it was, so shall it be.

Escalating Inequality

The sheer cost of modern campaigning connects to another vector of dismay – stark and rising inequality. Those with money can avail themselves of the latest technologies to protect their interests at the ballot box, although some campaigns have been able to raise substantial contributions through small donations. As political scientist Elmer Eric Schattschneider once wrote, "the flaw with the pluralist heavenly chorus is that it sings with an upper-class accent" (1960). Further, the influence of mega-donors is even being manifested at the local level, a negative corollary to James Madison's celebration of the virtues of an "extended republic." The perception that American elections and politicians are now being bought and sold is a troubling one, and political advertising lies at its very center.

For both Aristotle and Thomas Jefferson, the stability of the polity would be threatened by any sort of yawning inequality, an outcome that would sever the common class interest that facilitates harmonious political life. Today's economic inequalities have fueled cynicism and apathy, including the notion that leaders are selected on auction rather than by election. The result: angry politics across the ideological spectrum. With capital-intensive campaigning being fueled by big-data analytics and driven by big-dollar messaging, the ability of those with resources to fund political efforts creates a feedback loop wherein inequality begets inequality. The ailments of electoral democracy might be more sufferable if they did not so reinforce what observers for thousands of years have seen as the most central social and political schism: rich and poor.

To Madison's (2012) observation in *Federalist No. 51*, "but what is government itself but the greatest of all reflections on human nature," we might add, "but what is political advertising but the greatest of all reflections on politics." Like Madison, we may conclude that no remedy to alleviate the cause of the disease now exists and that we must therefore treat its effects. Fortunately, a myriad of reform proposals offers some promise of refreshing our politics.

Building a Better Ad Watch

Because we cannot control misinformation or its spread, inoculating voters and the body politic from its worst contagion is warranted. It is here, perhaps, that extant efforts are most encouraging. We are now decades into the existence of fact-checking organizations, built upon the pioneering work of Kathleen Hall Jamieson and a team of researchers at the Annenberg School of Communication at the University of Pennsylvania (Jamieson, 1992). In addition, Factcheck.org, PolitiFact, Snopes.com, and many news organizations now carefully check the factual claims made in campaign ads, speeches, and other forms of communication.

Fact-checking, unfortunately, is not without its limits. It can, for example, be a challenge to separate micromisstatements of truth from the overall validity of a message, and the journalistic penchant for mere "balance" can lead to false equivalency. Moreover, while fact-checkers have done much to scrutinize the textual claims made in ads, the same cannot be said of the implicit arguments constructed through audiovisual means. Soundtracks and special effects, distortions, and manipulations of images (even the use of super-slow-motion) can be critical parts of campaign communication and can often elude the interrogative lens of the ad watchers.

As a new generation of digital natives rises, it is possible that a more multifaceted approach to ad watching and fact-checking may take hold, using audiovisual/editorial tools to deconstruct the audiovisual claims being made (Richardson, 2012). So, for example, when ads mangle a chronological sequence of events, editing tools can now unmangle them and then re-present them in proper time order. Where audiovisual elements combine to form resonant narratives grounded in popular culture, counterediting can unpack and reveal unspoken linkages. Where visual effects distort, editing can retort.

Sharing the results of such analyses depends, to some degree, on the market for journalism, a market that has been roiled by disruption, leaving local journalism (especially) in tatters and forcing even the most powerful legacy media into a clickbait mentality when presenting the news. As suggested in this book (e.g., Chapters 16, 25, and 27), helping journalism may take a number of forms – for example, building civic networks and instituting public funding – to give news organizations the help they need to share ad watchers' findings.

Reduce the Electoral Incentives for Scorched-Earth Campaigns

Little, if anything, can be done legally to prevent candidates from smearing one another and spreading far and wide the very worst allegations and insinuations. Perhaps reframing the electoral space can accomplish what would otherwise be impossible. In particular, ranked-choice voting might at least marginally attenuate divisive appeals. With ranked-choice voting, candidates would have to seriously contemplate whether heated attacks against their opponent could deprive them of second- and third-choice votes that might prove decisive. Research has suggested that in jurisdictions with ranked-choice voting, campaign tone is less negative (see, for example, John & Douglas, 2017; Donovan et al., 2016), suggesting that "turning people on" is better choice in ranked-choice systems than is "turning people off."

Strengthen Political Parties

It might seem paradoxical to strengthen the very organizations that are so widely reviled as despoilers of democracy, but political parties are in fact democracy's sine qua non. Owing to the US Constitution's structure of single-member plurality district elections, American parties are broad based and coalitional. The weakening of parties and the rise of candidate-centered campaigns can foster negativity, as individual candidates find it easier to pillory their opponents and lack the broad and enduring responsibility of parties. While negative partisanship (opposition to the other side rather than support for one's own party) is prominent and may be rising, campaign attacks on a party carry risks that opponents may wish to avoid. Stronger parties might also strengthen the linkages between citizens and government and help political machines become more responsive and inclusive. Parties are imperfect vehicles, of course, having sustained and supported racism in the past. On the other hand, political parties also became the agents for dismantling segregation, so there are indeed two sides to the party coin.

Public Education to Inoculate Citizens

Absent some form of censorship, political trash talk will persist. Providing citizens with the intellectual and informational tools to better tame the tide of misinformation seems wholly appropriate. Informational and argumentative literacy should become part of school curricula at all levels. Public service announcements emanating from political literacy campaigns, supplemented by social media posts and memes, could warn against the tropes of misdirection. Thirty-second video segments could also be used to deconstruct the common types of political misdirection. No one of these will suddenly inoculate the citizenry, but together, they might change the calculations of political dissemblers and peddlers of disinformation. Even more importantly, they might provide citizens with the resilience needed to withstand the onslaught of indecorous political speech.

Public-Service Campaigns to Cajole Candidates

Changing a culture does not come quickly, but occasionally, it comes. Over the past half-century, public service campaign haves changed public attitudes about littering, drinking and driving, and social tolerance, among other noble goals. Might a similar concerted effort *directed at candidates themselves* nudge them away from plying the worst of their trade? And here might be the theme song: "Friends don't let friends destroy democracy!"

Strengthen Campaign Disclosure Requirements

A variety of recently passed laws and legislative proposals at both the federal and state levels have sought to enhance accountability through campaign disclosure requirements. Some (such as Maryland's 2018 Online Electioneering and Transparency Act) were aimed at identifying the organizations and individuals financing campaign communications, and others (such as Washington's 2018 DISCLOSE Act) include provisions on targeting and digital privacy. The bipartisan Honest Ads Act, first introduced in the 115th Congress and reintroduced in 2019 by Senators Amy Klobuchar, Lindsey Graham, and Mark Warner, would apply the same disclosure requirements to internet and social media ads that apply to radio, TV, and print ads. The bill would also help publicize key information about political ads, including how they are targeted and how money is being spent.

The reforms suggested here might marginally improve the caliber of political advertising. It is altogether possible, however, that making democracy safe for political advertising and dealing with the impact of Big Money will need institutional – and legal – support, a topic to which we now turn.

Amend the Communications Decency Act (CDA)

Major-party presidential candidates of both parties have supported repealing section 230 of the 1996 Communications Decency Act, sentiments that have attracted broader bipartisan support as well. The section shields technology platforms from the kind of liability that legacy media companies face for content posted on their sites by users. Opponents of repeal argue that doing so would limit freedom of expression, but that kind of freedom, like all constitutional rights, is not unbridled. It is hard to justify holding legacy media to one standard and tech giants to another. The costs to individuals and democracy from damaging and inflammatory content continue to mount. It is not inconceivable that compromise language could address the concerns of defenders of tech platforms while limiting the spread of harmful communication.

Break Up Big Tech

Today's tech behemoths have achieved market concentration beyond that which prompted the first wave of antitrust legislation during the Progressive era. Then and now, the economic clout of corporate titans led to unbridled political power as well. Moreover, their dominance is grounded in the data-driven modification of human behavior, constituting what Shoshana Zuboff (2019) has described as "a coup from above; an overthrow of the people's sovereignty." For Zuboff, "surveillance capitalism" claims "human experience as the free raw material for hidden commercial practices of extraction, prediction, and sales" (2019, p. vii). Surveillance capitalism has produced searing inequity and concentration of wealth and power, creating a startling challenge to democracy as traditionally conceived. Without reform, Big Tech will continue to hoover-up our most intimate personal experiences, sell them for profit, and foster ever-more-advanced forms of behavior modification wholly inconsistent with democratic self-determination. In such an unregulated world, the potential for political advertising to undermine liberal democracy is palpable and destabilizing.

Progressive Taxation for the 21st Century

We can have complete freedom of speech, and we can have the unfettered accumulation of great wealth, but in the capital-intensive world of modern politics, we cannot have both and expect democracy to emerge unscathed. Sharply progressive taxation aimed at curbing the largest of private fortunes would provide the public funding needed to secure the public infrastructure of democracy, including broad public education, while reducing the capacity of a handful of financial elites to dominate the democratic process.

Conclusion

Social media have been celebrated for their democratizing potential. That potential is real and realizable. Alexandria Ocasio-Cortez started her campaign for Congress with 300 Twitter followers. Today, she has a followership of 9.4 million, much of which has been organically driven. Ocasio-Cortez may be an outlier, but she also shows what can happen when people share information with one another. The alternative to such grassroots efforts is corporate algorithms optimized for "engagement," which often devolves into feeding users more and more extreme versions of content that had previously galvanized their attention. Facebook and Alphabet (including Google and You Tube) dominate online advertising, and they embrace a top-down model of behavioral modification. The basic infrastructure of Twitter, by contrast, offers a model of organic, user-driven sharing that might provide the infrastructure for a truly democratic environment in the 21st century.

Political advertising encapsulates democratic politics in all its peril and promise. Technological change may have helped drive concentration not only of wealth but of political power too. For democracy to prevail, it may be necessary to counter the sweep of surveillance campaigning in ways large and small, helping ensure that Abraham Lincoln's government of the people, by the people, and for the people shall not perish from the earth.

Note

1. https://about.fb.com/news/2020/05/investments-to-fight-polarization/

Bibliography

Donovan, T., Tolbert, C., & Gracey, K. (2016, June). Campaign civility under preferential and plurality voting. *Electoral Studies*, *42*, 157–163.
Jamieson, K. H. (1992). *Dirty politics: Deception, distraction, and democracy*. New York: Oxford University Press.
John, S., & Douglas, A. (2017, Spring). Candidate civility and voter engagement in seven cities with ranked choice voting. *National Civic Review*, *106*(1), 25–29.
Richardson, G. W., Jr. (2012). Ad Watch 3.0: Developing audiovisual and narrative techniques for engaging the audiovisual content of political advertising. *Poroi*, *8*, 1. https://doi.org/10.13008/2151-2957.1089
Schattschneider, E. E. (1960/1975). *The Semi-Sovereign people: A realist's view of democracy in America*. Boston: Wadsworth.
Zuboff, S. (2019). *The age of surveillance capitalism: The fight for a human future at the new frontier of power*. New York: Public Affairs.

24 Let's Outperform Super PACs

Robert Klotz

Writing in 81 A.D., Tacitus described the importance of information novelty to an effective communicator: "He saw that the public ear was formed to a new matter; and eloquence, he knew was to find new approaches to the heart" (Murphy, 1830, p. 19). Tacitus wasn't thinking of super PACs and probably would be disappointed with modern political campaigns. Indeed, few aspects of the modern political campaign are as stale as the negative 30-second television advertisement. In this chapter, I examine the evolving landscape of video during political campaigns, with particular attention to the visibility of super PACs. Systematic evidence from multiple campaigns suggests that the social media landscape is less hospitable to super PACs than the television landscape and that a more diverse online video market can improve campaign discourse.

The Problem

One fundamental problem for American politics in the media age is the quality of video communication, with the most visible manifestation being the 30-second television ad, which is hardly the ideal length of time needed to address the issues facing the nation. It is, however, ample time to denigrate somebody, and so negative ads proliferate in competitive campaigns. In presidential elections, for example, the percentage of negative ads increased from about 10 percent in 1960 to more than 50 percent in 2012 and 2016. The negativity of candidates' ads is far exceeded by those produced by special-interest groups, which are routinely 90 percent negative or higher (Iyengar, 2019). While there is nothing inherently wrong with negative ads – which can be informative and which are often needed to beat advantaged incumbents – the 30-second format is not well suited to fostering rich campaign dialogue. In practice, the coarseness of negative political ads stands apart from other advertising. *Advertising Age* columnist Bob Garfield summarizes: "By and large, advertising is essentially truthful, except political advertising which . . . is just the artful assembling of nominal facts into hideous, outrageous lies" ("Persuaders," 2004).

DOI: 10.4324/9781003212515-30

Negativity of this sort has its consequences, one of which is increased polarization. In landmark experimental research, for example, Stephen Ansolabehere and Shanto Iyengar (1995) demonstrated that negative ads can both increase political alienation and reduce voter turnout. Since the time of their research, the problem has become worse. And the greatest danger is this: Negative ads are increasingly being produced by people who cannot be held accountable for their communications.

That is possible because money, not accountability, is the driving force behind television content, whose media ecology is determined by the market. Federal campaign law, for example, requires television stations to provide the same opportunity to candidates to buy advertising time at the station's lowest rate. Beyond that, television stations sell time at market rates to those who can afford to buy it. Candidates and political parties are limited in how much they can raise from individual donors and often face scarce resources. On the other hand, some outside interest groups, particularly super PACs funded by unaccountable and wealthy individuals, face few resource constraints. This enables super PACs to play a substantial role in the video landscape of political campaigns, and in some local races, super PACs may be the only actors with any substantial resources.

Under the law, little can be done to prevent super PACs from independently spending as much as they want on political ads as long as television stations sell them the requested time. As interpreted by the Supreme Court, campaign spending is the functional equivalent of speech. Beginning with *Buckley v. Valeo* (1976), the Supreme Court has drawn a sharp distinction between contributions to candidates, which can be regulated to prevent corruption or its appearance, and expenditures, which are protected by the First Amendment. Although the Supreme Court upheld some focused regulation of campaign spending in the aftermath of 2002 campaign finance reform legislation, a majority of the court became uncomfortable with distinctions that were harder to interpret in the internet age. Ultimately, in *Citizens United v. FEC* (2010), the Supreme Court ruled that independent expenditures, including spending by labor unions and corporations, were protected by the First Amendment and hence beyond the reach of government regulation.

In practice, much independent spending is undertaken by interest groups that depend on large donors and that do nothing other than spend independently. A small number of wealthy individuals believes that the market rate for a television spot is a small price to pay for the opportunity to share their political views with the public. Indeed, some wealthy individuals have come to view this as a charitable contribution to the political education of the polity, an eventuality that has been described by some as "ideological philanthropy." Such philanthropy is typically undertaken through the legal entity of a super PAC or 501(c)(4) social welfare organization. Studies show that 11 wealthy donors accounted for

20 percent of super PAC funding from 2010 to 2018 (Lee, 2018). While ideological philanthropists have a right to spend their money as they see fit, the overall quality of the communications they subvent is often poor.

Another way to think about the problem is to make a list of those individuals whose communication would be most helpful to you when making a well-informed decision at the ballot box. Most likely, candidates would be at the top of your list. Another top source might be the news organizations covering the candidates. Others on the list might include political parties, public officials, membership groups, compelling political commentators, union leaders, and your favorite, local political scientist. Such a list might also include your friends, faith leaders, neighbors, or celebrities. When making your list of "communication helpers," how far down the list would you have to go to find "random rich person?"

Nevertheless, a substantial part of the video communication received in political campaigns on television essentially comes from just such people. By mid-2016, for example, one study found that interest groups underwrote 49 percent of the over 280,000 ads displayed in Senate races. As a percentage of interest group ads, the study found that super PACs accounted for 47 percent of Senate group ads, 68 percent of House group ads, and 90 percent of the ads run by interest groups in the presidential race (Wesleyan Media Project, 2016). Many group ads also originated from social welfare organizations that do not have to disclose their donors, organizations that appear to be funded disproportionately by a small number of wealthy individuals. In many campaigns, then, "random rich people" are effectively shaping the campaign video landscape, despite their providing campaign information that is sometimes of minimal value.

In short, many of the political ads on television that coarsen political dialogue are produced by wealthy individuals accountable to no one. In contrast, when candidates or parties run irresponsible ads, they may face the people's wrath. Too, in the realm of social media, people who insist on issuing political diatribes can be defriended; indeed, Pew Research Center (2014) found that 26 percent of Facebook users have blocked someone because they disagree with a given political post. In the world of televised advertising, however, a world often overseen by super PAC supporters, "defriending" is not an option. Such supporters have, after all, paid real money to "accidentally expose" you to their messages. As a result, your only recourse is to ignore their ads . . . if you can do so.

Ignoring such ads becomes easier in the realm of social media, but social media present their own concerns. Public opinion polls show that while social media have their advantages, their impact on political campaigns is not altogether positive. In October 2019, a national sample of 1,000 Americans (margin of error ±3) in battleground states was asked to assess blame for political problems. One question was: "For each one, please tell me if you think this item is very, somewhat, a little, or not at all responsible for the increase in bad behavior in American politics: Social media like Facebook and Twitter?" Social media received more blame than any of the other choices, including the news media, special interests, party leaders, and then-president Donald Trump. With more than 80 percent of US voters declaring that social media are more than a little to blame for bad political behavior, polls show an amazing – and rare – bipartisan agreement. The highest blame category of "very responsible" was assigned to social media by 52 percent of Republicans, 55 percent of independents, and 52 percent of Democrats. Ironically, social media are being blamed for a great many of the country's political problems (Tarrance Group, 2019), even though these very same online tools have become increasingly central to our day-to-day lives.

Solution

Despite their inadequacies, social media, and especially YouTube, can become part of the solution for improving campaign dialogue. Social media offer the potential for better video communication for several reasons. First, the 30-second time block, which is based on the economic imperatives of television, is easily superseded in social media, with YouTube allowing varying lengths and formats. Second, in the world of YouTube, features other than money influence which videos will be seen. Those factors include (1) the quality of the video displayed (i.e., TV's negative, cookie-cutter ads would fare poorly on social media) and (2) the size of the social network supporting the content producer (i.e., while it is possible to "purchase" friends online, organic networks – networks consisting of your own friends – are much more powerful). In short, social media offer real promise for both greater diversity of political information and greater political competitiveness.

Empirical research has revealed the comparative disadvantage faced by super PACs on social media. During the 2016, 2018, and 2020 election cycles, I researched US Senate campaigns on YouTube. I chose to study the Senate as a nationally representative sample of campaigns large enough to produce meaningful statistics. I chose YouTube as the most prominent video-sharing site, a source of news for 21 percent of Americans (Shearer & Matsa, 2018) and the second-most-visited website in the world (Alexa, 2020). My research was designed to identify the most popular video associated with every general-election, major-party Senate candidate on YouTube.

Operationally, a YouTube search was conducted for the candidate's name along with that candidate's "most viewed" video posted during the last year. With 68 candidates in 2016, 71 candidates in 2018, and 70 candidates in 2020, a total of 209 videos collectively representing the most viewed video for each candidate was secured. The "producers" of the videos were identified based on their content and not on who uploaded

Table 24.1 Producers of Most-Viewed Senate Campaign Videos on YouTube

Producer	2016	2018	2020
Candidates	41	27	24
TV Stations	32	52	44
Interest Groups	16	8	17
Political Parties	0	1	0
Other	11	12	14
	100%	100%	100%
	(n = 68)	(n = 71)	(n = 70)

them. That is, if an average citizen uploaded a campaign event that had been aired on Fox News, the video producer was identified as the television station, not as the citizen-voter.

Table 24.1 shows the producer of the winning videos. As can be seen, candidates and television stations were the most common sources of the videos by a wide margin, with political parties being almost invisible. There was only a small number of videos from nontraditional political participants as well.

Interest groups, in contrast, produced an average of 14 percent of the winning videos over the three cycles. Although significant, this is lower than their relative presence on television. The interest group videos were split between super PACs and other groups. In 2016, super PACs accounted for 4 of the 11 videos. Social welfare 501(c)(4) organizations – through which wealthy individuals often funnel their support – accounted for an additional three videos in 2016. In 2018, super PACs produced 3 of the 6 winning interest group videos. In 2020, super PACs produced 11 of the 12 winning interest group videos, including five from the Lincoln Project and four from Americans for Prosperity Action.

I also found that the brief ad of less than one minute is by far the most common format of the winning videos, representing about one-third of all winning videos over the three election cycles. This more than doubled the frequency of any other format. Not surprisingly, most of the brief ads came from candidates themselves. The super PAC videos were almost all 30-second negative ads.

Despite the potential for more creativity online, then, the most prominent campaign videos on YouTube were originally shown on television. TV's most-used formats also dominated the YouTube sample. *News interviews*, for example, were often directly transferred from television to YouTube. *Event speeches* appearing on television also were repurposed, as were *candidate debates*. Similarly, *congressional proceedings* previously aired by C-SPAN showed up on YouTube, as did *comedy skits* purloined from *Saturday Night Live* or other popular shows.

But other, fresher alternatives also exist, some of which are longer video ads produced by the candidates themselves that blend biography with policy. These videos use YouTube's minimal time restraints to offer distinct alternatives to campaign communication that open up the possibility for more substantive campaign dialogue. YouTube's longer time blocks counter the short time blocks provided through television advertising, brief video social media platforms like TikTok, and, ironically, through paid advertising on YouTube itself, which did a brisk business during the 2020 election.

Videos are also being produced by citizens from across the ideological spectrum. Here, citizens behave like ersatz journalists, doing on-the-scene filming and then posting the results on You Tube along with their own running commentaries. User-friendly video-editing software is now available to those with modest technical skills, thereby returning campaigns to the grassroots level, at least in part. In short, social media offer more people greater access to the campaign by tapping their creativity, giving them a sense of control, and thus offsetting the booming voice of super PACs.

Conclusion

Since the first systematic study of Internet political communication, researchers have examined whether new technologies might facilitate genuine information novelty in politics. Are political communicators using the internet to restate a message heard elsewhere or to bring new substance to political discourse? At the moment, the answer seems to be the former. One reason is that the logistical hurdles of online communication have limited the pool of content creators for independent websites. It took the advent of user-friendly social media such as Facebook, Instagram, and YouTube to bring large masses to online content creation. As technology changed, uploading videos to the web has become accessible to the average person and candidate. All of that is wonderful, of course, but it does not mean that *novelty* has yet thrived in the world of online politics. Most of the winning online videos in Senate campaigns had been repurposed from television even though social media have neither the gatekeepers nor the institutions overseeing the 30-second TV spot. Although I found a marginal increase in the diversity of formats and producers of video content on YouTube versus television, the real possibilities of social media have not yet been tapped.

The potential exists for much greater change, however, simply because video has become such a fundamental means of communication in modern life. User-friendly software to capture and edit video is readily available. Freed as they are from the economic structures of television, voters now have the ability to take the encouragement of a Tacitus and find new ways to connect through video. The landscape of campaign video communication can get better if new voices and new techniques enter the arena.

As video communication increasingly moves from television to social media, the role of money in shaping campaign video content may well decline. Rather than leverage money to force people to watch their videos on television, super PACs will have to compete on quality, size of social network, and other factors. Unlike the "gotcha" ads currently forced on television viewers, online videos may decrease their supply. But if the impact of unrepresentative and unaccountable super PAC ads communications is to be reduced, everyday voters must step up and make videos that provide a distinct alternative. Will they rise to the occasion? That is a question for the future.

Bibliography

Alexa. (2020, October 30). *The top 500 sites on the web*. Alexa. www.alexa.com/topsites

Ansolabehere, S., & Iyengar, S. (1995). *Going negative: How political advertisements shrink and polarize the electorate*. New York: Free Press.

Buckley v. Valeo. (1976). Available in *Oyez*. www.oyez.org/cases/1975/75-436

Citizens United v. Federal Election Commission. (2010). Available in *Oyez*. www.oyez.org/cases/2008/08-205

Iyengar, S. (2019). *Media politics: A citizen's guide* (4th ed.). New York: W.W. Norton.

Lee, M. Y. H. (2018, October 27). One-fifth of all super-PAC money, from just 11 pockets. *Washington Post*, A14.

Murphy, A. (Ed.). (2011/1830). *The works of Cornelius Tacitus*. Charleston, SC: BiblioLife.

"Persuaders." (2004). *Frontline*. PBS. www.pbs.org/wgbh/frontline/film/shows/persuaders/

Pew Research Center. (2014). *Political polarization & media habits*. Washington, DC: Pew Research Center.

Shearer, E., & Matsa, K. E. (2018). *News use across social media platforms*. Washington, DC: Pew Research Center.

Tarrance Group. (2019). *Battleground 65*. Alexandria, VA: Tarrance Group.

Wesleyan Media Project. (2016). *Over 2 million political ads aired this cycle*. Middletown, CT: Wesleyan Media Project.

Part 6
Reimagine Traditional Journalism

25 Address Journalism's Crisis Boldly

Regina G. Lawrence

Theorists of democracy have long assumed a critically important role for a robust and independent press. The free flow of quality information and vigorous exchange of ideas are considered essential to support the most fundamental democratic value: the ability of the people to govern themselves. On this view, the news media become the eyes and ears of the public, providing it with facts and perspectives that allow for generally shared knowledge about current events and the policy agendas of elected representatives – in other words, a picture of the world upon which citizens can act (Lippmann, 1977). Underlying this idealized vision has been an often unarticulated expectation that the public will trust the news media enough to accept the information it provides as a legitimate starting place for public debate.

According to many scholars, the American news media have often failed to meet that ideal because of several factors, one of which is the corporate structure of most American news outlets, leading them to maximize lowest-common-denominator information or outright ignore the information needs of their communities. These problems have become more acute as the traditional media business model has been destabilized, causing dramatic levels of cutbacks, layoffs, and newspaper closures across the country (Stonbely et al., 2015; Waldman, 2011; Center for Innovation & Sustainability in Local Media, 2018), further lowering the quality of public affairs news. But as I will explore briefly in this chapter, legacy journalism's problems run deeper than its failing business model. Journalism is experiencing a profound crisis of authority that must be addressed with bold innovations.

Journalism's Contemporary Crisis in Context

The era of mass media has given way to a "hybrid" media system in which legacy journalism (the model that came of age in the mid-20th century) now competes with a variety of digital and social media for a shrinking share of public attention (Chadwick, 2017; Prior, 2007). Technological transformations over the past two decades disrupted journalism's business model and gave rise to numerous alternative channels for information and commentary, dissolving journalists' gatekeeping powers (Williams & Delli Carpini, 2011).

In this new ecosystem, information gains currency through online "credibility cascades" of likes and shares, rather than from the presumed legitimacy of news organizations (Munger, 2020). Those who do seek out the news do so through personalized "curated flows" of information shaped not just by journalists but by automated algorithms and individuals' personal social networks (Thorson & Wells, 2015). Many people avoid the news altogether, assuming that the news will "find" them if it is truly important; otherwise, they can "just Google it" when necessary (Toff & Nielsen, 2018). What is left of the traditional audience often relies on partisan news sources, thereby engaging in selective exposure (Stroud, 2011; Benkler et al., 2017). The result: greatly diminished prospects for a shared, coherent picture of the world upon which an engaged public can act.

Meanwhile, public trust in the mainstream media has been declining for decades (Lewis, 2020), part of a more general decline in public trust of institutions (Bennett & Pfetsch, 2018) but also the product of unabated criticism from conservative politicians (Jamieson & Cappella, 2010). Trust in the media took an additional downward turn during the 2016 presidential election (Brenan, 2019), stoked by a Republican candidate whose style of politics heavily depended on undermining the press's legitimacy (Meeks, 2019; Scacco & Wiemer, 2019; Vernon, 2018).

This decline in media trust coincided with the rise of disinformation widely shared through social media and other channels. The Knight Foundation recently warned, for example, that "low levels of public trust in the nation's polarized media environment have left open the possibility for dangerous false narratives to take root in all segments of society," particularly as the country faced the COVID-19 pandemic and the racial reckoning stirred by the Black Lives Matter movement (Knight Foundation, 2020). Indeed, the US may have joined the ranks of "disrupted public spheres." "While political institutions and press systems continue to operate," scholars observe, "they often face serious problems engaging or representing citizens meaningfully" (Bennett & Pfetsch, 2018, pp. 243–244). Deep political divisions amplified by selective news exposure and rampant disinformation have contributed to a rising sense that the United States has entered a "posttruth" or "postdemocracy" era (Crouch, 2004; McIntyre, 2018) in which journalists have little authoritative voice. All these forces have roiled the information ecosystem, leaving journalism's place in the world profoundly in question. What, then, is the role of journalism in this new era? Indeed, what *can* it be?

The Crisis of Authority Versus the Problem of Trust

According to journalism scholar Matt Carlson, journalists are now struggling to "position their practices as legitimate means for generating knowledge about the world and their organizations as the legitimate venues for this to occur" (Carlson, 2017, p. 76). From this perspective, journalism's crisis centers on *who* gets to create and distribute authoritative knowledge about public affairs. In contrast, practicing journalists, who are heavily invested in saving legacy journalism, are plaintively asking a different question: "Why don't they trust us anymore?" It is important to note that while journalists talk about *regaining* public trust, whole swaths of the public, particularly minority communities, have long distrusted the mainstream media (Wenzel, 2017). That said, as journalism scholar Seth Lewis recently put it, "the dilemma of public trust is the dilemma of journalism writ large: how to find some semblance of stability in an entirely unstable media moment?" (2020, p. 346).

The Challenge of (Re)Gaining Trust

Trust will be difficult to reestablish for several reasons. For one, trust in the news has become a highly partisan issue, and distrust is especially pronounced among self-identified Republicans (Brenan, 2019; Knight Foundation, 2020), a problem exacerbated by the Trump presidency (Lawrence & Moon, 2021). Add to this the increasingly important role of Fox News, conservative talk radio, and right-wing social media sites (Levendusky, 2013; Pew, 2020), and the prospects for winning back self-identified conservatives would appear dim.

Moreover, traditional defenses of journalistic authority are less authoritative today than in the past. For many journalists, the solution to the crisis is simple: "People have forgotten what we do and how well we do it. We just need to remind them." That is exactly what many newspapers around the country did in the summer of 2018 when joining a coordinated campaign of editorials denouncing Donald Trump's "fake news" and "enemy of the people" attacks, language that polls at the time showed was highly resonant for Republican voters. The editorials reminded people of the hallowed values of journalism: political independence, professional detachment, objectivity, and the importance of watchdogging the government. It is doubtful, though, that the editorials had much impact given the accumulated distrust of the media. In fact, one study concluded that the sharp language used in the editorials may have reinforced the president's claims that the media are deeply tainted and hence cannot be trusted (Lawrence & Moon, 2020).

Some Trust-Building Innovations

In the book *The Logic and Limits of Trust*, sociologist Bernard Barber (1983) examined the trust dynamics associated with an array of public institutions and concluded that trust is based on two key dimensions of institutional performance: technical competence and fiduciary responsibility. That is, the public trusts institutions that perform according to professional standards of competence and that act in the public interest. Seen through this lens, declines in media trust may signal that they do not seem to be acting professionally or that they have fallen short on ethical standards. In fact, surveys indicate that the media's trustworthiness can be mapped precisely against these two major concerns (2020 Edelman Trust Barometer, 2020).

Increasing confidence in the media means acknowledging the various dimensions of distrust. The first dimension, what Barber called *rational distrust*, occurs when the media are seen as failing to live up to professional standards. To explain such perceptions, one need only look at the growth of tabloid-style television news, particularly on cable TV, featuring the sort of opinion-laden "news" and heated discussions that many Americans find distasteful. The mainstream media's routine discounting, stereotyping, and marginalizing of non-White communities can also lower trust, as can the "second trauma" visited on cities and towns where tragedy has struck. In such instances, journalists flock to the scene, eager to "get the story," but often distort local realities and subject citizens to additional distress when so doing.

A second variant, *reputational distrust*, occurs when the public comes to believe that the media are untrustworthy through repeated exposure to that message. Ladd's (2011) research on why Americans "hate" the media uncovered how elites (especially conservative elites) constantly beat the drum of distrust.

Identity distrust is something different, occurring when members of some social groups come to associate distrust in the media with their own belonging to the group. Various polls suggest, for example, that just like attitudes about climate change and COVID-19 public health measures, negative views of the news media have become part of many Republican voters' political identity (e.g., Brenan & Saad, 2019).

To rebuild trust, then, one must understand the different kinds of distrust and then ask if and whether each might be overcome. Identity distrust, for example, probably cannot be undone by the journalistic establishment itself. After years of being warned to distrust the "lamestream" media, and now with access to an entire set of alternative channels tailored to conservative voters, it seems unlikely that this particular segment of the American public can be won back to traditional journalism. The same may be true of reputational distrust. If Ladd's findings are correct, it is unlikely that the effects of elite antimedia rhetoric can be undone quickly, particularly by the very journalists working for the news organizations being targeted.

All this leaves only one type of distrust amenable to change: rational distrust. As it happens, many journalists at outlets around the country (along with nonjournalists who care about their communities' information needs) are working right now to build trust by changing how journalism is practiced.

Community-Centered Journalism

Journalism's crisis, as profoundly destabilizing as it has been, has also offered opportunities for innovation in practice and mentality around new ways of building deeper relationships with communities (Lawrence et al., 2019). On the scholarly side, Lewis (2020, p. 346) has urged journalists to seize the moment by practicing "relational journalism" that is "focused on better understanding, listening to, and engaging with people in ways that are mutually beneficial, solutions oriented, and fundamentally relationship driven." And on the journalistic side, among the leading recommendations in a 2019 Knight Foundation report was the recommendation that journalists "develop strategies to better engage with the public and reflect the interests of their communities" (Knight, 2019).

One example of this relational approach is found in the firm Hearken (https://wearehearken.com/), which provides tools for journalists to allow their audiences to help shape the news agenda – what it calls "people powered journalism." Some limitations of Hearken's approach have been uncovered by researchers – notably the reluctance of some newsrooms to fully embrace such a reorientation (Schmidt et al., 2020). But the growth Hearken reports in its client list suggests that this approach has been appealing to newsrooms struggling to find ways of rebuilding trust.

Other examples focus on building direct relationships with communities themselves. Organizations like the Listening Post Collective (www.listeningpostcollective.org/), Internews (https://internews.org/), and Free Press (www.freepress.net/) are partnering with news outlets from Omaha to New Orleans and from Minneapolis to Philadelphia, offering them resources to support local-level journalism. Also, practitioners like jesikamaria ross of Sacramento's Capitol Public Radio have created tools such as a "participatory journalism playbook" that teach journalists how to listen to and "report with" their communities (ross, 2020). Similarly, Southern California Public Radio has debuted a practice of including mission statements with their news stories, along with a call for public input into their reporting, all in an attempt to "narrow the gap between our newsroom and the communities we serve, and to find stories that matter to people" (Online News Association, 2020). And Spaceship Media (https://spaceshipmedia.org/?home=true) has pioneered the use of online platforms, like private Facebook groups, to practice "dialogue journalism" designed to bridge divides around divisive issues like gun control and partisan elections.

This community-centered journalism (Wenzel, 2020) may not "scale" to larger cities or to the nation itself. The challenges of trust are especially hard to grapple with for national-level media, such as the network news, cable TV news, and major newspapers like the *New York Times* and the *Washington Post*, outlets whose audiences are much broader and more dispersed geographically, outlets that are also seen as vulnerable to charges of "liberal media bias." But the importance of building or rebuilding local information ecosystems should not be minimized. Recent research by Darr et al. (2018) has shown that when local media fail economically, citizens fill the news gap with more polarized national news, thereby depressing existing levels of local civic engagement even further.

Conclusion

This chapter has argued that the legacy press cannot defend its authority merely by leaning into conventional journalistic norms (e.g., objectivity) or by attempting to win back the trust of increasingly distrustful conservative voters. But journalists can rebuild their informational authority with other segments of the public through bold experiments in building deeper connections with the individual communities they serve. Given the extent of the crisis, radical reinvention is now required, not just in modes of delivery, but also in ways of reconceptualizing journalism. Nothing less than the public's ability to understand and govern itself is at stake.

Bibliography

2020 Edelman Trust Barometer. (2020). www.edelman.com/trustbarometer

Barber, B. (1983). *The logic and limits of trust.* New Brunswick, NJ: Rutgers University Press.

Benkler, Y., Faris, R., Roberts, H., & Zuckerman, E. (2017, March). Study: Breitbart-led right-wing media ecosystem altered broader media agenda. *Columbia Journalism Review.* www.cjr.org/analysis/breitbart-media-trump-harvard-study.php

Bennett, W. L., & Pfetsch, B. (2018). Rethinking political communication in a time of disrupted public spheres. *Journal of Communication,* 68(2), 243–253.

Brenan, M. (2019, September 26). Americans' trust in media edges down to 41%. *Gallup.* https://news.gallup.com/poll/267047/americans-trust-mass-media-edges-down.aspx

Brenan, M., & Saad, L. (2019, March 28). Global warming concern steady, despite some partisan shifts. *Gallup.* https://news.gallup.com/poll/231530/global-warming-concern-steady-despite-partisan-shifts.aspx

Carlson, M. (2017). *Journalistic authority: Legitimating news in the digital era.* New York: Columbia University Press.

Center for Innovation & Sustainability in Local Media. (2018). *The expanding news desert.* University of North Carolina-Chapel Hill. www.usnewsdeserts.com/

Chadwick, A. (2017). *The hybrid media system: Politics and power* (2nd ed.). Oxford: Oxford University Press.

Crouch, C. (2004). *Post-democracy.* New York: Polity.

Darr, J. P., Hitt, M. P., & Dunaway, J. L. (2018). Newspaper closures polarize voting behavior. *Journal of Communication,* 68(6), 1007–1028.

Jamieson, K. H., & Cappella, J. N. (2010). *Echo chamber: Rush Limbaugh and the conservative media establishment.* Oxford: Oxford University Press.

Knight Commission on Trust, Media and Democracy. (2019). *Crisis in democracy: Renewing trust in America*. The Aspen Institute. https://csreports.aspeninstitute.org/Knight-Commission-TMD/2019/report

Knight Foundation. (2020). *American views 2020: Trust, media and democracy*. https://knightfoundation.org/reports/american-views-2020-trust-media-and-democracy/

Ladd, J. M. (2011). *Why Americans hate the media and why it matters*. Princeton: Princeton University Press.

Lawrence, R. G., Gordon, E., DeVigal, A., Mellor, C., & Elbaz, J. (2019). *Building engagement: Supporting the practice of relational journalism*. Agora Journalism Center, University of Oregon. https://dl.orangedox.com/building-engagement

Lawrence, R. G., & Moon, Y. E. "We aren't fake news": The information politics of the 2018 #FreePress Editorial Campaign. (2021) *Journalism Studies*, 22(2), 155–173. www.tandfonline.com/doi/full/10.1080/1461670X.2020.1831399?utm_medium=email&utm_source=EmailStudio&utm_campaign=JOE09650_3934328

Levendusky, M. (2013). *How partisan media polarize America*. Chicago: University of Chicago Press.

Lewis, S. C. (2020). Lack of trust in the news media, institutional weakness, and relational journalism as a potential way forward. *Journalism*, 21(3), 345–348.

Lippmann, W. (1977). *Public opinion* (Re-issue ed.). New York: Free Press.

McIntyre, L. (2018). *Post-truth*. Cambridge, MA: MIT Press.

Meeks, L. (2019). Defining the enemy: How Donald Trump frames the news media. *Journalism & Mass Communication Quarterly*, 97(1), 211–234.

Munger, K. (2020). All the news that's fit to click: The economics of clickbait media. *Political Communication*, 37(3), 376–397. doi: 10.1080/10584609.2019.1687626

Online News Association. (2020). *Engaged journalism*. https://awards.journalists.org/entries/southern-california-public-radios-engaged-journalism/

Prior, M. (2007). *Post-broadcast democracy*. Cambridge: Cambridge University Press.

ross, j.m. (2020). *JMR's participatory journalism playbook*. https://internews.org/sites/default/files/2020-07/JMR_playbook_07-10-20_V3.pdf

Scacco, J. M., & Wiemer, E. C. (2019). The president tweets the press: President-press relations and the politics of media degradation. In D. Taras & R. Davis (Eds.), *Power shift? Political leadership and social media* (pp. 18–32). New York: Routledge.

Schmidt, T., & Lawrence, R. G. (2020). Engaged journalism and news work: A sociotechnical analysis of organizational dynamics and professional challenges. *Journalism Practice*, 14(5), 518–536.

Schmidt, T., Nelson, J., & Lawrence, R. G. (2020). Conceptualizing the active audience: Rhetoric and practice in "engaged" journalism. *Journalism*. https://journals.sagepub.com/eprint/YGRFDMYTBZD3ZY9NRZ3V/full

Stonbely, S., Napoli, P. M., McCullough, K., & Renninger, B. (2015, March 27). *Assessing the health of local journalism ecosystems: Toward a set of reliable, scalable metrics*. TPRC 43: The 43rd Research Conference on Communication, Information and Internet Policy Paper. SSRN. https://ssrn.com/abstract=2586115 or http://dx.doi.org/10.2139/ssrn.2586115

Stroud, N. J. (2011). *Niche news: The politics of news choice*. Oxford: Oxford University Press.

Thorson, K., & Wells, C. (2015). Curated flows: A framework for mapping media exposure in the digital age. *Communication Theory*. doi: 10.1111/comt12087

Toff, B., & Nielsen, R. K. (2018). "I just Google it": Folk theories of distributed discovery. *Journal of Communication, 68*, 636–657.

Vernon, P. (2018). A climate of hate toward the press at Trump rallies. *Columbia Journalism Review*. www.cjr.org/the_media_today/trump-acosta-rally.php

Waldman, S. (2011). *The information needs of communities: The changing media landscape in a broadband age*. Federal Communications Commission. www.fcc.gov/general/information-needs-communities

Wenzel, A. (2017). Public media and marginalized publics: Online and offline engagement strategies and local storytelling networks. *Digital Journalism*, 1–18. http://doi.org/10.1080/21670811.2017.1398594

Wenzel, A. (2020). *Community-centered journalism: Engaging people, exploring solutions, and building trust*. Champaign, IL: University of Illinois Press.

Williams, B. A., & Delli Carpini, M. X. (2011). *After broadcast news: Media regimes, democracy, and the new information environment*. Chicago: University of Chicago Press.

26 Measure Newsroom Effectiveness Differently

Natalie (Talia) Jomini Stroud and Yujin Kim

Gawker, a popular website from 2003–2016, was known for many things: salacious coverage, questionable techniques, and an unabashed focus on metrics. The site's "Big Board," a digital display of the best-performing stories on the site, adorned the receptionist's desk and attained iconic status. In an interview with *The New York Times*, Gawker founder Nick Denton said: "Sometimes one sees writers just standing before it, like early hominids in front of a monolith" (Peters, 2010, July 18).

Although Gawker met its demise from a Hulk Hogan invasion-of-privacy lawsuit, the dominance of digital metrics remains part of its legacy. Other sites like Upworthy and BuzzFeed capitalized on metrics using related strategies. The influence of metrics extends far beyond a few prominent digital startups, however. Attend news meetings at a few newsrooms, and you are bound to see data from CrowdTangle, Parse.ly, or one of the many other analytics vendors. At any moment of any day, one can see which stories are attracting more page views, unique visitors, or time on page. According to communication scholar Hong Tien Vu (2014), news editors take web metrics into account when they make journalistic decisions, both in the news-selection process and in determining how to present the news, such as making high-traffic stories more visible on the front page of a news site.

In this chapter, we evaluate the influence of news metrics through the lens of "connective democracy," or the linkages between the public and institutions that promote well-functioning societies (Overgaard et al., in press). Connective democracy sees journalism as critical in building linkages between the public and institutions such as the government and the scientific community. For journalism to serve this role, however, there must be connections between audiences and news organizations whereby audiences trust the news media to provide reliable and relevant information. Yet people's trust is fragmented by ideology for national news sources, and local news does not consistently form connections with the local community, according to surveys from the Pew Research Center (2019, 2020). The lack of such a connection makes it difficult for the news media to fulfill its traditional democratic role.

DOI: 10.4324/9781003212515-33

Metrics could be seen as one way to establish stronger connections. They provide insights about those accessing a newsroom's journalism and could allow news organizations to better tailor their products to meet the public's information needs. But as we outline in the pages that follow, there are reasons to see metrics as problematic, in part because they are designed to serve advertisers and not the public. Yet we contend that metrics – despite their problems – could be part of the solution to establishing connective democracy, especially if they are used to help build relationships between news audiences and newsrooms.

The Problem With Metrics

Newsroom metrics are not new; they have existed for decades in other forms, with newspapers having tracked their circulation figures and television stations their Nielsen ratings. These data help newsrooms understand how the public consumes their product, yet they are "not of direct help in guiding the countless choices" involved in producing the news (Shoemaker & Reese, 1996, p. 105). But digital metrics are different. They are immediately known, they can be tied to specific forms of content, and they can be quickly changed using digital marketing strategies. They also have made it easier for advertisers to reach audiences with enviable precision.

The digital metrics revolution comes at a particularly challenging moment for the news industry, with the revenue model for news having fallen apart. Local advertising increasingly has gone to Facebook and Google, where audience reach is greater and where people can be targeted even more precisely. Paid classified ads have gone to Craigslist and other vendors. Print circulations are down as people consume news for free online. Digital paywalls work well for large, national media organizations, but the case for their efficacy is far less clear for smaller outlets. Further, margins on digital advertising are far lower than print ads. Local broadcast news has fared somewhat better in terms of maintaining viewers, but a generational audience analysis portends difficult times ahead. In this context, metrics are heralded by some as a savior, a way to discover audience trends and pummel out more content that increases revenue via digital advertising. Metrics, in this version, can save the news.

Yet we argue that newsrooms are missing the mark when using metrics to solve revenue problems by catering to advertising goals, as opposed to using metrics to establish deeper connections with communities. As we review in the subsequent pages, metrics can be problematic when focusing attention on journalism as it currently exists instead of on what it might become, when conflating advertising and audience goals, and when obscuring the firewall between the business and reporting functions of news organizations.

Metrics Can Distract Us From Societal Needs

Metrics are important because they dictate focus. As soon as you start measuring something – whether it is grades in school or fat in food – it affects how people behave. Grades can divert attention from learning and heighten concern about earning an "A" whether or not the material has been truly mastered. Searching for low-fat food can take the focus away from salt and sugar, both of which are problematic if not consumed in moderation and both of which are frequently used in low-fat food to infuse flavor. In newsrooms, a focus on metrics can detract from other important outcomes, such as informing the public or addressing their information needs.

The most readily available news metrics are those that assess whether and for how long people look at content; other popular measures examine whether people engage with content by, for example, sharing or commenting on it. These metrics yield a focus on maximizing behavioral responses by audiences – scrolling, clicking, liking, etc. They most certainly do not ask whether journalists are meeting a community's information needs.

Recently, the Center for Media Engagement at the University of Texas at Austin conducted a national survey along with a content analysis of Facebook posts by local newsrooms about the coronavirus in mid-2020. The results revealed gaps in what the public wanted and what newsrooms provided. In particular, local news Facebook posts covered the economic and business implications of the coronavirus more frequently than the public thought was warranted. These stories can be seen as aligning with the interests of advertisers versus those of news consumers. The public craved fact-checking, a form of coverage that evaluates whether messages are true or false. Fact-checking was almost entirely absent from local news' Facebook posts. These findings highlight the problem of relying on traffic metrics: If a newsroom fails to produce fact-checked stories, it will have no data to show that the public wants to consume this content. Traffic metrics react to journalism as it exists rather than on what it might become.

Metrics Can Conflate What Advertisers Want With What Audiences Want

Clicks are often interpreted as a sign of the audience's interest in the news – the more clicks, the more interest. This interpretation makes sense, in part, and matches what advertisers want: More clicks means more advertising impressions. The opposite scenario, however, illustrates how interpreting metrics in line with advertising goals is not always in the audience's best interest. Using in-depth interviews, journalism scholars Tim Groot Kormelink and Irene Costera Meijer (2018) examined what "not clicking" means to users. An undersupply of clicks, they found, can indicate monitoring and browsing patterns and correspond with headlines that are sufficiently informative and thus do not require a click. Although the absence of clicks is bad for advertisers, it may not mean that audiences are disinterested in the content.

Metrics Can Obscure the Editorial/Business Firewall

The dominance of digital news metrics is concerning for yet another reason. An oft-cited hallmark of journalism is a division between the reporting and business sides of a news organization. Reporters, the logic goes, are detached, objective, and unburdened by financial considerations. When digital metrics infiltrate a newsroom, journalists begin thinking about the business of news, because bringing more clicks to a site means more revenue from digital advertising and, for some outlets, more chances to get people to become subscribers, donors, or members. When reporters consider the business implications of their work, they stop focusing on what matters and instead are lured by lowest-common-denominator content that maximizes traffic.

There is merit to that fear; communication scholars Eugenia Mitchelstein and Pablo Boczkowski (2013) found that digital editors privilege hard news content, even though the public generally prefers softer fare. If metrics dictate content, celebrity news will easily supersede foreign affairs. Even Gawker was concerned about such matters. The site abandoned the strategy of rewarding writers who achieved high levels of page views after concluding that page views were too easy to manipulate. They observed, for example, "editors resorting to galleries and click-bait headlines" (Sternberg, 2013). Gawker's solution, however, was not to move away from a metrics-based reward system. Instead, it used the number of unique visitors, as opposed to page views, to measure the impact of their journalism. This modest shift encouraged reporters to find ways to attract more people, as opposed to more clicks, yet it also continued to prioritize metrics.

The overarching problem with metrics-based digital journalism is this: Instead of resuscitating news, metrics can kill it. Used in ways to game attention, metrics can yield short-term wins such as an article with a high number of page views. In contrast, long-term sustainability derived from adequately serving news consumers would not benefit from such a strategy. But *Fixing American Politics* is not a book about problems; it is a book about solutions. To fix "the metrics problem," we need solutions that are in large part cultural. That is, we must rethink how newsrooms might best use metrics.

Metrics as a Solution

Without question, there are reasons to be concerned about metrics, but there are also reasons for optimism. That is, metrics could be interpreted differently, used differently, and conceived of differently. When approached with goals like these in mind, metrics can help build connective democracy.

Metrics Could Be Interpreted Differently

News organizations' ability to respond to their audiences has always been constrained by a lack of data. Without metrics, it's difficult to think of a reliable feedback mechanism that allows audiences to convey their thoughts to journalists. Journalists can, of course, ascertain public sentiment from the vocal minority who leave comments or write letters and emails. They could also extrapolate from the feedback of those around them in the newsroom or in their personal lives. But neither method is likely to provide generalizable insights.

Traffic metrics, however, could provide a less biased way of learning about audiences. Gawker's focus on unique visitors, for example, has implications for reporting in general since it rewarded reporters who wrote content attracting lots of people (and hence gaining lots of advertising impressions). It is no wonder, then, that celebrity gossip was common on the site. But standard metrics could be helpful in meeting audiences' information needs. Journalists could, for example, gain valuable feedback by examining how far people get through the articles they have written, known as scroll depth. If very few people make it more than halfway through an article, a journalist could become productively introspective: What happened at the halfway point that I might have conveyed in a better way? Seen as genuine feedback from their audiences, metrics might become far more valuable to an enterprising journalist.

Metrics Could Be Used Differently

Metrics also do not have to be used in a stagnant way, especially if news sites are open to experimentation (or A/B testing in the language of newsrooms). For example, we analyzed a newsroom's Facebook posts during an election, experimentally evaluating whether *issue-framed* or *strategy-framed* posts attracted more clicks and engagement (Stroud & Muddiman, 2019). Issue-framed posts focused on the candidates and the issues they championed were contrasted with strategy-framed posts emphasizing who was ahead or behind in the race and how candidates were maneuvering to secure additional votes. The results showed that issue-framed posts attracted more comments and reactions, whereas strategy-framed posts attracted more clicks. A newsroom wanting to increase community conversation could use these results to prioritize issue-framed posts (a decision we would heartily endorse).

As another example, the Center for Media Engagement partnered with the Graham Media Group to analyze how to include links to additional news content on their websites. Across seven different local television news stations, we randomized aspects of the links such as the content of the links (whether to topically related content or to content that was popular on the site), where the links were positioned, and whether the links were presented with images. All of these factors made a difference in whether people clicked to read more news. In general, when the links were topically related, were positioned at the bottom of articles, and included an image, click-through rates became higher (Collier et al., in press).

A final example, one having direct application to the current ideological divides in news trust: Newsrooms might evaluate how those on the political Left and the political Right respond to the news they consume. In collaboration with ProPublica, the Center for Media Engagement investigated which types of social media posts attracted liberals and conservatives. Although some strategies (such as changing the headlines in an effort to appeal to liberals' and conservatives' distinct moral foundations) reduced clicks across the ideological spectrum, using real-world images (as opposed to illustrations) increased clicks from both ideological groups. Each of these examples illustrates an audience-focused use of metrics employing real-world experimentation.

There are several important components of such metrics-based testing. For one thing, it requires a newsroom's inventiveness. Brainstorming new approaches, or figuring out two or more ways of doing something, takes time. In addition, such experimentation requires newsrooms to define a metric of interest. Just as social scientists determine dependent variables for their studies, newsrooms must figure out what is most worthy of being evaluated – for example, click-through rates or scroll depth. Further, some tests may need to be conducted more than once. For instance, if a newsroom is interested in contrasting problem-based versus solution-based news stories, a single test may find that the former approach garners more clicks. Yet there may have been something about the topic or the timing that produced those results. By doing repeated tests, however, a newsroom could resolve those ambiguities, perhaps even identifying an overall trend. For instance, Center for Media Engagement research has found that solutions-framed headlines tend to garner more clicks than problem-framed headlines, although that was not the case in all of the studies we conducted.

Metrics Could Be Conceptualized Differently

Right now, the most easily accessible metrics are traffic data. But one could imagine alternative metrics that could help newsrooms build connections with audiences. Several years ago, for example, the Center for Media Engagement hosted a workshop for digital news innovators. One of the participants, Tom Negrete, then the director of innovation and news operations for *The Sacramento Bee*, proposed that newsrooms should measure comprehension – whether or not people understood what they were reading. Indeed, Norway's NRKbeta once required people to complete a quiz question prior to being allowed to comment. In another instance, the Civic Signals project conducted focus groups and surveys in countries around the world to try to understand what people wanted from their digital experiences. They identified needs such as a sense of belonging, the availability of reliable information, and the resilience of a community when faced with tragedy. Each of these could be new metrics and could reveal what forms of journalism best further these goals.

To make advances in this kind of real-world testing, articulating a precise series of goals must be the starting point. Afterward, identifying how to measure the desired outcomes becomes critical. By taking an audience-centered approach to measurement and by expanding the repertoire of considered metrics, newsrooms can better establish more enduring links with the communities they aim to serve.

Conclusion

Using metrics blindly can lead newsrooms to provide more of the same old thing or, even more problematically, to resort to trickery such as clickbait headlines that garner clicks but fail to deliver substantive journalism. More optimistically, metrics can be used to aid in the development of connective democracy by helping newsrooms learn what information people most desire. The pressing need for revenue has motivated the use of metrics catering to advertisers. But what is the real purpose of the news? And how often will audiences return to it if it lacks what they desire, especially with so many other kinds of content competing for their attention? Using metrics for societal goals can help solve the revenue and trust problems newsrooms currently face and, in doing so, help journalism fulfill its important democratic role.

Bibliography

Collier, J. R., Dunaway, J., & Stroud, N. J. (in press). Pathways to deeper news engagement: Factors influencing click behaviors on news sites. *New Media & Society*.

Groot Kormelink, T., & Costera Meijer, I. (2018). What clicks actually mean: Exploring digital news user practices. *Journalism*, 19(5), 668–683.

Mitchelstein, E., & Boczkowski, P. J. (2013). *The news gap: When the information preferences of the media and the public diverge*. Cambridge, MA: MIT Press.

Overgaard, C. S. B., Dudo, A., Lease, M., Masullo, G. M., Stroud, N. J., Stroud, S. R., & Woolley, S. (in press). Building connective democracy. Interdisciplinary solutions to the problem of polarisation. In H. Tumber & S. Waisbord (Eds.), *The Routledge companion to media misrepresentation and populism*. Oxfordshire, UK: Taylor & Francis/Routledge.

Peters, J. W. (2010, July 18). In a world of online news, burnout starts younger. *The New York Times*. www.nytimes.com/2010/07/19/business/media/19press.html

Pew Research Center. (2019). *For local news, Americans embrace digital but still want strong community connection*. www.journalism.org/2019/03/26/for-local-news-americans-embrace-digital-but-still-want-strong-community-connection/

Pew Research Center. (2020). *U.S. media polarization and the 2020 election: A nation divided*. www.journalism.org/2020/01/24/u-s-media-polarization-and-the-2020-election-a-nation-divided/

Shoemaker, P. J., & Reese, S. D. (1996). *Mediating the message: Theories of influences on mass media content*. White Plains, NY: Longman.

Sternberg, J. (2013). Pageview journalism gets a reset. *Digiday*. https://digiday.com/media/pageview-quota-pay-per-click/

Stroud, N. J., & Muddiman, A. (2019). Social media engagement with strategy- and issue-framed political news. *Journal of Communication, 69*(5), 443–466.

Vu, H. T. (2014). The online audience as gatekeeper: The influence of reader metrics on news editorial selection. *Journalism, 15*(8), 1094–1110.

27 Publicly Subsidize Journalism

David M. Ryfe

After more than a decade, the deterioration of local and regional news systems in the United States is barely newsworthy. In that time span, 25 percent of daily journalists have lost their jobs, and ever-growing swaths of the country are no longer served by a professional news organization (Abernathy, 2018). Yet many Americans don't even realize that their local news outlets are dying (Pew Research Center, 2019a). We should pay more attention. When journalism ceases to function well, democracy suffers, and the most charitable view today would agree that the profession is in disarray. The editor of this volume has asked authors to identify one concrete action Americans might take today to improve their polity. For me, the answer to this question is simple: Provide direct public subsidies to journalism. Democracy needs journalism, and if journalism is to survive, public subsidies are necessary.

Journalism and Democracy

Discussion of journalism's contributions to democracy is older than the profession itself and much older than the earliest academic studies of the occupation (Keane, 1991; McNair, 2000). Until recently, much of this discussion has been more theoretical than empirical. Enlightenment thinkers associated newspapers with reason, rationality, progress, and, ultimately, democracy itself (Habermas, 1989; Thompson, 1996; Tocqueville, 1835/2004). As journalism began to professionalize at the turn of the 20th century, sociologists like Tarde (1969/1901) and Tönnies (1971/1923) pondered its role in emerging modern societies. In the United States around the same time, public conversations about journalism mostly centered on its relation to democracy (Dewey, 1927; Lippmann, 1922). However, as professional journalism has faced increasing pressures, these discussions have become more practical. Can we concretely specify journalism's contributions to democracy? It turns out that we can.

Scholars have shown, for instance, that journalism is associated with the development of social capital in communities. A vibrant local news ecosystem means less political polarization (Darr et al., 2018), stronger

DOI: 10.4324/9781003212515-34

attachment among citizens (Yamamoto, 2011), higher levels of civic efficacy (Kim & Ball-Rokeach, 2006), and, most broadly, a deeper sense of community (Buchanan, 2009; Hess, 2012). As Lewis Friedland (2001, p. 384) argues, journalism "contributes to a sense of place ... and this sense of place is necessary for democratic action."

A collective feeling of belonging is a precursor to more direct civic engagement. Journalism enhances these activities as well. For instance, Shaker (2014) examines levels of engagement in Denver and Seattle just before and just after the closing of the *Rocky Mountain News* and the *Seattle Post-Intelligencer* in 2008. By civic engagement, he means contacting local officials, participating in local civic organizations, and talking to one's neighbors. Using data from the 2008 and 2009 Consumer Population Survey, he finds that, after the loss of the newspapers, most measures of civic engagement declined in these cities. Nearly a dozen other studies produced in the past decade support these conclusions (Local News Lab, 2018). Generally, this research has shown that less journalism in communities means lower voter turnout, less political competition, and less participation in civic life.

The presence of strong and independent journalism has other salutary effects. For example, it reduces levels of actual and perceived political corruption (Brunetti & Weder, 2003; Camaj, 2013). Researchers have found a relationship between journalism and levels of corruption in many countries around the world (Freille et al., 2007; Tulchin & Espach, 2000; Waisbord, 2000). Indeed, in a study that included data from 100 countries, Alícia Adserá and colleagues (2003, p. 479) report that "the presence of a well-informed electorate in a democratic setting explains between one-half and two-thirds of the variance in the levels of governmental ... corruption." The link between press freedom and political corruption is relatively simple to understand (Themudo, 2013). When public officials feel that their actions are closely monitored, they are less likely to engage in dishonesty. Similarly, a strong system of external control also tends to increase public knowledge and enhance citizens' feelings that officials are acting in accordance with the law.

Journalism also makes government work better. In places where journalism is strong, officeholders tend to work harder on behalf of their constituents and to be more responsive to their concerns (Strömberg & Snyder, 2008). Government activities also tend to be more efficient and less costly (Gao et al., 2020). Media economist James Hamilton (2016) has quantified journalism's impact on good governance. Though costly to produce, Hamilton concludes, every dollar spent on investigative journalism produces hundreds of dollars in social benefits.

We should not oversell journalism's benefits to democracy. As Schudson (1998) reminds us, the framers of the American Constitution thought little of journalism's role in society. But we should not undersell journalism's importance, either. There are strong, intuitive reasons to believe that better journalism promotes better democratic functioning (Gans, 2004; Schudson, 2013). The empirical evidence is sufficient enough to support this broad conclusion. Thus, if we want a robust democracy, journalism must stay healthy.

The Deterioration of Journalism

Unfortunately, today, American journalism is anything but healthy, and its illnesses have been well documented (Ryfe, 2012). Space allows me to discuss only two of the most important.

First, journalism has lost its business model. Historically, professional journalism was supported by a three-legged stool of advertising subsidies: national advertising, local advertising, and classifieds (Picard, 2008). Together, these subsidies made the industry one of the most profitable in the economy. Indeed, for decades, newspaper advertising revenue closely tracked the rise and fall of the country's gross domestic product (GDP). And as Picard (2008, p. 707) reports, from 1950 to 2005, GDP in the United States grew from $293 billion to $12,445 billion. Thus, into the early 2000s, it was not uncommon for the larger chain newspaper companies, like Gannett, McClatchy, and Knight-Ridder, to make profit margins of 20 percent and higher. For journalists, this meant that they were mostly insulated from economic considerations, left to pursue their public-service mission as they understood it.

Then, of course, the economic realities of news abruptly changed. The advertising-only website Craigslist was founded in 1995. In just a few years, it essentially took the business of classified advertising away from most large to mid-sized newspapers. As the internet became more pervasive, national advertisers began to see news outlets as an inefficient way of reaching consumers, and so they took their business elsewhere (first to television and mailers, later to Google and Facebook). The loss of two legs of the advertising stool left newspapers with local advertising as a primary subsidy for public-service journalism. However, in most communities, this revenue source is not sufficient to support a newsroom of any great size. By the 2010s, the business model for most large and midsized news organizations had simply collapsed.

The result has been horrific: Droves of daily journalists have lost their jobs. Pew Research Center (2019b) reports that newsroom employment has dropped 25 percent since 2008 and that close to 50 percent of newspaper employees have been let go. Today, 1 in 5 journalists now works in New York, Los Angeles, or Washington, D.C. (Pew Research Center, 2019c). In an analysis of all counties across the country, Abernathy (2018) finds that 200 of the 3,143 counties in the nation are now served by no newspaper at all. An additional 1,449 counties are served by only one – typically a small weekly – what Abernathy refers to as "ghost" newspapers. In a study of 16,000 news stories across 100 communities,

Napoli and colleagues (2018) find much the same thing: Local stories account for only about 17 percent of the sample. So-called "news deserts" also appear to be expanding across the country.

The industry's economic turmoil is bad enough, but intense criticism of journalism (especially by conservative Republicans) has reduced journalism's legitimacy in many people's eyes. Hemmer (2018) has tracked the growth of a network of conservative radio programs, publishing houses, magazines, and television shows that grew alongside conservative political groups beginning in the 1940s and 1950s. Delegitimizing traditional journalism was a key mission of this network. Eventually, its criticisms made their way into mainstream media and politics, often through Fox News, a national broadcast company that functions as something like a modern-day version of the party newspaper. These criticisms have culminated in the presidency of Donald Trump, whose Twitter feed constantly decries journalists as liars and traitors.

This effort to delegitimize journalism has perhaps been more successful than its early participants could have imagined. A 2018 poll conducted by Gallup and the Knight Foundation discovered that a majority of Americans had "lost trust" in journalism, largely because people believed reporters did not report the truth (Ingram, 2018). This view is felt most strongly by self-described conservatives. An Axios/Survey Monkey poll, for instance, found that 92 percent of Republicans believe that "journalists intentionally report fake news" (Fischer, 2018). But suspicion of journalism is now widespread.

Given its reduced circumstances and the wounds inflicted to its reputation, journalism can hardly keep up. It is easy to become hyperbolic when discussing these trends. One commentator (Pollgreen, 2019), for instance, describes them in terms of the "collapse of the information ecosystem," one that is "wreak[ing] havoc on our politics . . . undermin[ing] our democratic elections . . . shak[ing] basic trust in institutions . . . and threaten[ing] to fundamentally destabilize the existing social order." This conclusion may be a bit extreme, but the situation in which journalism finds itself is clearly worrying – worrying enough to consider new solutions.

Public Subsidies

It is sometimes said that the idea of subsidizing the press is anathema to the American experience, but this is untrue. In fact, through the 19th century, the United States subsidized the news at a much higher rate than any other country in the world (Starr, 2004). Mostly, these subsidies were indirect, taking the form of preferred postal rates, tax breaks, and other accommodations in the law. However, they were enough to produce a vibrant journalistic culture. By the 1850s, the United States had more newspapers per capita than any other country in the world – double its closest competitor, the United Kingdom. It is true that in the 20th century, American interest in subsidizing the news lagged, eventually falling behind many of its European counterparts. For instance, according to one comparison (Nielsen & Linnebank, 2011), the per capita public subsidy of journalism in the United States amounts to only £5.2 today, nearly £20 less than the lowest European subsidies (in Italy), and an astounding £125 less than the highest subsidies in Europe (in Finland). But even today, the United States continues to subsidize the press. Neither the idea nor practice of subsidies, in other words, is foreign to the American experience.

One might argue that other revenue streams may prop up journalism without the need for public subsidies. Examples like *Minnpost* and *The Texas Tribune* suggest that a combination of subscriptions, donations, and foundation support may be enough to support local news. It is true that these and other nonprofit news organizations are financially stable and providing valuable service to their communities. However, it is not true that their model is easily duplicated elsewhere. Most stable nonprofit news sites exist in markets with large populations and, equally important, with large foundations. By definition, most states do not fit this definition. For instance, the state in which I live, Iowa, has a population of only 3 million people and has no foundations with resources sufficient to support a news operation of any size. The model exploited by *Minnpost* and others is simply not duplicable in most other places.

To my mind, then, the issue is not whether to provide more public subsidies to journalism but how. Suppose for a moment that Americans agreed to increase public subsidies for the news. How should it be done? Answers to this question are difficult to come by (Murschetz, 2013; Pickard, 2020). Historically, financial support for the news has taken one of three forms: direct subsidies that fund *public service news* organizations (like the BBC); *indirect subsidies* for private news organizations that mostly involve preferential treatment in tax law but that sometimes also include grants for journalistic training and research, state loans, public notice laws, and the like; *lump sums* of public money provided to private news organizations also exist but are rarely employed.

Each of these arrangements presents difficulties. Direct subsidies to public news outlets may engender political backlash. Moreover, public service media may push private news organizations out of the market. For their part, indirect subsidies are typically anchored to circulation and advertising numbers – the higher circulation goes, the more the subsidy is worth to a news organization. But circulation and advertising are precisely what private news organizations are losing today. Indirect subsidies thus are of less and less help to news organizations. Direct subsidies provided to private news organizations may seem like a sensible alternative. However, these funds are mostly captured by legacy news outlets and so fail to support the increasingly hybrid media system emerging across digital platforms (Chadwick, 2013). And, of course, these news organizations are also supported by indirect subsidies.

How, then, should a public subsidy of journalism work? There is likely no one right answer to this question, and space prohibits a deep discussion of any particular one. However, let me outline a few features that will likely be intrinsic to any successful scheme. In a review of public funding structures across 12 Western democracies, Rodney Benson and his colleagues (2017) suggest a first: Public subsidies should be dedicated, generous, and supplied over multiyear periods. Each of these elements is important. Revenue sources need to be dedicated in the sense that they should be an automatic, ongoing governmental expense rather than, say, a tax that is periodically voted upon (and therefore at risk of political backlash). Subsidies need to be generous because otherwise, journalists may not possess adequate resources to do the job well (and therefore risk public backlash). In addition, subsidies need to be set over multiple years to allow for longer-term planning.

A second feature: Funds should be used to pay for local, on-the-ground reporting. This is, after all, the kind of journalism that is most at risk of going away. Fewer journalists are covering government agencies at local, state, and regional levels. This means that there is less of the day-to-day, incremental coverage that, over time, builds better public understanding and official accountability (Kovach & Rosenstiel, 2001).

A third feature naturally arises from the preceding two: If adequate public money is made available, and we wish to subsidize local journalism, then we must create an oversight system of charters, agencies, and boards to ensure that the system does what we hope it will do. This system likely will operate across several layers and include policy experts, scholars, technologists, journalists, and, perhaps most importantly, members of the public. As Pickard (2020, p. 173) writes, if we want a true publicly owned media system, one that conforms to public values, it must include the perspectives of ordinary people.

A generous and steady revenue stream provided over multiple years, a focus on on-the-ground, local reporting, and an oversight network that ensures that money flows from the national to the local level to serve public ends: To my mind, these are the necessary conditions for any successful system of subsidies.

Conclusion

Given the space provided, I have left many details of a public subsidy system unaddressed. However, I hope to at least have convinced you of this: If we believe professional journalism is integral to a healthy democracy, then public subsidies will be necessary to ensure its existence. There is simply no other way to ensure a steady supply of local, professional journalism. And that is important, is it not?

Bibliography

Abernathy, P. (2018). *The expanding news desert.* The Center for Innovation and Sustainability in Local Journalism, University of North Carolina, Durham, NC.

Adserá, A., Boix, C., & Payne, M. (2003). Are you being served? Political accountability and quality of government. *The Journal of Law, Economics, & Organization, 19*(2), 445–490.

Benson, R., Powers, M., & Neff, T. (2017). Public media, autonomy, and accountability: Best and worst policy practices in 12 leading democracies. *International Journal of Communication, 11*, 1–22.

Brunetti, A., & Weder, B. (2003). A free press is bad news for corruption. *Journal of Public Economics, 87*, 1801–1824.

Buchanan, C. (2009). Sense of place in the daily newspaper. *Aether: The Journal of Media Geography, 4*, 62–84.

Camaj, L. (2013). The media's role in fighting corruption: Media effects on governmental accountability. *The International Journal of Press/Politics, 18*(1), 21–42.

Chadwick, A. (2013). *The hybrid media system: Politics and power.* New York: Oxford University Press.

Darr, J. P., Hitt, M. P., & Dunaway, J. L. (2018). Newspaper closures polarize voting behavior. *Journal of Communication, 69*(6), 1007–1028.

Dewey, J. (1927). *The public and its problems.* New York: Holt.

Fischer, S. (2018). 92% of republicans think media intentionally report fake news. *Axios.* www.axios.com/trump-effect-92-percent-republicans-media-fake-news-9c1bbf70-0054-41dd-b506-0869bb10f08c.html

Freille, S., Hazue, M. E., & Kneller, R. (2007). A contribution to the empirics of press freedom and corruption. *European Journal of Political Economy, 23*, 838–862.

Friedland, L. A. (2001). Communication, community, and democracy: Toward a theory of the communicatively integrated community. *Communication Research, 28*(4), 3580–3591.

Gans. H. (2004). *Democracy and the news.* New York: Oxford University Press.

Gao, P., Lee, C., & Murphy, D. (2020). Financing dies in darkness? The impact of newspaper closures on public finance. *Journal of Financial Economics, 135*(2), 445–467.

Habermas, J. (1989). *The structural transformation of the public sphere: An inquiry into a category of bourgeois society* (T. Burger, Trans.). Boston: MIT Press.

Hamilton, J. T. (2016). *Democracy's detectives: The economics of investigative journalism.* Cambridge: Harvard University Press.

Hemmer, N. (2018). *Messengers of the right: Conservative media and the transformation of American politics.* Philadelphia: University of Pennsylvania Press.

Hess, K. (2012). Breaking boundaries: Recasting the "local" newspaper as "geo-social" news in a digital landscape. *Digital Journalism, 1*(1), 48–63.

Ingram, M. (2018, September 12). Most Americans say they have lost trust in the media. *Columbia Journalism Review.* www.cjr.org/the_media_today/trust-in-media-down.php

Keane, J. (1991). *The media and democracy.* London: Polity Press.

Kim, Y. C., & Ball-Rokeach, S. J. (2006). Civic engagement from a communication infrastructure perspective. *Communication Theory, 16*, 173–197.

Kovach, B., & Rosenstiel, T. (2001). *The elements of journalism: What newspeople should know and the public should expect*. New York: Three Rivers Press.

Lippmann, W. (1922). *Public opinion*. New York: Macmillan.

Local News Lab. (2018). How we know journalism is good for democracy. https://localnewslab.org/2018/06/20/how-we-know-journalism-is-good-for-democracy/

McNair, B. (2000). *Journalism and democracy. An evaluation of the political public sphere*. London: Routledge.

Murschetz, P. (2013). State aid for newspapers: First theoretical disputes. In P. Murschetz (Ed.), *State aid for newspapers* (pp. 21–46). New York: Springer.

Napoli, P., Weber, M., McCollough, K., & Wang, Q. (2018). *Assessing local journalism: News deserts, journalism divides, and the determinants of the robustness of local news*. DeWitt Wallace Center for Media & Democracy, Duke University.

Nielsen, R., & Linnebank, G. (2011). Public support for the media: A six-country overview of direct and indirect subsidies. In *Reuters Institute for the Study of Journalism*. Oxford, UK: University of Oxford. reutersinstitute.politics.ox.ac.uk.

Pew Research Center. (2019a). *For local news, Americans embrace digital but still want strong community connection*. www.journalism.org/2019/03/26/for-local-news-americans-embrace-digital-but-still-want-strong-community-connection/

Pew Research Center. (2019b). *U.S. newsroom employment has dropped by a quarter since 2008, with greatest decline at newspapers*. www.pewresearch.org/fact-tank/2019/07/09/u-s-newsroom-employment-has-dropped-by-a-quarter-since-2008/

Pew Research Center. (2019c). *One-in-five U.S. newsroom employees live in New York, Los Angeles or D.C.* www.pewresearch.org/fact-tank/2019/10/24/one-in-five-u-s-newsroom-employees-live-in-new-york-los-angeles-or-d-c/

Picard, R. (2008). Shifts in newspaper advertising expenditures and their implications for the future of newspapers. *Journalism Studies, 9*(5), 704–716.

Pickard, V. (2020). *Democracy without journalism: Confronting the misinformation society*. New York: Oxford University Press.

Pollgreen, L. (2019, November 19). The collapse of the information ecosystem poses profound risks for humanity. *The Guardian*. www.theguardian.com/commentisfree/2019/nov/19/the-collapse-of-the-information-ecosystem-poses-profound-risks-for-humanity

Ryfe, D. (2012). *Can journalism survive? An inside look in American newsrooms*. New York: Polity.

Schudson, M. (1998). *The good citizen: A history of American civic life*. New York: Free Press.

Schudson, M. (2013). *Why democracies need an unlovable Press*. London: Polity.

Shaker, L. (2014). Dead newspapers and citizens' civic engagement. *Political Communication, 31*, 131–148.

Starr, P. (2004). *The creation of the media: Political origins of modern communications*. New York: Basic Books.

Strömberg, D., & Snyder, J. M. (2008). The media's influence on public policy decisions. In R. Islam (Ed.), Information and public choice: From media markets to policy making (pp. 17–32). Washington, DC: The World Bank.

Tarde, G. (1901/1969). *Gabriel Tarde on communication and social influence* (T. Clark, Ed.). Chicago: University of Chicago Press.

Themudo, N. S. (2013). Reassessing the impact of civil society: Nonprofit sector, press freedom, and corruption. *Governance: An International Journal of Policy, Administration, and Institutions, 26*(1), 63–89.

Thompson, J. (1996). *Media and modernity: A social theory of media*. Palo Alto: Stanford University Press.

Tocqueville, A. (1835/2004). *Democracy in America* (A. Goldhammer, Trans.). Washington, DC: Library of America.

Tönnies, F. (1971/1923). The power and value of public opinion. In W. J. Cahnman & R. Heberle (Eds.), *Ferdinand Tönnies on sociology: Pure, applied and empirical*. Chicago: University of Chicago Press (pp. 251–265).

Tulchin, J. S., & Espach, R. H. (Eds.). (2000). *Combating political corruption in Latin America*. Washington, DC: The Woodrow Wilson International Center for Scholars.

Waisbord, S. (2000). *Watchdog journalism in South America: News, accountability, and democracy*. New York: Columbia University Press.

Yamamoto, M. (2011). Community newspaper use promotes social cohesion. *Newspaper Research Journal, 32*(1), 19–33.

28 Report on Terrorism Responsibly

Scott L. Althaus

Terrorism has been a problem in the United States for more than a century and a half. Terrorists use spectacular acts of violence to draw particular kinds of attention to themselves, attention that they hope will pressure targeted political leaders into giving them what they want. And from the terrorists' point of view, the opportunities for getting it have never been better.

Social media is now the main way many people find out what is going on in the world, and today's news system is so cash starved that ratings-chasing coverage has become the standard formula for reporting breaking events. The dual tendency for social media users to share unfiltered (and often factually incorrect) information conveying strong emotions like fear and outrage (e.g., Lewandowsky et al., 2017; Sobieraj & Berry, 2011) and for dramatic styles of news reporting to carry the day (Hindman, 2018; Munger, 2020; Mutz, 2015) means that the United States is more vulnerable than ever before to the threat of terrorism. Ironically, the easiest way for journalists to report on terrorist attacks is exactly how social media users talk about them: Focus on what is dramatic, outrageous, in ways that elevate the perceived threat and that raise uncertainty about what will happen if the terrorists are not stopped or if their concerns are not addressed. This is exactly the kind of coverage terrorist groups hope to attract.

Breaking this vicious cycle has been the goal of the Responsible Terrorism Coverage Project, a program linking researchers in Germany, the Netherlands, and the United States, a project of which I have been a part for several years.[1] Because the information-transmission systems of the early 21st century are so finely tuned for unintentionally advancing the strategic goals that motivate terrorists to commit violence, the Responsible Terrorism Coverage Project was formed to help journalists provide citizens with the information they need without giving terrorists the attention they want.

We have learned a great deal from this work over the last several years. For example, we found clear evidence that the kind of sophisticated and sedate journalism traditionally practiced by leading news organizations

DOI: 10.4324/9781003212515-35

like the *New York Times* can effectively filter out many kinds of attention that terrorists hope to produce. But since quality news coverage is under threat from the same technological and economic forces that promote sensational journalism, any realistic fix for how social media and news organizations unwittingly play into the hands of terrorist groups must start somewhere else.

Fortunately, there are several simple steps that journalists and social media users can take to deny terrorists the attention they desire. Instead of amplifying the psychological impact of terrorist attacks, responsible citizens and journalists who follow these recommendations can increase societal resilience to terrorist threats and reduce the strategic incentives that lead terrorists to commit violent acts in the first place.

To understand why widespread adoption of these simple steps can be so powerful, it is important first to distinguish terrorism from other kinds of violence and then to identify the specific communication goals that terrorists are pursuing when attacking unsuspecting targets. With clarity on those important points, we can then see why having journalists and social media users follow rather simple guidelines when deciding what to say (and what not to say) about terrorist attacks can helpfully remove the incentives that lead terrorists to do what they do.

What Is Terrorism?

Defining what terrorism is and is not helps clarify why terrorists seek particular kinds of public attention and why denying them that attention can be a powerful disincentive for terrorist violence. Following widely used academic definitions (e.g., Hoffman, 2006), the Responsible Terrorism Coverage project defines terrorism as *a tactic chosen by nonstate actors that uses violence to generate publicity in order to achieve political goals by exploiting fear and shaping the perceptions of multiple audiences.*

Terrorism is a tactical choice made by groups operating outside normal institutions of government (in academic parlance, these groups are called "violent nonstate actors"). In many cases, these nonstate actors could choose to deploy a broad repertoire of legitimate political behaviors for pursuing their goals, including lobbying and peaceful protest. But these groups specifically choose spectacular violence as a means of getting what they want, a tactic that they perceive to have a higher likelihood of success than the more conventional methods available to them.

Terrorism is different from other kinds of violence in that its aims are persuasive rather than criminal. Terrorists want to bring about political change of some kind, and the groups that choose terrorism as a tactic have decided that violence is the best way to draw attention to their cause. They also hope that violence will give them political leverage over the institutions that stand in the way of their getting what they want.

Publicity is the key ingredient that terrorists need to achieve both goals, but not just any kind of publicity. They use spectacular violence to generate strong emotional responses in target populations – particularly fear – presuming that scaring people will force political leaders to act in ways that ultimately advance the terrorists' own goals. Terrorists also use the publicity from their attacks to communicate with sympathizers, as well as with third parties who could help advance their goals.

A key insight follows from this way of thinking: terrorists use violence rather than more legitimate tactics because they expect a publicity payoff. If groups conducting attacks find that violence fails to produce the attention they need, then more legitimate political tactics might be pursued. Depriving terrorists of the attention they seek shifts the strategic calculus for using violence in the first place.

Violent nonstate actors can't achieve any of their communication aims without the help of news organizations and social media users who unwittingly distribute terrorists' desired messages in the intended ways. Identifying the kinds of attention terrorists seek holds the key for empowering journalists and social media users to take small steps to deprive terrorists of the fuel needed to sustain their campaigns of violence.

What Terrorists Want From Media Users

Different terrorist groups have different communication objectives, but all terrorists want three main things from journalists and social media users. The first and most important is *visibility*. Terrorist groups want to draw attention to their own demands and their capabilities as a necessary condition for producing the political outcomes they are after. If they don't achieve visibility in larger news and social media discourses within a target population, they are unlikely to achieve anything else they are after.

Besides visibility, terrorists also want *legitimacy*. They don't want to be called terrorists, a label that undermines their moral justification for resorting to violence in the first place. Terrorists want to be seen as legitimate actors with valid grievances, persons who should be taken seriously by mainstream political institutions. They want to legitimize these grievances within news coverage by getting people to talk about them and their concerns. The more they succeed at legitimizing themselves and their grievances, the greater the likelihood that targeted political institutions will respond with acts of conciliation or concession.

Third, terrorists want *prestige*. They want to be seen as a credible threat to public order and to look like they are being taken seriously by political institutions. But the intended audience for this prestige goal is different from the other two. Terrorists hope to boost their visibility and legitimacy within the populations they target but they want prestige to impress their own supporters and potential allies. When such cohorts begin to regard one terrorist group as more important than their other violent competitors, the group's fundraising prospects are improved as well as their ability to recruit new members. While visibility and legitimacy advance terrorists' political objectives, prestige keeps them in the fight.

Visibility, legitimacy, and prestige only lay the foundation for terrorists. They also need to create leverage to pressure political institutions into bringing about their desired change. Different strategies of violence will dictate which kinds of leverage a terrorist group needs to produce, but two are especially relevant for groups targeting the United States: strategies of attrition and strategies of provocation. Each strategy aims to produce a different kind of emotional response, and this is where two additional communication goals come into play.

The fourth thing that terrorists want is *to make us afraid*. Strategies of attrition aim at pressuring governmental leaders to give in to terrorists' demands by scaring a given population. Groups using this strategy hope that terrorist attacks will heighten the targeted population's sense of powerlessness and disunity. The more such a population fears that terrorists have the power to behave badly and that they cannot be stopped, the greater the political pressure on political leaders to do something about it.

The fifth communication goal is *to make us angry*. Terrorists using strategies of provocation hope to lure political leaders into overreacting by generating widespread feelings of outrage and solidarity within a targeted population. Instead of stopping with fear, terrorist groups try to draw targeted governments into a trap that, when sprung, will advance the terrorists' goals. These traps invite political leaders to overreact by demonstrating to their outraged constituents that they're doing something definitive to respond to the terrorist threat. Causing the targeted nation to bomb terrorist training camps, send military forces overseas, or violate the civil liberties of a terrorist group's co-religionists or co-ethnics are just some of the traps that, when sprung, can set victory in motion for terrorist groups using strategies of provocation.

How to Avoid Giving Terrorists What They Want

If terrorists hope to generate visibility, legitimacy, and prestige through violent attacks, then dropping a blanket of silence around their acts would certainly undermine their intended effects. But how to do so? Citizens in free societies, after all, need to know when terrorism is threatening their welfare or their liberty. Prohibiting citizens (or journalists) from sharing what they know about terrorist attacks would also violate the core tenets of free societies. As a result, reporting about terrorist acts in responsible ways becomes a complex business, giving the offenders some but not all of the attention they desire. The Responsible Terrorism Coverage Project offers six ways of doing so, methods that are easy to follow and that can frustrate terrorists ready to engage in acts of violence.[2]

Recommendations for Journalists and News Organizations

1. **You stand in the gap between what terrorists do and what terrorists want.** Unsuspecting citizens may be the primary targets of terrorist actions, but unsuspecting journalists are the primary targets of terrorist strategies.
2. **Adopt a clear definition of terrorism now.** The Responsible Terrorism Coverage Project's definition is a useful place to start, but your news organization may want to go further. For example, what counts as "violence" is a contested matter (e.g., Does violence against property count as terrorism?). Adopting a consistent way of identifying terrorism reduces the communication echo that terrorists hope to generate from news coverage.
3. **Call acts of violence that meet the definition terrorism but avoid using the term to describe other acts of violence.** Consistent use of delegitimizing language costs terrorists what they want. This is why defining terrorism is important: A clear definition teaches reporters when to employ delegitimizing labels like "terrorist" to describe an attack's perpetrators. Delegitimizing language should be used whenever the definitional elements are represented in a particular attack.
4. **Focus on what happened, where it happened, when it happened, who committed the act, and who was victimized by the act.** Reporting that emphasizes "who, what, where, and when" provides the best balance between giving citizens the information they need without giving terrorists the coverage they want.
5. **Avoid story topics exploring how or why the act was committed.** Overly interpretive reporting carries significant risks of advancing terrorists' strategic communication goals. Addressing "how they did it" makes terrorist groups appear more threatening, and explaining "why they did it" draws attention to their grievances and demands.
6. **Avoid story topics and reporting styles likely to stir up outrage or fear in news audiences.** Reporting that generates strong emotions of anger or anxiety is likely to play into the hands of terrorists' strategic communication goals.

Recommendations for Social Media Users and Platforms

1. **Your choices about what information to share can turn terrorist acts into political gains.** Your social media choices can also hinder terrorists in producing the political leverage they intend their violence to generate.
2. **Signaling you're safe immediately after a terrorist attack reduces fear or anxiety in a targeted population.** Letting others know you're safe not

only puts your friends and family at ease but also reduces the chance they will further circulate messages that stoke fear or anger in others.
3. **Before posting about a terrorist attack, confirm that any factual claim you're making has been verified by at least two credible news sources.** Terrorists thrive in a climate of fear and outsized concern about the potential threat they represent. Don't help them by passing along hearsay about terrorist tactics, goals, or capabilities.
4. **Offering messages of sympathy for terrorist victims and support for first responders strengthens a targeted population without giving terrorists what they want.** This is one of the best ways of countering terrorist messaging strategies because it both denies terrorists the communication echo they hope to generate from their attacks and increases the resilience of the targeted population.
5. **Demonstrating solidarity with people from the same religious or ethnic groups as terrorist perpetrators undercuts terrorists' efforts to stoke fear, suspicion, and overreactions.** When pursuing provocation strategies, terrorists want authorities to overreact in the aftermath of violence. Demonstrating solidarity with communities within the targeted population that share the religion or ethnic identity as terrorist perpetrators helps improve the resilience of the targeted population and increases the ability of governing leaders to respond appropriately to terrorist threats.
6. **Avoid naming particular terrorists, terrorist groups, or terrorist acts.** Terrorists thrive on attention and notoriety. Don't let them have it. If you have to say something, post about terrorists or terrorism in general terms.
7. **Never share terrorist manifestos, videos, or photos from a terrorist attack.** Don't do terrorists' work for them. Reproducing their propaganda can only advance their strategic communication goals.
8. **Avoid posting messages that express fear or a desire for retribution.** Terrorist groups can win by either scaring us or stoking our anger. Since either reaction advances their causes, it is important to deny terrorists the one thing they want most of all: Generating an extreme emotional response in a targeted population.

Conclusion

Terrorist attacks are acts of attention seeking as much as acts of political violence. Mostly, terrorists want to be seen as legitimate. They want to advance their grievances in ways that force targeted governments to take them seriously. They want to burnish their own prestige in the eyes of their supporters and in the eyes of third parties who can advance their political goals. They want to spread fear and uncertainty in the minds of a target population. But terrorists can do none of these things on their own. They need journalists and social media users to transmit and amplify their messages. Above all, they need your help, which is precisely why you should deny it to them.

Notes

1. The Responsible Terrorism Coverage project was funded by the Round Four Trans-Atlantic Platform "Digging Into Data Challenge," with support from the U.S. National Endowment for the Humanities (HJ-253500–17), the Netherlands Organization for Scientific Research (463–17–004), and the German Research Foundation (WE 2888/7–1). The views, findings, conclusions, or recommendations expressed in this chapter do not necessarily represent those of the three funding agencies. A more elaborated version of the material presented in this chapter can be found at www.responsibleterrorismcoverage.org.
2. These lists of recommendations can be found in more elaborated form at www.responsibleterrorismcoverage.com.

Bibliography

Hindman, M. (2018). *The Internet trap: How the digital economy builds monopolies and undermines democracy.* Princeton, NJ: Princeton University Press.

Hoffman, B. (2006). *Inside terrorism* (Revised and enlarged ed.). New York: Columbia University Press.

Lewandowsky, S., Ecker, U. K. H., & Cook, J. (2017). Beyond misinformation: Understanding and coping with the "Post-Truth" Era. *Journal of Applied Research in Memory and Cognition,* 6(4), 353–369. https://doi.org/10.1016/j.jarmac.2017.07.008

Munger, K. (2020). All the news that's fit to click: The economics of Clickbait media. *Political Communication,* 37(3), 376–397. https://doi.org/10.1080/10584609.2019.1687626

Mutz, D. C. (2015). *In-your-face politics: The consequences of uncivil media.* Princeton, NJ: Princeton University Press.

Sobieraj, S., & Berry, J. M. (2011). From incivility to outrage: Political discourse in blogs, talk radio, and cable news. *Political Communication,* 28(1), 19–41. https://doi.org/10.1080/10584609.2010.542360

29 Challenge Fox News

Jeffrey P. Jones

American democracy has faced numerous threats in the nation's history but few with more immediate and long-term danger from internal sources than the one faced after the 2020 presidential election. Tens of millions of citizens came to believe – without a scintilla of credible evidence – that the 2020 presidential election contest had been stolen or rigged or that it was the product of mass fraud, resulting in the electoral loss of President Donald Trump (Sheth, 2020). Such critics called into question the very legitimacy of democratic elections and the peaceful transfer of power because they believed that electoral fraud had occurred across multiple state voting systems, eventually resulting in a riot and the takeover of the US Capitol by pro-Trump forces in an attempted coup to stop Congress from certifying that Democrat Joe Biden was the president-elect. How did so many people come to believe such lies, to the point of attempting to violently overthrow the legislative branch of their own government?

The answer is clear: President Trump refused to accept defeat and simply asserted that the election had been stolen from him, that he had actually won the election, and that his supporters should "Stop the Steal." After Electoral College votes were submitted and after Congress met to declare Biden the winner, Trump called on his supporters to march down Pennsylvania Avenue to the Capitol and stop the legislative process, resulting in the worst internal attack on American democracy since the Civil War. But how did we arrive at a juncture at which millions of people believed whatever Trump said, however disconnected his remarks were from reality, however wrong, fallacious, and conspiratorial they were, however much they diverged from what major news outlets and state electoral systems had reported as true?

True according to all major news outlets except one – Fox News.[1] As has been shown repeatedly by journalists (Stelter, 2020; Poniewozik, 2019), scholars (Benkler et al., 2018), media watchdog organizations (Media Matters for America, 2010), and research institutes (Public Religion Research Institute, 2020), Fox News, more than any other right-wing media operation, was the most significant source of Trumpism, right-wing propaganda, and intentional disinformation on the American media landscape between 2000 and 2020.

Fox News not only exhibited fealty to Trump, but during the entire Trump presidency, the network was the generative force for constructing a systematic drumbeat of narratives that worked tirelessly to reinforce whatever Trump said at any given moment. Detailed (and humorous) comparisons of Fox News to North Korean state media became a commonplace on late-night comedy shows during the Trump administration.

Indeed, the lies emanating from the Trump administration and Fox News existed in a vicious circle, in which Trump would parrot what he heard on Fox programming while Fox would faithfully advance whatever fallacies Trump was peddling at the time. CNN's media correspondent, Brian Stelter, captured the warping influence of this co-dependency when observing:

> [Trump] relied on hyper-partisan media outlets that distorted his view of America, the world, his presidency and his own popularity. He watched and watched as his favorite TV shows deceived him and his base, further alienating Republican voters and deepening the country's divides. Trump followed Fox's lead. He parroted what he heard on TV. He lied and lied, but rather than suffer the consequences, his lies were excused and supported and even celebrated by his media enablers.
>
> (Stelter, 2021)

To be sure, Fox News is but one organ in a robust right-wing media ecosystem (Benkler et al., 2018) that also includes talk radio (Rush Limbaugh, Mark Levin, Glenn Beck), competing conservative cable news outlets (NewsMax, One American News Network), websites (Breitbart, InfoWars), social media (Facebook, Twitter, Instagram), and other outlets (evangelical media). This ecosystem is critical to furthering narratives of support for Trump and the Republican Party generally. Through years of overt pro-Republican, right-wing propaganda, these media outlets have constructed, in tandem, a completely alternative epistemic system (Roberts, 2017, 2019), one that rejects traditional, objective ways of arriving at facts, substituting instead a belief system more akin to religion, albeit a religion that is deferential to only certain voices of authority.

Fox News is arguably the most important such voice in the right-wing mediasphere (Benkler et al., 2018; Public Religion Research Institute, 2020). As conservative writer and former Republican presidential speech writer David Frum once put it a decade ago, "Republicans originally thought that Fox worked for us, and now we are discovering we work for Fox" (Media Matters for America, 2010).

Fox is not only the top-ranked cable news outlet but also the number-one cable *network* on television. As a 24-hour cable news channel, Fox is the center of gravity for talk and coverage of public affairs on television. Its prime-time hosts have loyal and dedicated followers, none more important than former President Trump himself (Poniewozik, 2019). Indeed, it has been repeatedly shown that Trump was a heavy Fox News viewer throughout the day and evening and would quite frequently Tweet orders and make policy changes (or issue recriminations and insults) minutes after watching Fox programs, such as the morning show *Fox & Friends*, as well as prime-time shows hosted by Tucker Carlson, Sean Hannity, and Laura Ingraham. This feedback loop between Fox and presidential action became even more robust and bizarre when Carlson, Hannity, and Ingraham effectively became a "shadow cabinet" for the president (Stelter, 2020), talking to him by phone almost every day (Hannity), counseling him on foreign policy issues (Carlson), and visiting the White House to tout supposed miracle cures for COVID-19 (Ingraham).

From its beginnings in 1996 under the leadership of former CEO Roger Ailes, Fox News counterprogrammed mainstream journalism outlets (Sherman, 2014). The network adopted the slogan "Fair and Balanced," wryly suggesting that all other media competitors were liberal and biased in comparison. And while other right-wing voices were also popular with conservative audiences at the time (in particular, on talk radio), Fox's labeling itself a "news" outlet (complete with traditional news tropes and conventions that were merged with the extraordinary mise en scène of bombastic patriotic graphics and sexy blondes in short skirts) was its most brilliant stroke in claiming legitimacy for its questionable reporting practices.[2]

Fox may call itself "news," but it rarely observes standard journalistic routines – reliance on evidence, verification of facts, neutral expertise, multiple sources, objective reporting, and demonstrable fairness to all sides in a policy debate. Instead, Fox relies on scripted talking points with heavily biased "experts" or extremist politicians to further a prechosen narrative. Fox uses on-screen interviews not for interrogating truth but for repeating its scripted talking points, for identifying its enemies (liberals, Democrats, African Americans, immigrants, etc.), for obfuscating facts, for highlighting trivial culture wars, for articulating petty grievances and endless recriminations, for crafting group victimhood, and for making audiences fearful enough and angry enough to come back for more.[3] The "facts" Fox News presents need not be true, only believable (Jones, 2009; Manjoo, 2008).

In many ways, Fox serves as a conservative pulpit, similar to that of evangelical preachment. Its sermons are always the same: Focus on this theme today, repeat these words in unison, parse this text and ignore all others, praise this and damn that, fear those people and exalt the chosen others. Secular and religious practices can be quite similar in affect and, not inconsequently, equally lucrative as well. As a result, viewers are thrust into one of two houses – belief or nonbelief.

Once such performances move from logic, facts, norms, and institutional processes to beliefs, faith, myth, and desires, the repeated themes become additive, while unsubstantiated facts are simply woven into the larger tapestry. One does not have to believe *all* the stuff, but the stuff adds up to a narrative worthy of belief – for salvation, for identity, for patriarchal obedience, for love of Trump, etc. The inerrancy of the Bible and the inerrancy of Trump/Fox work well together, so it is hardly surprising that White evangelicals number among Trump's most ardent constituents.

Trump's claims of "fake news" in the face of any media report or media organization that criticized him was a brilliant move for leading viewers away from mainstream media (Benkler et al., 2018). Given such strategies, it becomes easy to understand how more than 60 million American voters could believe that the 2020 election had been stolen: Nurtured by Fox from morning to night, who could imagine an alternative universe?

All of this brings us back to the crisis of American democracy. Today, the nation finds itself deeply divided not just about politics but about what constitutes truth and reality. Within the polity, one finds incommensurate worldviews between warring factions based not only on partisanship but also on habits of media consumption. Dave Roberts (2017) refers to the fundamental tension in this divide as *tribal epistemology*: "Information is evaluated based not on conformity to common standards of evidence or correspondence to a common understanding of the world, but on whether it supports the tribe's values and goals and is vouchsafed by tribal leaders. 'Good for our side' and 'true' begin to blur into one. Now tribal epistemology has found its way to the White House." In other words, the constant feedback loop between Trump and Fox News only deepens the chasm of common citizenship. And while Trump no longer holds the power of the presidency, adherence to the right-wing epistemology is maintained 24 hours a day, 365 days a year by Fox News programming.

In sum, there is little chance of fixing the dysfunctional state of American political culture as long as such a powerful organ of lies, disinformation, and propaganda continues unabated. Yet fixing the "Fox News problem" presents a vexing dilemma: How does one begin to regulate intentional disinformation when the channel that calls itself a "news" channel is protected by the First Amendment? What can a nation do when propaganda is not the product of government but of the market itself? And what if that channel is not only highly profitable to shareholders but is also the highest-rated cable television channel across all genres? How does a nation address disinformation networks when there is such a tremendous demand for it? And what do we do when the channel's viewers seemingly have little understanding of what constitutes legitimate journalistic practices or demonstrate little desire to believe that such practices are necessary for the establishment of shared facts and, even, of shared democracy?

There are issues of both supply and demand here, as well as of the norms and expectations that structure both of them. Clearly, there is no magic bullet for fixing Fox or for addressing the many followers whose citizenship is warped by its dictates. Only recently, for example, Fox News became a central propagator of coronavirus threat denialism (Ecarma, 2020), thereby becoming not only a threat to democracy but a threat to life itself.[4] To begin coping with such malignant forms of influence, we might follow the approach of Renee DiResta (2020), who advocated a "whole-of-society" method to counter the antivaccination movement. Using that approach to deal with the "Fox News problem" means enlisting the help of multiple political actors, including various segments of government, civil society, the education establishment, and informed individuals to mitigate the damage to democracy and the threat to human life that Fox News now represents.

An additional solution is to address those who ultimately control Fox News – Rupert Murdoch, the chairman of Fox Corporation; Lachlan Murdoch, his son and CEO of Fox Corp.; and shareholders of the corporation. What Fox places on the airwaves, ultimately, is a management decision. Despite the death of former Fox President Roger Ailes, the Murdoch family has shown little appetite for turning away from Ailes's successful formula of stoking fear and hatred while promulgating ideological orthodoxy to drive profits. Indeed, after the Trump-provoked coup attempt to overthrow the US Congress, prospects for change in this regard looked dim. The Murdochs doubled-down on their existing approach through two telling changes. They moved one of the network's more "journalistic" and less opinionated hosts from her 7 p.m. time slot to the afternoon dead zone of 3 p.m., opening the 7 p.m. hour exclusively for opinion talk (the true bread and butter for audiences).

Rupert himself was also behind the decision to fire the digital editor and Election Center decision desk editor who were responsible for the election-night prediction ("call") that Arizona's electoral votes would go to Joe Biden. In short, while one might hope that watching a mob overtake the Capitol and attempt to overthrow the legislative branch of government might moderate Murdoch's belief in capitalism over democracy, Murdoch himself proved once again that his primary interest in Fox ownership was self-interest.

Although Fox is protected by the First Amendment from overt government regulation, that does not mean that there are no avenues for exerting legal, economic, political, and societal pressure to influence daily management. Public shaming and intra-elite pressure might be an effective means for reaching the Murdoch family, or at least one could hope. The threat of defamation lawsuits has also recently produced retractions from Fox related to its lies about the role that certain voting machine manufacturers played in perpetrating fraud in the 2020 election (Smith, 2020b). Lawsuits over the role Fox played in denying COVID-19 as a societal threat have already occurred. While such suits may not be successful, they very well might engender some degree of accountability from management that has typically turned a blind eye to the network's most egregious lies about COVID, lies that may well have contributed to thousands of deaths (O'Neil, 2020).

Shareholders, too, could find a moral conscience and emphasize democracy over profits, although that, too, seems rather a blind alley. But economic pressure could derive from other sources – advertiser boycotts (which have been short-lived and typically ineffectual); cable companies dropping Fox from their slates of channels; or non-Fox viewers removing it from a la carte cable channel selections (when that option becomes more widely available).

In short, while pressuring Fox's management would be the most effective way of toning down Fox's antidemocratic tendencies, it is unlikely to succeed given the network's astounding balance sheet. On the other hand, a whole-of-society approach might work. After the 2020 coup attempt, for example, the idea of cable carriers dropping Fox and other right-wing media from their lineups became a more common topic of discussion, as did increased pressure on Fox's advertising partners.

Another tough nut to crack is *audience demand* for the type of programming Fox perpetuates. If, for example, Fox suddenly changed its programming to a more moderate tone, many members of its audience could and would find other outlets to provide the diet of red meat nourishing them. In fact, that is exactly what happened to Fox in the weeks following the network's Decision Desk calling the 2020 election for Joe Biden. Audiences quickly began to migrate to two of Fox's right-wing cable competitors – NewsMax and OANN – outlets that flatly refused to concede the election, asserting an array of wild-eyed conspiracies that even Fox had not stressed so vehemently (Smith, 2020a).[5]

Right now, it is unclear whether the audiences moving rightward are simply drawn to Donald Trump's cult of personality or whether Fox (and its right-wing brethren) is building a cult of disinformation, producing what one national security expert has called the "mass radicalization" of the American polity (Allam, 2020). If such audiences believe that democracy has been truly "stolen" from them and that Democrats are the enemies of the people and not their political opponents, why should they maintain faith either in their government or in the nation's media institutions? Indeed, given such belief systems, what stands in the way of broad-based societal violence or calls for the declaration of martial law or even civil war?

Some experts believe that the coup attempt at the nation's capital on January 6, 2021, was just the first of what could be persistent efforts by radicalized insurrectionists to engage in violence against the institutions of government. If that happens, there will be little doubt that Fox News has played and continues to play a role in that radicalization. At the very least, Fox has given full-throated support to the culture wars now being fought in the homeland (such as attacks on "cancel culture" and support for Mr. Potato Head and Dr. Seuss) that often serve as distractions from actual policy debates (Viser, 2021).

Adopting a whole-of-society approach to counteract these dire consequences requires multiple ways of addressing delusional audiences and their tribal epistemologies. To begin, audiences must relearn what constitutes legitimate journalism. It is rarely satisfying to say "we need more education," but it is nonetheless true that a great many citizens do not know what journalism is or how that hallowed institution unearths important facts day in and day out. Citizens also do not know the difference between objectively collected information and outright propaganda or will even fathom how tribal trust networks like Fox put them and their neighbors in peril.

Journalists themselves must also get into the game, taking greater pains to explain their craft and why it is so vital to the nation's heartbeat. But citizens must return the favor, reaching out to journalism to regain an appreciation for how hard it is to produce a collection of common facts. Once they have done so, citizens must show their friends, family, and peers how often Fox and its compatriots consistently fail to meet the standards of journalism and how their very lives are endangered when that happens.[6]

Reengaging one's conservative relatives and friends in discussions of public affairs is hard work indeed. Donald Trump's election deepened social and political divisions already underway in American society, and in the social media sphere, "unfriending" quickly followed. In reality, it is not the most vocal (and annoying) ideological combatants who most matter in such public exchanges. They may already be a lost cause. What really matters is the much greater number of moderates, people open to less radical perspectives, who are not caught up in any particular echo chamber. Reengaging such people means that we must talk to them and argue with them and, above all, listen to them.

But how to cope with devoted Fox fans? One suggested avenue is to approach them as if one were deprogramming a cult member (Lincoln & Owen, 2020). One can't simply tell Fox viewers that they are wrong or deluded. Instead, one must remind them of who they used to be and what they have lost in recent years. One must remind them of what America once was, what values its people shared, and what has already been lost by the zero-sum, scorched-earth thinking prized at Fox. They can be reminded as well that Fox's radical propaganda is not new in American history. Radio demagogue Father Charles Coughlin of the 1930s and the John Birch Society of the 1960s sang these hymns as well. Above all, Fox viewers need to be made aware that political moderation, shared epistemology, and a set of common values have larger, longer, and deeper traditions in the United States and that they, above all, constitute the enduring threads of the American fabric.

Conclusion

In short, to find a workable present, we must resurrect our gloried past. That history, combined with our assorted commonalities and a whole-of-society approach, must work together to wrest audiences away from Fox's embrace and the network's deeply cynical emphasis on profiteering and drive toward authoritarianism. What we are as a nation and who we are as individuals hang in the balance.

Notes

1. To be fair, Fox News's election Decision Desk reporters did declare Democrat Joe Biden the presumptive election winner on November 7, 2020, after all the other television news outlets had already done so, dedicating the program's coverage that Saturday and Sunday morning to this fact. But by Monday morning, the network was back to its role in supporting Trump's claims of electoral fraud across all of its talk programming.
2. Roger Ailes, who began in Republican politics with Richard Nixon, produced Rush Limbaugh's short-lived television program (1993–94) then the cable channel America's Talking (1994–96), which modeled itself after conservative talk radio. Only when Ailes created a "news" program for Fox did he find a successful formula to spread the Republican gospel (Sherman, 2014).
3. Lest one think this description is unfair, Brian Stelter (Sullivan, 2020) reports that a large number of Fox staffers "acknowledge the harm the network has done and its frequent failure to meet basic standards for truth telling."
4. One could make this critique of Fox News as an *existential threat* all the more damning by highlighting its overt propaganda about guns, police violence, war, shoddy health care, and, of course, climate change. Indeed, the uptick in racial violence against immigrants, people of color, and antiracism demonstrations suggests Fox likely plays an important role in encouraging bodily threat and harm in these regards as well.
5. In the three weeks after the election, Fox lost nearly 30 percent of its prime-time audience, while NewsMax nearly tripled its audience numbers.
6. Unfortunately, Fox has no interest in journalism (or in its audience recognizing what constitutes journalistic practices), so we can be assured that it will continue to tell its audience that no other media can be trusted and that only it provides the way and the truth and the light.

Bibliography

Allam, H. (2020, December 14). Ex-national security officials warn of mass radicalization. Morning Edition, *National Public Radio*. www.npr.org/2020/12/14/946189613/ex-national-security-officials-warn-of-mass-radicalization

Benkler, Y., Faris, R., & Roberts, H. (2018). *Network propaganda: Manipulation, disinformation, and radicalization in American politics*. Oxford: Oxford University Press.

DiResta, R. (2020, December 20). Anti-vaxxers think this is their moment. *Atlantic Monthly*. www.theatlantic.com/ideas/archive/2020/12/campaign-against-vaccines-already-under-way/617443/

Ecarma, C. (2020, September 24). Fox News' COVID Denial hasn't aged well. *Vanity Fair.* www.vanityfair.com/news/2020/09/fox-news-covid-denial-hasnt-aged-well

Jones, J. P. (2009). Believable fictions: Redactional culture and the will to truthiness. In B. Zelizer (Ed.), *The changing faces of journalism: Tabloidization, technology and truthiness* (pp. 127–143). Abingdon, UK: Routledge.

Lincoln, R. A., & Owen, P. (2020, November 20). Maher says Trump's MAGA Cult should be deprogrammed the same way NXIVM was. *The Wrap.* www.thewrap.com/maher-says-trumps-maga-cult-should-be-deprogrammed-the-same-way-nxivm-was/

Manjoo, F. (2008). *True enough: Learning to live in a post-fact society.* New York: Wiley.

Media Matters for America Staff. (2010, March 23). Frum: "Republicans originally thought that Fox worked for us, and now we are discovering we work for Fox". *Media Matters for America.* www.mediamatters.org/abc/frum-republicans-originally-thought-fox-worked-us-and-now-we-are-discovering-we-work-fox

O'Neil, C. (2020, May 21). Fake news v. the first amendment: Fox news gets sued for alleged "campaign of deception" & disseminating of disinformation to deny & downplay the danger of Coronavirus. *Syracuse Law Review.* https://lawreview.syr.edu/fake-news-v-the-first-amendment-fox-news-gets-sued-for-alleged-campaign-of-deception-disseminating-of-disinformation-to-deny-downplay-the-danger-of-coronavirus/

Poniewozik, J. (2019). *Audience of one: Donald Trump, television, and the fracturing of America.* New York: Liveright Publishing Corporation.

Public Religion Research Institute. (2020, November 18). Trumpism after Trump? How Fox news structures republican attitudes. www.prri.org/research/trumpism-after-trump-how-fox-news-structures-republican-attitudes/

Roberts, D. (2017, May 19). Donald Trump and the rise of tribal epistemology. *Vox.* www.vox.com/policy-and-politics/2017/3/22/14762030/donald-trump-tribal-epistemology

Roberts, D. (2019, November). With impeachment, America's epistemic crisis has arrived. *Vox.* www.vox.com/policy-and-politics/2019/11/16/20964281/impeachment-hearings-trump-america-epistemic-crisis

Sherman, G. (2014). *The loudest voice in the room: How the brilliant, bombastic Roger Ailes built Fox News – and divided a country.* New York: Random House.

Sheth, S. (2020, December 7). 83% of republicans polled after the 2020 election said they didn't believe Joe Biden won. *Yahoo News.* https://news.yahoo.com/83-republicans-dont-believe-joe-152545118.html?guccounter=1

Smith, B. (2020a, November 29). The King of Trump TV thinks you're dumb enough to buy it. *The New York Times.* www.nytimes.com/2020/11/29/business/media/newsmax-chris-ruddy-trump.html

Smith, B. (2020b, December 20). The "red slime" lawsuit that could sink right-wing media. *The New York Times.* www.nytimes.com/2020/12/20/business/media/smartmatic-lawsuit-fox-news-newsmax-oan.html?searchResultPosition=1

Stelter, B. (2020). *Hoax: Donald Trump, Fox News, and the dangerous distortion of truth.* New York: One Signal Publishers.

Stelter, B. (2021, January 14). "He could never tell the truth:" Trump's presidency was kneecapped by his lies. *CNN.com*. www.cnn.com/2021/01/13/media/trump-presidency-reliable-sources/index.html

Sullivan, M. (2020, August 23). Trump is "Fox's Frankenstein," insiders told CNN's Brian Stelter – and here's the toll it's taken. *Washington Post*. www.washingtonpost.com/lifestyle/media/trump-is-foxs-frankenstein-says-cnns-brian-stelter-and-heres-the-toll-its-taken-on-the-network/2020/08/21/d3af1288-e3ad-11ea-b69b-64f7b0477ed4_story.html

Viser, M. (2021, March 5). Early in Biden's presidency, GOP shows the places they'll go. *Washington Post*. www.washingtonpost.com/politics/gop-seuss-muppets-neanderthal/2021/03/05/9d4e92b6-7dd8-11eb-a976-c028a4215c78_story.html

Conclusion

30 Enliven Your Civic Capacities

Susan Nold

Every book has a history, and this book is no exception. In April of 2000, the Annette Strauss Institute for Civic Life was inaugurated at the University of Texas at Austin. To get things going, the institute sponsored a research conference that brought to Austin 24 young scholars from communication and political science who were asked to identify research agendas for the upcoming century. In the years after the conference, the authors became leaders in their respective disciplines. To celebrate the institute's 20th anniversary, they and other scholars were presented with a second challenge: to analyze the problems affecting modern politics and to identify plausible solutions. Hence this book.

I write as the current director of the Annette Strauss Institute for Civic Life. An attorney by training, I served for many years as general counsel to an influential Texas state senator, an attorney for the Texas Sunset Advisory Commission, and a government-relations professional and fundraiser. The mission of the Strauss Institute drew me back to the University of Texas, where I received my law degree. In addition to running the institute, I am a senior lecturer in communication studies and teach the course "Communicating to Government." Because of the broken politics of our day, *Fixing American Politics* speaks to my soul.

The preceding chapters have discussed myriad problems now besetting American democracy. In this chapter, I describe how the Strauss Institute works day in and day out to flesh out ideas for strengthening democracy and putting them into practice – through applied research, community outreach, working with K–12 educators on curricular matters, and engaging college students in focused discussions about civic life. Our highly engaged activities generally track what the contributors of this book have laid out in the preceding chapters:

* We **ask important questions**, as have Bethany Albertson (How can political emotion be made safe for democracy?) and Sharon E. Jarvis (How should we discuss the role of voters?).
* We **examine existing institutions**, as Vanessa Beasley, Bartholomew H. Sparrow, and Jeffrey P. Jones did when urging a fundamental rethinking of the presidency, the FCC, and Fox News.

DOI: 10.4324/9781003212515-38

- We **risk being unconventional**, as Jill A. Edy did with her encouragement to make old politics new again, and as my predecessor, Regina G. Lawrence, did when imagining how journalism in the US might be reframed and refreshed.
- We **broaden social networks**, an increasingly important objective given the polarization now stalking the United States, in part by listening to people who are different from us and by actively seeking out groups that have long been ignored, as Shawn J. Parry-Giles, Nicholas A. Valentino, and others have urged.
- We **pursue everyday fairness** – a central mission for the institute, given the profound disparities that now define our politics, by encouraging young people to reckon with economic differences and appreciate how social media can turn people against one another, as Eunji Kim and Emily Sydnor have described.
- Above all, the institute **tries bold experiments**. We are excited about innovation in campaign communication, as Robert Klotz has envisioned, and in modes of reporting the news, which Natalie (Talia) Jomini Stroud and Yujin Kim have discussed.

In short, the ideas explored in *Fixing American Politics* are the very ideas we put into practice at the Annette Strauss Institute. The contributors urge us to shake ourselves loose of stale and unproductive political practices, a goal to which the institute aspires each and every day. To wit:

Ask Important Questions

The Annette Strauss Institute still bears the stamp that Dr. Roderick P. Hart, this volume's editor, left as its founding director, and we still pursue the probing questions that have defined his career. In the 1970s, for example, he and his co-authors (Hart et al., 1980) developed a metric to measure what they called rhetorical sensitivity – the degree to which communicators adapt their language to the audience and circumstances confronting them. Such sensitivity is in tragically short supply today, yet the need for it is clearer than ever. Hart also raised important questions about the role of popular television in civic life and its disconnecting, disengaging effects on the nation (Hart, 1994).

Hart's curiosity, especially regarding political communication, provides essential context for the institute's goals. It was founded on the premise that "active engaged citizens, are made not born," and that they are made quintessentially through communication. For Dr. Hart and many of his protégés, our collective civic experience can best be judged by the quality and content of what we say to one another and how we say it. The civic lives we aspire to will be shaped to no small degree by what we see and hear.

Dr. Hart is a fine mentor and friend whose words leave an impression. Those words often take the form of a question that stays with you long after your conversation ends. Once, when offering me advice, he noted that I was prematurely focused on solutions. "Instead," he recommended, "ask yourself the most important question that needs to be asked." This is something I've never forgotten – the search for the right answer starts with the right question.

For Hart, questions are a natural way of becoming unstuck, of imagining new possibilities. Having been educated in law and having worked in public policy for much of my career, I know that asking the right question often leads to the right solution. Hart knows that too; hence the specific parameters he outlined to the authors of this book: Make the title of your chapter succinct – no more than six words; include an imperative verb; and end with a concrete suggestion. So, yes, solutions certainly have their place. But we will all be better off if we start by asking the right questions, which is exactly what the contributors to this book have attempted throughout.

Examine Existing Institutions

The Strauss Institute named our flagship citizenship award after Shirley Bird Perry. Her long resumé of service to the University of Texas at Austin included stints as senior vice president, vice president of development and university relations, vice chancellor for development and university relations for the University of Texas system, and director of the student union. She served, led, and mentored thousands of students over the years and made people's lives better throughout the State of Texas. She believed in institutions; she shaped them; and, in the process, she became one herself.

This notion of "institutions" has been powerfully devalued by modern politics, as a raft of polling demonstrates (Gallup, 2007). And to be sure, examining institutions means asking hard questions of them. But it also requires recognizing the vital importance of healthy, accountable institutions for communities, democracy, and society at large. Institutions exist because people need them; big institutions exist because people confront big problems.

Institutions bring order and process to society, even as they shift to reflect it. Institutions endure beyond a given generation to help the next one thrive. With institutions, civic action becomes meaningful and impactful, scaling up to the needs of a community, city, state, or nation. Without institutions, civic life shrinks. Strong institutions amplify, and are bound by, democratic principles and virtues. Weak ones lack meaning and purpose. At their worst, institutions become indecent, insidious, and corrupt oppressors – purveyors of lies and perpetrators of injustice. All citizens have a stake in strong institutions.

Unfortunately, as Yuval Levin (2020) notes, vital institutions such as the mass media, Congress, and even the presidency are increasingly viewed as platforms not for strengthening society but for building personal brands and increasing one's celebrity. In such cases, an institution can bestow power on people who neither appreciate nor respect it, even as they leverage its scale and resources:

> When we don't think of our intuitions as *formative* but as *performative* – when the presidency and Congress are just stages for political performance art, when a university becomes a venue for vain virtue signaling, when journalism is indistinguishable from activism – they become harder to trust. They aren't really asking for our confidence, just for our attention.
>
> (Levin, 2020, p. 34)

Supporting institutions is fundamental to the mission of organizations like the Annette Strauss Institute. Our 20th anniversary (in 2020) was supposed to be a celebratory one, but it shifted dramatically as the COVID-19 pandemic engulfed the world. Almost predictably, revered and vital institutions – such as the nation's electoral and public health systems – came under attack. As the crises deepened, the institute's focus of discussion shifted as well, from answers we helped find during the last generation to questions that will define the next one:

- Is public faith in our institutions still merited?
- What are the attributes of strong institutions?
- What lessons do they offer for leadership and for citizenship?
- Should respect for institutions be taught in the nation's schools?
- What tensions are inherent in our strongest institutions?
- What steps must be taken to preserve private and public institutions?
- What narratives surround our institutions? Are they based in reality? How might they be reimagined?
- Who impacts institutions – as defenders, detractors, or disruptors – and what are they trying to say to us?
- How can institutions become antidotes to polarization?

The fate of American society and democracy rests in no small part on how we answer these questions. None of the answers will be easily found, but the questions – always the questions – will guide the institute's path for years to come.

Risk Being Unconventional

While those of us at the Annette Strauss Institute revere institutions, we resist conventionality. We know how urgent our work is, and we try to approach it in creative ways. As a result, I often describe the institute as a living laboratory; we do not merely observe civic engagement but must be committed to solving the problems we study.

That was the impulse driving our *Texas Civic Health Index*. The index creates objective, standardized metrics to evaluate the civic health of communities, regions, and populations. Communities with strong indicators have higher employment rates, stronger schools, better physical health, and more responsive governments. This effort, launched in 2013 and updated in 2018, has prompted partnerships that have restructured government processes, affected classroom civics education, redirected investments in civic health, informed national and local conversations about civic life, and helped build a network of civic leaders across the country.

The Index grounds the concept of "civic engagement" in three specific categories:

* *Political engagement* includes voting and emailing elected officials – it describes what citizens can do to influence governmental decisions and actions.
* *Community service* includes volunteering, donating to charities, and joining organizations – it describes actions people can take to address the needs of others in their communities.
* *Neighborliness* considers the degree to which people know and trust those immediately surrounding them; it describes actions citizens can take to help one another. Given the succession of natural disasters that has befallen Texas in recent years, this is an increasingly important window into the life-and-death effects of civic health.

The Strauss Institute conducted the Civic Health Index in partnership with the National Conference of Citizenship. In both 2013 and 2018, the index drove wide-ranging conversations in the media and in communities about the troubling state of civic health in Texas, which ranked last among all states in political engagement in 2013 and generally fared poorly on other measures as well.

Beyond these headlines, the index helped direct the institute's work to improve civic communication and education. It did so by challenging convention, looking at civic health in new ways, and being brave enough to ask how communities are really doing and how they might do better.

We have also used the Civic Health Index across a spectrum of activities. Students in our Texas Civic Ambassador Program, for example, have become proficient in using the index to guide their training and community outreach. We have also created several engaging lesson plans and interactive exercises to help more Texans become familiar with the index's insights. Ideally, the index will continue to offer people a way to expand their own civic practice and civic identity, leading them to become more regular voters, better neighbors, and more generous donors.

There are many such opportunities to rethink how we talk about civic values. Most require breaking out of conventions, especially those that increasingly disregard institutions and equate compromise with weakness. As we tackle these thorny questions, we constantly ask ourselves where a less conventional approach might lead. What if we did not know what we currently know? Is there another way of moving forward?

Broaden Social Networks

My first conference as director of the Annette Strauss Institute was the 2016 Frontiers of Democracy convening by the John Tisch College of Civic Life at Tufts University. I arrived feeling honored, excited, and, honestly, a bit overwhelmed. It was a shock to find that many of the more experienced conferencegoers confessed to similar feelings. In 2016, and in the years leading up to it, the United States and other democracies around the world were experiencing massive disruption. Many civic experts were caught off guard, unnerved by the pace of the social and technological transformation taking place – just as millions of Americans were.

New, unprecedented connections are helping to drive this disruption. Technology platforms and social networks allow people to spread information – and misinformation – with alarming speed. These technological accelerants shape our impressions of each other and society, our thoughts, our behavior, and even our offline experiences. To the degree that these connections are helping to drive the problem, they just might help drive the solution as well.

It is no coincidence that the Strauss Institute resides in the Moody College of Communication at UT Austin. Our institute and others like it have a new and vital role in helping citizens understand the quickly transforming communications landscape and what it means for people, communities, and democracy. We need to ask critically important questions about the benefits – and the threats – that social media platforms pose for society. And we need to integrate new educational practices into the broader framework of civic health.

The Civic Health Index embodies this approach. Its framework and the three categories it measures – political participation, civic involvement, and social connectedness – are all fundamental to how people approach societal issues. And all of them are increasingly driven by social media.

There now exists a fast-growing body of research that examines how to minimize the problems social platforms create and instead use them to strengthen connections within communities and between neighbors. The Strauss Institute and Moody College are proud hubs for this research, which is also happening at similar institutions around the world. By improving the character and quality of the communications that social media facilitates, we can work to strengthen and safeguard democracy. We cannot afford not to try.

Pursue Everyday Fairness

I have mentioned the first part of the Annette Strauss Institute's tagline: "*Active engaged citizens are made, not born.*" The second part is just as important: "*Society benefits when more citizens take part.*" For 20 years, the institute has tried – through research and education – to ensure that more Americans have the opportunity to acquire skills for constructive civic engagement. As discussed earlier, we believe schools, churches, governments, and universities are only as strong as the people who show up, take part, and contribute. Increasing the number of people who do so is central to the institute's mission.

Wider participation, we believe, creates a fairer political system. When more people participate, electoral and policy outcomes create wider benefits. Right now, economic and social disparities increasingly permeate American life. One of the best ways to address such imbalances is to bring more of those affected into the political process itself.

Much of the institute's work focuses on students – we create outlets for their service and learning opportunities to help them become more engaged citizens. As discussed, our strong ties to the Moody College of Communication fortify a fundamental understanding that communication lies at the heart of civic education and individual transformation. Our programs include:

- **Speak Up Speak Out,** the institute's research, problem-solving, and public-speaking program for students in grades 3 through 12. Since its inception in 2002, more than 10,000 young Texans have taken part in our civic education programs, culminating in an annual State Civics Fair, where students present ideas for strengthening engagement. Some of these ideas have been taken up by local elected officials and state officials and been turned into public policy.
- **TX Votes** is a UT Austin student organization that works on campus to create more voters, increase electoral participation, and inspire citizenship. TX Votes' work is entirely nonpartisan, offering all students a way to participate on campus in registration drives, volunteer voter registrar deputization, and training sessions supported by the county voter registration office. It also connects students with similar efforts on other campuses through voting networks, summits, and conferences.
- **RU Ready Texas** is a course launched first by Rutgers University's Eagleton Institute of Politics. Back in Austin, the institute offers the Eagleton program in partnership with the Moody College's communication and leadership degree plan and the Ann Richards School for Young Women Leaders. Students in the course are immersed in civic learning and communications theory, and

they apply what they know by teaching civics to local high school students.
- **New Politics Forum** is a statewide program that hosts nonpartisan and bipartisan youth-focused events and workshops. These events aim to enhance students' understanding of democratic principles while teaching civic skills and highlighting civic values, especially as they are manifested in state and local politics.
- **Campaign Bootcamp** convenes a bipartisan group of political professionals to train students on the basics of election campaigns. It equips students with the nuts and bolts of campaign work and empowers them to consider the ethical and democratic implications of elections.
- **Great Conversations** brings together institute supporters, friends, and students of all political stripes every year for an evening of civil dialogue about shared values and ideals.

These programs show how the institute works to make active, engaged citizens. Since its inception in 2000, tens of thousands of students have benefited from these programs and others like them. More than 1,200 student staff and volunteers have received appointments or funding to produce these programs and conduct research in conjunction with the institute.

The institute supports these wide-ranging activities – and more besides – with an eye toward a more robust political system. As more people become involved in government, more people will benefit from its policies and, thus, gain a sense of ownership in the government that governs them.

Try Bold Experiments

The Annette Strauss Institute is rooted in the conviction that one can always find better ways of making more citizens, although doing so means questioning assumptions, trying new things, failing, learning, and trying again. We are proud of this spirit of adventure. To that end, the boldest experiment of all might be the institute itself.

That is true for others in the civic-engagement space as well. All of us are swimming against a current of misinformation and cultivated cynicism. We work every day to transform the cultural forces that increasingly define modern life in hopes of building a healthier democracy. We are both committed and creative, constantly seeking out any new partnerships, ideas, or angles to help us build a more inclusive and substantive approach to political engagement.

It is especially appropriate that so much of this experimentation is taking place in the communications realm. New communications styles and techniques are shaping political life in powerful, even dominant ways. Clearly, we also must learn how to leverage the power of these platforms for the benefit of society.

Fixing American Politics has brought together a compelling set of musings offered by thinkers and doers from across the United States. Organizations like the Annette Strauss Institute depend on such people for ideas that can be translated into action, creating a new generation of engaged citizens. Democracy is an attractive and resonant form of government, but it can also be taken for granted, an unacceptable outcome indeed.

Conclusion

My work at the institute has offered me the opportunity to collaborate with – and to learn from – an incredible range of people, organizations, and initiatives from across the country and around the world. All of us share basic goals that reflect our values: to combat political division, expand civic engagement, and improve civic education.

More fundamentally, we all share the aim reflected in this book's title: to fix American politics and to preserve America's principles of democratic self-governance. The stakes of this work can feel overwhelming at times. They require:

- a refusal to take the permanence of American democracy for granted;
- the day-to-day certainty that democracy cannot produce desired outcomes without the engagement of active, informed citizens; and
- regular, often difficult examinations of our history, policies, and assumptions – a process modeled by the contributors to this book.

Current trends – visible online, in the headlines, in our communities, and even within our own families – make this democratic discipline even more difficult. In nearly every direction, we see fragmentation and division in politics and government, all fueled by a global pandemic, increasing economic inequality, a warming climate, aging infrastructure, and rapid technological change. All of these things test American democracy. They also prompt the question: Will our system of democratic self-government press through these challenges or be subsumed by them?

Yet despite the stark challenges and massive stakes involved, almost everyone I've encountered in this field of democracy preservation has been fundamentally hopeful and pragmatic. Their work is rooted in the faith that if citizens are educated and prepared for what citizenship requires, self-governance will prevail. We may differ on how to best deliver this education – *how* to prepare people for their roles as citizens – but we share the belief that it is possible and essential to do so.

Respected scholars and civic visionaries have examined this question for centuries – it is gratifying that such exploration continues to yield new answers. Here, to me, are some of the most exciting projects:

- In 2012, the National Task Force on Civic Learning and Democratic Engagement published *A Crucible Moment: College Learning and Democracy's Future*.[1] The publication was accompanied by a national call to action by the US Department of Education: to make civic learning a fundamental part of the student experience at colleges and universities. The report (available at www.aacu.org/civiclearning/crucible) prompted the formation of regional action networks, and their work still continues today.
- The 2021 Educating for American Democracy (EAD) Roadmap offers an important framework for K–12 civic learning. It weaves together history and civics in a way that teaches students about America's constitutional democracy, cultivates a sense of civic patriotism, and inspires involvement. The multiyear initiative represents a collaboration by some of the brightest stars in our field: Danielle Allen of Harvard University, Paul Carrese of Arizona State University, Louise Dubé of iCivics, Jane Kamensky of Harvard University, Kei Kawashima-Ginsberg of CIRCLE, Peter Levine of Tufts University, and Tammy Waller of the Arizona Department of Education (explore and interact with the EAD roadmap at www.educatingforamericandemocracy.org/).
- Between 2018–2020, the American Academy of Arts & Sciences Commission on the Practice of Democratic Citizenship – co-chaired by Professor Allen, Stephen B. Heintz of Rockefeller Brothers Fund, and Eric P. Liu of Citizen University – surveyed people across the US. Their essential goal: to discover the best ways of responding to the weaknesses and vulnerabilities of political and civic life. Its final bipartisan report, *Our Common Purpose: Reinventing American Democracy for the 21st Century*, includes six strategies and 31 recommendations to help the nation emerge as a more resilient democracy by 2026, the nation's 250th anniversary (find *Our Common Purpose* at www.amacad.org/ourcommonpurpose/report).
- In 2019, the Institute for Citizens and Scholars' president, Rajiv Vinnakota, published a landscape analysis of civic organizations and initiatives. Titled *From Civic Education to a Civic Learning Ecosystem: A Landscape Analysis and Case for Collaboration*, the analysis reveals far more agreement about the aims of civic engagement than current political debates and rhetoric might suggest (it can be found online at https://rbw.civic-learning.org/).
- The CivXNow coalition, the nation's largest cross-partisan civic education cooperative, is in the trenches every day, helping schools fulfill their civic mission. It is led by iCivics and does inspiring work to help educators improve civic education from kindergarten through

high school graduation – in and out of school (learn more at www.civxnow.org/).
- The John Tisch College of Civic Life at Tufts University, Center for Information and Research on Civic Learning & Engagement (CIRCLE), and Institute for Democracy & Higher Education (IDHE) are all wellsprings of research and initiatives to support civic scholarship and engagement. These programs have demonstrated an impact far beyond campus boundaries, providing an interdisciplinary model for institutions to emulate (see https://tischcollege.tufts.edu/ for more).
- National Conference of Citizenship is a congressionally chartered nonprofit organization that spotlights national initiatives to expand civic engagement and civic health in communities across the country. This group continues to be a source of work and resources that strengthen the nation's civic life (learn more at https://ncoc.org/).
- And Philanthropy for Active Civic Engagement (PACE Funders) is a member-based organization that brings together some of the more active philanthropic foundations in the civic space. This collaboration creates a "philanthropic laboratory" that helps funders strengthen American democracy and civic life (see www.pacefunders.org/ for more).

This is a very short list, one that barely scratches the surface of all that is happening in civic work. It certainly does not capture the tens of thousands of regional, state, and local efforts and initiatives that are happening right now to create a healthier civic life.

More than anything, the programs listed here simply demonstrate how much creative work is going into our nation's civic health at this moment and why such work is so important. They show virtuous cycles and positive multipliers that are revealed when committed citizens inspire others to get engaged. All of these efforts deserve their own unique chapter in our shared civic story.

These initiatives lean on inquiry and collaboration and do not try to prescribe every solution. Rather, they reach out to other people, inviting and inspiring them to become part of the national civic story. Behind each one are respected civic heroes – people drawn to the hard work of fixing American politics not out of self-interest but rather out of a sense of patriotism, public service, and commitment to be part of something larger and more lasting than themselves. Such leaders are made and not born. Perhaps you will choose to join their company.

Note

1. The National Task Force on Civic Learning and Democratic Engagement. 2012. *A Crucible Moment: College Learning and Democracy's Future*. Washington, DC: Association of American Colleges and Universities. To download a copy of the report, see www.aacu.org/crucible.

Bibliography

Gallup Poll. (2007). *Confidence in institutions.* https://news.gallup.com/poll/1597/confidence-institutions.aspx

Hart, R. P. (1994). *Seducing America: How television charms the modern voter.* New York: Oxford University Press.

Hart, R. P., Carlson, R., & Eadie, W. (1980). Attitudes toward Communication and the Assessment of Rhetorical Sensitivity. *Communication Monographs*, 47, 1–22.

Levin, Y. (2020). *A time to build: From family to community to congress and the campus, how recommitting to our institutions can revive the American dream.* New York: Basic Books.

Index

Abernathy, P. 237
Academy of Motion Pictures Arts and Sciences 81
Adam 4
Adserá, Alícia 236
advantaged party 21
Advertising Age 209
affective polarization 180, 202
African Americans 30
AIDS activists 38
Ailes, Roger 253, 255
Ali, Muhammad 34
"All Cops are Bastards" (ACAB) 68
Alphabet 208
Amazon 162
Amazon Prime 73
American Council on Graduate Medical Education 150
American Idol 74
American national identity 13–14; cosmopolitan memory concept of 19; patchwork approach to 18–19
American Press Institute 166
Americans for Prosperity Action 213
Ameritech 165
anger generating, terrorists and 247
Annette Strauss Institute for Civic Life 186, 263–271; experimentation and 270–271; Hart and 264–265; ideas explored 264; institutions and 265–266; programs 269–270; social networks and 268; *Texas Civic Health Index* 266–268
Ansolabehere, Stephen 210
Anthony, Susan B. 30
Apple 162
Apter, Emily 83
Arbery, Ahmaud 31, 84
Arceneaux, M. 108

Arendt, Hannah 29
Aristotle 203
Asian American vote 82
Asian vote 81
asymmetry, frame diversion and 132–133
Atlantic, The 59
AT&T 162, 165
attention economy, hybridity and 131–132
Austin Bulldog, The 198
authoritarianism 118
authority *vs.* trust journalism problem 220–221
Axios/Survey Monkey poll 238

Bambara, Toni Cade 40, 42
Barber, Bernard 221–222
Barber, William 33
Bartels, Larry 186
Batson, C. D. 119
Bell Companies 165
Bell South 165
Bennett, Lance 105
Benson, Rodney 240
Berry, J. M. 67
Bezos, Jeff 73
Biden, Joe 28, 61, 78, 121, 124, 155, 251
big data, campaigns and 178
Big Tech, political advertising and 207
Black Joy and Resistance (Waheed) 42
Black Joy Project 42
Black Joy Zine 42
Black Lives Matter 42, 69, 84, 193, 220
#BlackLivesMatter 31
Black Lives Matter Global Network Foundation, Inc. 83
Blasian 82

Boczkowski, Pablo 230
Brady, Tom 75
Breen, Lorna 150
broadband 167
broadcast localism 164
Brookings Institution Policy 2020 196–197
Brown, Adrienne Maree 40, 42
Brown, Nannie 40
Brown, Scott 25
Brueggemann, Walter 33
Bryant, Kobe 13
Buckley v. Valeo, 1976 210
Bush, George H. W. 21, 178, 194
Bush, George W. 22, 24–25
Butler, Judith 114
BuzzFeed 227

cable news; *see also* Fox News: most-watched 74; outrage programming on 66–67; with political slants 131
Caillois, Roger 38
Campaign Bootcamp 270
campaign disclosure requirements 206
campaign discourse, improving *see* super PACs
Campbell, Karlyn Kohrs 101, 103
cancel culture 108–114; democratic deliberation and 110–111; expressions of 108; overview of 108–109; political equities and, advancing 111–113; roots of 109–110
Capitalism and Freedom (Friedman) 168
Capitol Public Radio, Sacramento 223
Carli, Linda 59
Carlson, Matt 220–221
Carlson, Tucker 253
Carney, Dave 175–176, 179
CBS News 162
censorship 157
Center for Media Engagement 229, 231–232
Chappell, David 31
Charter Communications 161, 162
Chauvin, Derek 31, 84
Chavez, Cesar 31
Chávez, Karma 83
Chicago Defender 32
Chicago Tribune, The 60
Chomsky, Noam 74
citizen journalists 197
Citizens United 95

Citizens United v. FEC, 2010 210
Civic Health Index 267
civics education 196–197
Civic Signals project 233
civil engagement 196–197; *see also* Annette Strauss Institute for Civic Life; community service 267; components of 267; neighborliness 267; political 267
"Civility in America 2019" (poll) 68
CivXNow 197
Clay, Henry 23
Cleveland, Grover 21, 23
climate change 52–53
Clinton, Bill 21, 24, 29, 178
Clinton, Hillary 60, 109, 181
Clubhouse 76
CNN 252
coalitions 80–86; overview of 80; quantitative representation and 81–82; race and 81–82; unexceptional 83–85
Coke, J. S. 119
Colter, Ann 108
Combahee River Collective 84
Comcast 161, 162
Commager, Henry Steele 13–14
Committee to Protect Journalists 166
Common Cause 166
Communications Decency Act (CDA) 206–207
Communication Workers of America 166
community-centered journalism 223–224
community service 267
Condon, Meghan 76
conflict-of-interest problem, government 137; *see also* Watchdog Journalism Branch (W.J.B.) of government
Conn, K. M. 123
connective democracy 227
consensus, polarization and 49–55; overview of 49–50; partisan divide and 51–54; public opinion and 50–51
conservative nostalgia: American politics and 14–16; described 15; social identities and 15–16
Consumer Population Survey 236
Coolidge, Calvin 161, 167–168
Corporation for Public Broadcasting 161

Cortéz, Ricardo Antonio 3
Cosby Show, The 75
cosmopolitan memory 19
Coughlin, Charles 257
COVID-19 pandemic 52–53;
  caretakers and, toll on 150–151;
  economic inequality and 77–78;
  health care decision-making and
  147, 149; outgroup empathy and
  121–122; populations hardest hit
  during 149–150
Craigslist 228, 237
Crenshaw, K. 84
Crick, Bernard 96, 98
Crisis (NAACP) 32
Crossing the Quality Chasm (Institute
  of Medicine) 147
CrowdTangle 227
Cruz, Kleaver 42
Cruz, Ted 176
culture, politics and 6–7
cynicism 7

Daily Texan, The 60
Darr, J. P. 223
Darsey, James 30
Daum, Meghan 110
Davis, M. H. 119
deGrasse Tyson, Neil 57
democracy and journalism 235–237
Democracy Fund 187, 188
Democracy Matters 34
democratic integrity, described 154
democratic norms, outgroup empathy
  and 121
Democrats, beliefs of 51–54
Denton, Nick 227
Diaz, Francy Luna 121–122
Digital First Media 162
digital media 131, 153, 155; *see also*
  election apps for democratic
  integrity; stock market valuation
  162–163
digital metrics 227–233; audience
  interest *vs.* advertiser wants and
  229–230; conceptualizing 232–233;
  editorial/business firewall and
  230, Gawker and 227; influence
  of 227–228; interpretation of 231;
  problem with 228; societal needs
  and 229; as solution for newsrooms
  230–231; use of 231–232
digital sexism 68
direct subsidies 239

DiResta, Renee 255
disadvantaged party 21
disinformation: political advertising
  and 201–202; redesigning
  circulation of 157–158
Disney 162
Doss, E. 15–16
Douglas, William O. 57
Douglass, Frederick 30, 93
DREAMers 67
Du Bois, W. E. B. 32
Duffield, Gladys 39

Eagly, Alice 59
economic inequality 73–78;
  COVID-19 pandemic and 77–78;
  media coverage of 78; overview
  of 73–74; reality TV programs
  and 74–75; social media and
  76–77; solutions to 77–78; sports
  broadcasts and 75
Edwards, George 22
Ehrenreich, Barbara 40
Eisenhower, Dwight 21, 26–27
election apps for democratic
  integrity 153–159; circulation
  of disinformation, redesigning
  157–158; democratic integrity,
  described 154; overview of
  153–154; political message
  transparency and 154–157
election threats, communicating about
  185–191; balancing threat/solution
  communications 188–189; electoral
  participation study 189–190;
  overview of 185–186; rigged
  elections study 187–188; solutions
  for 186–187
Electorally Speaking Project 186
electorate studies 175–183; big
  data and 178; campaign research
  176–177; investments suggested
  for 182–183; issue debates and
  182; overview of 175–176; political
  bias and 180; political parties
  and 180–181; polling and 177;
  qualitative data and 178–179;
  social media and 179; swing
  voting and 181; voter attitudes and
  179–182
Emergency Alert System 161
emotion 56–61; consequences for,
  in politics 59–60; embedded in
  politics 57–58; overview of 56;

truths about, and politics 57–60; as valuable political resource 56–57
empathic concern items 119
empathy 19; defined 119
Engels, Jeremy 29
Environmental Protection Agency 53
Eve 4
expectations gap, presidency 23
expertise concept, medicine and 148

Facebook 76, 95, 153, 155, 158, 162, 202, 208, 214, 228
Fact Checker 133
fact-checking 229; organizations 204–205
FactCheck.org 133, 204
fairness doctrine, mediated listening and 93–96; diversity of views and 95; information quality and 96; polarization and 96; public accountability and 96; quantity over quality equation and 95–96; time limitations and 95
family separation policy 32
FCC *see* Federal Communications Commission (FCC)
fear, terrorists and 247
Federal Communications Commission (FCC) 94–95, 161–168; media economy and 162–163; media mergers and 161; media policy and 163–165; neoliberalism and 161, 162–163; overview of 161–162; ownership diversity and 164–165; policy changes needed 166–167; reforming 165–167; structure changes needed 165–166
Federalist Paper: No. 49 56; No. 51 204
First Amendment 91–98; fairness doctrine, mediated listening and 93–96; overview of 91–92; right to listen and 92–93
Fitzgerald, Ella 34
Floyd, George 31, 84
focus groups 178–179
Ford, Christine Blasey 110
Fox & Friends 108, 253
Fox News 17, 70, 74, 108, 162, 213, 238; challenging 251–258; COVID-19 and 255–256; mass radicalization role of 256–257; Murdoch family and 255; Trumpism and 251–253

fractured media system 130–131
frame-checking 129
frame diversion 132–133
"Freedom Budget for All" 33
Free Press 223
Friedland, Lewis 236
Friedman, Milton 168
Frum, David 252
"Fuck 12" 68

Gallup 238
Game of Thrones 75
Gannett 237
Garber, M. 59
Garfield, Bob 209
Garner, Jennifer 52
Garrison, William Lloyd 93
Garza, Alicia 83
GateHouse Media 162
Gawande, Atul 149
Gawker (website) 227, 230
gay liberation movement 38
gender, incivility and 66, 68
General Social Survey 52
Gerber, Alan 175
Get Out the Vote (Gerber and Green) 175
Gibbs, Nancy 29
Gillis, Shane 108
Gimpel, Jim 175
Ginsburg, Ruth Bader 113–114
Google 153, 162, 202, 228
Graham, Lindsey 206
Graham Media Group 231–232
Grant, Ulysses 21
Great Conversations program 270
Great Depression 24
Great Pilgrimage 39
Green, Donald 175–175
Group Empathy Index (GEI) 119
group identity 118

Hamilton, James 236
Hanks, Tom 51
Hannity, Sean 253
Harding, Warren G. 24
harmony 111
Harris, Kamala 82, 83, 124
Harrison, Benjamin 22
Harrison, William Henry 21, 23
Hart, Kevin 81
Hart, Roderick P. 31, 104–105, 264–265
hate radio 94

health care decision-making 147–152; COVID-19 pandemic and 147, 149; expertise and 148; overview of 147–149; patient experience and 148; physicians as people and 150–151; populations receiving health care and 149–150; value/efficiency and 147
Hearken 223
Help America Vote Act, 2002 178
Hemmer, N. 238
Henricks, Thomas 38
Herbst, Susan 66
Herrick, James 114
Hersch, E. 58
Heschel, Abraham Joshua 32
Hitler, Adolph 7
Holmes, Oliver Wendell, Jr. 202
Honest Ads Act 206
Hong Tien Vu 227
Hu, E. 60
Hudson, Valerie 111
Hughes, Charles Evans 57
Hulu 73
hybridity, attention economy and 131–132
hybrid media system 219
hyperlocal news 197–198

Idealism, politicians and 5
identity 19; American politics and 13–14; cultural 14; national 14
identity distrust 222
ideological polarization 202
inaugural address, functions of 102
incivility 64–70; affective polarization and 65; gender and 66, 68; motivated reasoning and 65; vs. outrage 66–68; outrage programming and 66–67; overview of 64; polarization and 64; public-level 65; in social media 8; solutions for 68–70; understanding of 64–66
Independent, The 108
indirect subsidies 239
inequality, political advertising and 203–204
Ingraham, Laura 253
Inhofe, Jim 17
injustice, prophetic revelation of 32
Innerarity, Daniel 86
Innocents Abroad, Roughing It, The (Twain) 123
Instagram 74, 76, 95, 153, 214

Institute for Local Self Reliance 166
Institute for Nonprofit News (INN) 198
institutional listening 103–105
institutions 265–266
intensive-care checklist 149
Internews 223
Interpersonal Reactivity Index (IRI) 119
intersectionality 84
Investigative Reporters and Editors 166
issue-framed posts 231
Iyengar, Shanto 210

Jackson, Andrew 21
Jackson, Samuel L. 52
Jamieson, Kathleen Hall 101, 103, 204
Jayapal, Pramila 60
Jefferson, Thomas 203
Jeremiah (prophet) 34
Jesus 3
Jet (magazine) 32
John Birch Society 257
Johnson, Lyndon 26, 27, 194
Jones, Rosalie 39–40
journalism: authority *versus* trust problem 220–221; community-centered 223–224; contemporary crisis, context of 219–220; crisis, addressing 219–224; democracy and 235–237; deterioration of 237–238; public subsidies for 235–240; re-gaining trust challenge 221; subsidizing 238–240; trust-building innovations 221–222; volunteer/citizen 197
journalist advocacy groups 166
journalists, terrorism and 248
Joy Revolution (Rivera) 42
justice: prophetic imagination and 33–34; prophetic scope of 33

Kalmoe, N. 57
Kam, Cindy 52
Kansas-Nebraska Act 23
Kavanaugh, Brett 110
Kennedy, Edward 25
Kennedy, John F. 22, 26, 27
Key, V. O. 185–186
Key & Peele (comedy duo) 59
Kim, E. 75
Kinder, Donald 58

King, Martin Luther, Jr. 16–17, 29–31, 33–34, 122, 124–125
Klobuchar, Amy 206
Knight Foundation 196, 220, 223, 238
Knight-Ridder 237
Kondabolu, Hari 80
Kormelink, Tim Groot 229

Ladd, J. M. 222
Latino vote 81, 82
LBGTQ+ rights 113, 120
legacy journalism 219
legitimacy, terrorists and 246
Lehman, Mattias 84
Lepore, Jill 15
Levin, Yuval 265–266
Lewinsky, Monica 29
Lewis, John 113, 122
Lewis, Seth 221, 223
Liberator, The 93
Limbaugh, Rush 94
Lincoln, Abraham 21
Lincoln Courier 64
Lincoln Project 213
Lippmann, Walter 137, 138
Listening Post Collective 223
local election voting 193–199; civics education and 196–197; hyperlocal news and 197–198; midterm elections 194–196; nonprofit news and 198; overview of 193–196; structural changes and 198–199
Locke, John 14
Logic and Limits of Trust, The (Barber) 221
Lorde, Audre 40, 42
lump sums 239

Madison, James 56, 92, 203, 204
mainstream media, trust in 220
Main Studio Rule 164
March on Washington, 1963 33
Martin, Trayvon 83
Marwick, Alice 157
mask wearing 52–53
Mason, Lilliana 13, 57
mass communication 94; *see also* fairness doctrine, mediated listening and; media effects
mass radicalization 256
McCain, John 25, 180
McCarthy, Joseph 109
McClatchy 237

media effects 129–134; asymmetry, frame diversion and 132–133; fractured media system and 130–131; hybridity, attention economy and 131–132; overview of 129–130; preexisting preferences within 130–131; reporting *vs.* reacting of 129
Media Law Resources Center 166
media policy, FCC and 163–165
media-related public-interest organizations 166
media trust, decline in 220
media users, terrorism and 246–247
Meijer, Irene Costera 229
Mercieca, Jennifer 103
metrics *see* digital metrics
midterm elections 194–196
Mill, John Stuart 93
Minnpost 239
misreading context, presidents 22–24
Mitchelstein, Eugenia 230
Mo, C. H. 123
Moonves, Leslie 168
Morgan, Joan 42
Moses 3
Muddiman, Ashley 64–65
Murdoch, Lachlan 255
Murdoch, Rupert 255
Musk, Elon 73, 78

Napoli, P. 238
National Amusements 162
National Digital Inclusion Alliance 166
National Opinion Research Council 52
Negrete, Tom 232–233
neighborliness 267
Nelson, Dana 104
neoliberalism 162–163; *see also* Federal Communications Commission (FCC); described 161
Netflix 73
net neutrality 161–162, 167
New, Alice 41
New Deal 26–27
New Democrat faction 24
New Politics Forum program 270
News-Corp 162
News deserts 162
NewsMax 256
news organizations, terrorism and 248
Newspaper/Broadcast Cross-Ownership Rule 164

newspapers 162, 168
newsroom effectiveness, measuring 227–233; *see also* digital metrics; editorial/business firewall and 230; metrics and, problem with 228–230; metrics as solution 230–233; overview of 227–228
New Voices 198
New York Daily News 144
New Yorker, The 149
New York Post 144
New York Times, The 65, 74, 92, 144, 188, 223, 227, 245
New York Young Lords 38
Nixon, Richard 27, 29
"No Justice, No Peace" 68
nonprofit news 198
nostalgia, described 15
NRKbeta 233
NYNEX 165
Nzoughe, Lydie Oyanem 3

OANN 256
Obama, Barack 22, 25, 59, 60, 66, 83, 108, 181
Ocasio-Cortez, Alexandria 61, 207–208
Occupy Wall Street 83
Omar, Ilhan 112
Onate, Juan de 17
opposition presidents 21, 22
opposition president-to-restoration president patterns 24–26; Clinton-Bush 24–25; Obama-Trump 25–26
Organisation for Economic Cooperation and Development (OECD) 194
O'Rourke, Beto 176
#OscarsSoWhite 81
outgroup caring 118
outgroup empathy 117–125; COVID-19 pandemic and 121–122; cultivating 122–123; defined 119; democratic norms and 121; identifying 120; links to 118–119; measuring 119; naivete of 120; overview of 117–118
outrage programming 66–67

Palin, Sarah 66
Parks, Rosa 59
Parler 95
Parse.ly 227
participatory journalism playbook 223

partisan identities, American politics and 13–19; American national identity and 13–14; conservative nostalgia and 14–16; overview of 13; progressivism and 16–18
partisanship; *see also* partisan identities, American politics and: American politics and 13–19; consensus and 51–54
Parton, Dolly 51
Patch service, AOL 197
Peck, Annie 41
Peck, Reece 17
PEN America 166
performance, politics and 6
Perot, Ross 178, 180
Perry, Rick 175
Perry, Shirley Bird 265
personnel, politics and 6
perspective-taking items 119
persuasion 53, 91, 155
Pew Research Center 211, 227, 237
Phoenix, Davin 59
physician burnout 150
physicians as people 150–151
physician suicide 150, 151
Picard, R. 237
Pickard, Victor 165, 240
Pierce, Franklin 23
Pinker, Steven 190
Pittsburgh Courier 32
play, defined 38
playful protest 37–42; Black suffragists and 41; as disrupting power systems/social structures 38; play, described 38; racial equity and 41–42; suffragist examples of 37–41; in United States 38
polarization: affective, between partisans 57, 180, 202; consensus to overcome 49–55 (*see also* consensus, polarization and); expectations gap and 23; ideological 202; incivility and 64, 65; mediated listening and 96; misread context and 24–26
polarized division, political advertising and 202–203
political advertising 201–208; ad watch for 204–205; Big Tech and 207; campaign disclosure requirements and 206; Communications Decency Act and 206–207; disinformation and

201–202; inequality and 203–204; overview of 201; polarized division and 202–203; political parties and, strengthen 205; progressive taxation and 207; public education and 205–206; public service campaigns and 206; ranked-choice voting and 205; surveillance campaigning and 202
political engagement 267
political message transparency 154–157
political time 22
politicians: Idealism and 5; power and 4–5; reporters and 6
politics: coalitions and 80–86 (*see also* coalitions); culture and 6–7; emotion embedded in 57–58; fixing American (*see* partisan identities, American politics and); and healthcare (*see* health care decision-making); imperfections 5–7; introduction to 4–5; partisanship and 50–51; passionate about 3–10; performance and 6; personnel and 6; reasons for dismissal of 5–7; socialization and 7; substance *vs.* 5–6; throughout history 3–4; time and 4; as trauma 3
PolitiFact 133, 204
Polk, James K. 22, 23
polling, campaigns and 177
Pomper, Gerald 186
posttruth society 29
poverty *see* economic inequality
Powell, Michael 164
power, politicians and 4–5
president categories 21–22
presidentialism 104
presidential rhetoric 100–106; listening for what is different 101–103; listening to president institutionally 103–105; overview of 100–101
president's moment in time 21–28; misreading context of 22–24; opposition president-to-restoration president patterns 24–26; understanding 21–22
prestige, terrorists and 246–247
progressive taxation, political advertising and 207
progressivism: American politics and 16–18; examples of 16–17

Pronovost, Peter 149
prophetic rhetoric 29–34; Black 30; imagination and justice 33–34; overview of 29–30; revelation of injustice 32; scope of justice 33; speaker-centered commitment of 30–32
prophetic voices 30–31
ProPublica 232
Proud Boys 84
public-level incivility 65
public opinion, nature of 50–51
public service news organizations 239
public subsidies for journalism 235–240; democracy and 235–237; described 238–240; deterioration of journalism and 237–238; overview of 235

qualitative data, campaigns and 178–179
quantitative representation, coalitions and 81–82
queer migration politics 83

race, coalitions and 81–82
racial equity, playful protest and 41–42
racial identity, essentializing 81–82, 84
radicalism 30
Radio Act, 1927 93
Radio/Television Cross-Ownership Rule 164
Randolph, A. Philip 33
ranked-choice voting 205
rational distrust 222
Rayburn, Sam 26
Reagan, Ronald 21, 23, 29, 94, 194
reality TV programs, economic inequality and 74–75
regime builders 21, 22
regime managers 21, 22
reporters, politicians and 6
Republicans, beliefs of 51–54
reputational distrust 222
Requiem for the American Dream (Chomsky) 74
Responsible Terrorism Coverage Project 244, 245, 247–248
restoration presidents 21–22
rhetoric: as civil or uncivil 65–67; in health care 147–149 (*see also* health care decision-making); presidential 100–106 (*see also* presidential

rhetoric); prophetic 29–34 (*see also* prophetic rhetoric)
rhetorical sensitivity 264
Rivera, Gabby 42
Roberts, Dave 254
Rochdale, Lady 41
Rock, Chris 81
Rocky Mountain News 162, 236
Rogers, Will 180
Romano, Aja 108
Romney, Mitt 49, 181
Roosevelt, Franklin 16, 21, 23, 105
Rosenzweig, Roy 18
ross, jesika maria 223
Ross, Loretta 110
Roth, Michael 114
Rothman, Aviva 111
Rude Democracy (Herbst) 66
Rule of Eight 164
Rule of Four 164
RU Ready Texas program 269–270
Rustin, Bayard 33
Ruth, Babe 75

Sacramento Bee, The 233
Sandel, Michael 92
Sanders, Bernie 59
Sasse, Ben 123
Saturday Night Live 108
"Say His Name" 68
SBC Communication 165
Scalia, Eugene 114
Schattschneider, Elmer Eric 203
Schiavo, Terri 25
Schroeder, Pat 60
Schudson, M. 236
Seattle Post-Intelligencer 236
Seeing Us in Them: Social Divisions and the Politics of Group Empathy (Sirin, Villalobos, and Valentino) 119
separation-of-powers system 21
September 11, 2001 terrorist attacks 25
Serazio, Michael 75
Shaker, L. 236
Shark Tank 74
Shelby County vs. Holder, 2013 112–113
Shepard, Benjamin 39, 40
Sioux City Journal 64
Sirin, Cigdem 119
60 Minutes 73
Skowronek, Stephen 22
slavery, intellectual inferiority and 30

Sloterdijk, Peter 6–7
Smith, Lily 37
Snopes.com 204
Sobieraj, Sarah 67, 68, 70
social dominance orientation 118
social fragmentation 31
socialization, politics and 7
social media: clinical services and 148; democratic functions served by 153–154; disinformation, redesigning circulation of 157–158; economic inequality and 76–77; electorate studies and 179; First Amendment questions regarding 95; incivility in 8; media system and 131; terrorism and 248–249; transparency in political messages 154–157
social networks, broadening 268
societal needs, metrics and 229
Southern California Public Radio 223
Southern Christian Leadership Conference 34
Southwestern Bell 165
Spaceship Media 223
Speak Up Speak Out program 269
Spivak, Gayatri 81
sports broadcasts, economic inequality and 75
Stelter, Brian 252
Stewart, Maria 30
Strachan, J. C. 67
strategy-framed posts 231
Strauss Institute 267
substance *vs.* politics 5–6
suffragist playful protest 37–40
Sunrise Movement 83, 84–85
Super Bowl 74, 75, 77
super PACs 209–215; overview of 209; problem with 209–212; solution to problem with 212–214
surveillance campaigning, political advertising and 202
Survey Sampling Inc. (SSI) 187
Suskin, A. 114
Swingus Americanus 181
swing voting 181
symbolic racism 118

Tacitus 209
Tampa Tribune, The 162
Tarde, G. 235
Taylor, Breonna 31, 84
Tea Partiers 15

Tea Party 59, 83
Tech Workers Coalition 166
Telecommunication Act 161
terrorism 244–250; definitions of 245–246; journalists/news organizations and, recommendations for 248; media users and 246–247; overview of 244–245; reporting on 247–248; social media users/platforms and, recommendations for 248–249
Texas Civic Ambassador Program 267
Texas Civic Health Index 266–268
Texas Tribune, The 239
Thelen, David 18
Thorson, Emily 75
Through the Labyrinth: The Truth About How Women Become Leaders (Eagly and Carli) 59
TikTok 76, 214
Till, Emmett 32
Till-Bradley, Mamie 32
Time 29
Tocqueville, A. D. 100
To Err Is Human report (Institute of Medicine) 147
Tönnies, F. 235
Top-Four Prohibition 164
Traister, R. 59
transparency in political messages 154–157
tribal epistemology 254
Trudeau, Pierre 57
Truman, Harry 21
Trump, Donald 23, 25–26, 29, 51, 69, 100, 102–103, 108–109, 118, 154, 155, 166, 168, 181, 185, 238, 251
trust: *vs.* authority journalism problem 220–221; building innovations 221–222; re-gaining journalism 221
Twain, Mark 123, 180
2042 demographic shift 80–81
Twitter 68, 70, 95, 108, 131, 158, 208, 238
TX Votes program 269
Tyler, John 23

UHF Discount 164
unexceptional coalitions 83–85
unexceptional politics 83
Unite the Right 104
UNITY: Journalists for Diversity 166
Upworthy 227

USA Today 188
U.S. Commission on Civil Rights 113
U.S. Election Project 193
US military 52–53

Van Buren, Martin 21
Verizon 161, 165
Villalobos, Jose 119
visibility, terrorist groups and 246
Voice of San Diego 198
volunteer journalists 197
voter suppression 60–61
Vox 108

Waheed, Adreinne 42
Waiting for 2042 (Kondabolu album) 80
Wall Street Journal, The 144
Warner, Mark 206
Washington Post 37, 188, 223
Watchdog Journalism Branch (W.J.B.) of government 137–145; candidates 142; described 137–138; design overview for 138–139; elections 142; ethics 143; formatting 143–144; funding for 139–140; guidelines 138–139; immunity 143; internal competition 144; Jury 141–142; privileges 141; reporting 143; responsibilities 140–141; seats for 140; trustees 142–143
Watchdog Jury 141–142
Weber, Max 38
Weber Shandwick 68
Weinberger v. Wiesenfeld, 1975 113
Wells-Barnett, Ida B. 30, 32
West, Cornel 34
White House Office of Faith-Based and Community Initiatives 24–25
White minority 80
Whiteness of Hollywood 81
Whitmer, Gretchen 112
Wichowsky, Amber 76
Wilson, Woodrow 24
Wolf, M. R. 67
Wong Chin Foo 30
World Press Freedom Index 163, 164
Writers Guild of America 166

Yippies 38
YouTube 74, 76, 212, 214

Zimmerman, George 83
Zuboff, Shoshana 207